MASS MEDIA AND COMMUNICATION IN GLOBAL SCENARIO

MASS MEDIA AND COMMUNICATION IN GLOBAL SCENARIO

Ratnesh Dwivedi

KALPAZ

ISBN: 978-81-7835-948-9

Price : ₹ 790

First Published 2013

Published by

Kalpaz Publications
C-30, Satyawati Nagar,
Delhi - 110052
E-mail: kalpaz@hotmail.com Ph.: 9212142040

Laser Typesetting: Rajender Vashist, Delhi
Printed at: G. Print Process, Delhi

Cataloging in Publication Data--DK
Courtesy: D.K. Agencies (P) Ltd. <docinfo@dkagencies.com>

Dwivedi, Ratnesh.
Mass media and communication in global scenario / Ratnesh Dwivedi.
p. cm.
Includes bibliographical references and index.
ISBN 9788178359489

1. Mass media. 2. Mass media--India. 3. Communication.
4. Communication--India. I. Title.

DDC 302.23 23

Contents

Preface

The idea behind putting these research papers and research articles in this book is to give various aspects of communication, a platform where from readers may go through them at one go. When I decided to start writing academic paper or more over compiling them in 2005,I had one thing in my mind and that was to cover all possible areas of communication and media studies. Hence forth I started my voyage to search out the possibilities where I can present my ideas and compiled references of other notable people in various international conferences and journals.

It was not an easy task to force your point of view in to journals and conferences as majority of international conferences and publication put forward a particular core area or subject on which an author may present a paper or his findings.

So, it was a matter of time, patience and rigorous effort that I found opportunities of the areas I did wish to cover. It is at glance that my readers of this book will find almost all possible social ,political and communication topics ,when they will go through one by one on these thirteen papers, which I either presented in an international conference or they got published in national or international journals or subject to be published.

Believe me, past eight years journey in academics has been adventurous, worthy and interesting for me as I got chance to put forward my opinion and to comment on other's opinion and then to compile them in form of an academic paper. I have honestly tried to touch all possible areas of my expertise in this book of compilation of my academic papers.

I am a little bit disappointed as I have not been able to include two of my best and first academic papers which I presented in a national conference at Purvanchal University. These two papers were related with the Economics of South Asian countries and efforts of world's biggest space science research organization -NASA.

However rest of my presentation and published papers are part of this book.

In my thirteen papers I have discussed about Community Radio, its current status and challenges before it in Indian atmosphere. This paper was published in proceeding of one of the biggest conferences organized by Hans Bredow Research Foundation at University of Hamburg,Germany.

Sanskrit is considerd as Language of Gods and is mother of many regional Indian languages as well as foreign language. Panini organized this language of Gods through the grammer he invented. A paper on Sanskrit and Panini is part of this book which is due to be presented in an international conference in Russia.

Organizational Communication is a new study in the area of communications science. A paper on organizational communication is presented here which was presented by author in an international conference organized by Russia's number to university by using vedio conferencing facility.

Media is accountable to public but it's a matter of debate if media has fulfilled its duty. A paper on Public Accountability of media was published by Press Council of India, the apex press body in India. Author's that very paper is also part of this book.

Keeping the need of research students in mind, a paper on research process and tools has been specially designed by author.

Higher education in India is facing many challenges. Our ancient past has been glorious but we have to work out on future. Hence a paper has been designed by author which deals with higher education in ancient India, challenges of today and a work plan for future.

Author has designed two papers on radio which deals with both coomercial and community wise aspect of radio in India. One paper deals with commericial radio while other deals with educational radio or community radio.

History of Communication is discussed right from origin of sign language up till invention of computers and internet thorough pigeon post and harkara systems in medieval India. The compilation of whole process was accepted and presented in form of a research paper at Tver State University, Russia.

Changing pattern in Television viewership and in programme making has been discussed with a case study of India's no 1 English news channel CNN-IBN and its special initiative of Citizen Journalism hosted and conceptualized by Anubha Bhonsle.This paper was published by an academic journal named 'Pragyan' of Institute of Management Studies ,Dehradun.

The challenges before traditional media in modern digital age and chances of its integration with digital media have been discussed in a separate paper. The paper was presented at International conference at Amity University,Rajasthan.

What role media can play in developing awareness during disasters and early warning system has been included keeping in view of disastrous events india has faced like tsunami 2004.

Coverage of issues like human rights by media has always been a matter of debate. This topic is discussed in a paper which is accepted in an international conference of India's apex press body, Press Council of India.

Michel Foucault is an acclaimed French Philosopher .His master piece 'The Archeology of Knowledge' need no introduction .A critical study of his work has been compiled in a paper which was accepted in an international conference at Tver State University, Russia.

Two of researches papers are dedicated to the issues which has shaken not only India but whole world-Wiki leaks and Radia tapes. It's a debate between 'Right to Publish' and 'Ethical Code of Conduct'. These two papers are due in International journals.

Another paper which deals with role of social media in generating public perception and its role in uprising in Tunisia and Egypt is published in and refreed Indian journal.

A comprehensive study of key terror organizations and working of it has been put in another paper. While medi's role in covering sensitive issues like terrorism is discussed in a paper which was published in a national journal.

I have also touced the global economic meltdown in brief.

The idea is to aware and inform my readers on all possible happening and aspect between these years.

It has been an eventful journey for me and the best thing I can quote is "....miles to go before I sleep" of Robert Frost.

In this journey and work of twenty research papers and articles I must thank to my parents who have been a guiding force for me during thick and thin. I also wish to thank my teachers and my friends for pushing me up to do good job at my work place. My elder brother who is source of inspiration for me deserves thanks from my side and so is my wife and little baby who always stood by my side..

Two of my friends in media has enormously helped me by giving me their valuable inputs whenever I needed. I extend my word of thanks to Mr Bhupendra Chaubey and Ms Anubha Bhonsle of CNN-IBN.

The story is uncomplete if I do not mention the name of Lyudmila Isaeva of Tver State University and Dasha Mileyaeva of RosNou, Moscow in Russia who provided me special facility to present some of my papers by using vedio conferencing facility from India.

And last I must convey my heartiest thanks to my publisher who has made this work possible to put these thirteen shades of communication at one place by giving it shape of a book.

10 January, 2012 **Ratnesh Dwivedi**
Noida, U.P.

Introduction

The days of metamorphosis in global media environment is triggering the rapid changes in academic scenario of Mass Media and Communication. Today one can not continue with same old curriculum which was taught ten years back. Academic institutions and universities continuously keep revising the syllabus and course curriculum keeping the needs of industry in mind. Same is applicable for academicians and researchers in the community of Mass Media and Communication. Research has been emphasized with core competence and both the educators and students are encourages to do valuable researches to obtain a key methodology in area of education and teaching to Mass Media and Communication.

We are living in the era of communication and in the days of 24*7 news channels, sharp PR and advertisement and internet newspapers. Just to cite an example how rapidly the news ,mass media and communication environment changing I will quote an example from U.S. media scenario.

In May, 2012 Warren Buffett's Berkshire Hathaway Company announced the purchase of 63 newspapers, including 23 dailies, from the debt-ridden Media General Company. The transaction was a course reversal for Buffett, who earlier had said he wouldn't buy newspapers, and created a major new player in the industry. It also left Media General-whose history with newspapers dates back to the mid-1800's-with only one remaining daily, the Tampa Tribune, which many predict it will still try to sell.

The purchase, seen as a rare vote of confidence in a struggling industry, also capped a period of intense change in U.S. newspaper ownership. In the last 18 months many better known newspaper companies divested most or all of their holdings while a number of new entities, including hedge funds and private equity firms, jumped in.

According to the investment banking firm of Dirks, Van Essen & Murray, which monitors newspaper transactions, a total of 71 daily newspapers were sold as part of 11 different transactions during 2011, the busiest year for sales since 2007.

And newspapers were not the only media to undergo major changes. The last 18 months also saw local television sales reach new heights, the merging of Newsweek and the Daily Beast, Comcast's acquisition of NBC Universal, the Huffington Post's movement into web TV and further reach among U.S. broadcast companies into the Hispanic market.

- In transactions other than the Buffett deal with Media General, The New York Times Company sold 14 daily newspapers to Halifax Media and Journal Register Company (with 20 dailies) was acquired by one of its investors, Alden Global Capital. The Times Company's sale of its Regional Newspaper Group left it with only three remaining dailies, the flagship New York Times, The Boston Globe and the Worcester Telegram & Gazette.
- The Chicago Sun Times was sold to a new company called Wrapports LLC, an organization led by technology executive Michael Ferro Jr. and former Newsday publisher Timothy Knight.
- The San Diego Union-Tribune was sold in November 2011 by the private equity firm Platinum Equity, which bought it in 2009, to a company owned by a local hotel developer.

And so far in 2012:

- Freedom Communications announced on June 11 the sale of its remaining dailies, including the Orange County Register (163,000 print circulation) to the investment group 2001 Trust LLC. That sale ended the company's almost 80-year history as a newspaper publisher. And as was the case with Journal Register, Freedom had recently emerged from bankruptcy protection.
- Once known as the crown jewel of the now defunct Knight Ridder chain, The Philadelphia Inquirer (along with its sister Philadelphia Daily News) was sold in April for the fourth time in six years. A group of local businessmen bought the company for a reported $55 million, roughly 10% of the $515 million the papers fetched in 2006 when they were purchased by another group of local investors led by advertising executive Brian Tierney.
- Hedge Fund Company Alden Global Capital bought the Journal Register Company with twenty papers including the New Haven Register (CT), the Oakland Press (MI) and the Daily Times (PA).

Alden Global has also invested in several other newspaper organizations.

- Versa Capital Management, which purchased a number of small dailies in Ohio in 2011, acquired the Times Leader in Wilkes-Barre, Pennsylvania in March of 2012.
- 53 stations were sold in 2011, which brought in a total of $307 million dollars in revenues. While the total value of station mergers and acquisitions was still minuscule compared to the decade before the recession hit, transactions topped a billion dollars for the first time since 2007 and were almost ten times the value of station sales the year before.
- Sinclair Broadcasting was the biggest player in 2011. It bought 15 stations from two ownership groups. In the single largest acquisition in four years, the company paid $385 million for the eight-station broadcast division of Freedom Communications, which had been on the block since the company declared bankruptcy in 2010. These 8 stations brought in $62 million in revenue in 2011. Sinclair also bought seven stations owned by Four Points Media Group for $200 million, whose stations earned $98 million in revenues in 2011.
- ABC and CBS affiliate stations, that produce news across markets, continued to lead in revenues. Both reported $2.9 billion in 2011, down from $3.2 billion in 2010. Fox affiliates followed with $2.2 billion in revenues for 2011, down from $2.3 in 2010.
- While stations in all market sizes lost revenue on average in 2011, the top 25 markets saw the greatest declines by far. The 176 stations in the top 25 markets averaged a 24% decline in revenues in 2011 ($48.5 million dollars). That compares to a 9% loss in midsize markets (26-50), 8% loss in markets 51-100, 12% in markets 101-150 and 9% in the 44 stations in the smallest markets (151+). Even with a 24% decline, though, the largest markets still bring in far more total revenue, an average of $49 million in 2011.
- Newsweek's website was integrated into The Daily Beast's site in August 2011, nine months following the merging of the two companies. Combining the two websites was supposed to boost traffic; instead traffic has fallen significantly. When the deal closed, The Daily Beast's audience was 2.2 million, while Newsweek drew 3.1 million unique monthly visitors, according to Compete.com. Combined traffic for the two sites for the five months following

the August 2011 website merger averaged 2.5 million; in January 2012, that inched up to 2.9 million. Newsweek used to have an online partnership with MSNBC since 2007, which generated more than 50% of its online traffic. But the partnership ended in February 2011, a few months after the merger of Newsweek and The Daily Beast companies.

Cable Television

- Comcast increased its total revenue by 47% in 2011, thanks to the acquisition of NBC Universal and Universal Orlando. Apart from the impact of those deals, company revenues increased 5%. Comcast's cable communications businesses such as video and high-speed internet (up 5%) performed slightly better than NBCUniversal segments, which together rose 4%. Within NBCU, aside from 24% growth at the relatively small theme parks division, it was cable programming, which includes MSNBC and CNBC that experienced the strongest revenue growth at 11%.
- For News Corp., the phone-hacking scandal in Britain and the associated legal proceedings and parliamentary investigation, including closing of the News of the World tabloid (Britain's largest paper) hung over the company in 2011. In its August 2011 annual report, News Corp. noted, "it is possible that these proceedings could damage our reputation and might impair our ability to conduct our business." Revenue projections at Fox News Channel, a key News Corp. holding, continued to climb. One Morgan Stanley analyst estimated the value of Fox News Channel at $12.4 billion.

Network Television

- Comcast's merger with NBC Universal in January 2011 was the first ownership change for the network since General Electric acquired NBC from its original owner, RCA in 1986.[1] Comcast now has a 51% stake in NBCUniversal, making it a majority owner. Perhaps the most notable change so far has been an effort to bring in more diversity, both in ownership and programming. As part of its commitment to the FCC, in February 2012, Comcast/NBCU announced the scheduled release of the first four minority-owned channels as the first of 10 new independently-owned and operated channels established by 2018. Comcast/NBCU also agreed to allocate $20 million to these channels.

- In addition, the FCC imposed several other conditions on Comcast in order for the merger to go through:
    - It would have to expand its existing broadband network to reach 400,000 more homes and six additional rural communities.
    - It would have to provide free video and high-speed internet service to 600 new schools or libraries in underserved and low-income areas.
    - It would have to make broadband available for less than $10 a month to 2.5 million low-income households. The same households must also be given the option of buying personal computers or netbooks for less than $150.
- The Huffington Post took several steps in 2012 to expand its brand into new formats. It announced that in July it would begin offering the first web-only 24 hour news network in the same spirit as CNN or Fox News. The "network," originally called Huffington Post Streaming Network but re-christened Huffpost Live, is projected to carry 12 hours of live video each weekday, with the content replayed for the other 12 hours of each day. In June, the Huffington Post launched a new iPad-only publication called "Huffington" that has the look and feel of a traditional print magazine in a digital form. Huffington hit the Apple store on June 14th priced at 99 cents per issue, $1.99 for a monthly subscription, or $19.99 per year. The publication features both repackaging of Huffingtonpost.com content and content exclusive to the iPad as well.
- Yahoo in the last year struck two partnerships aimed at expanding its news content, particularly in video. In the fall of 2011 Yahoo announced a partnership with ABC News. Yahoo News, the most popular online news destination in the United States according to Nielsen, comScore, and Hitwise has in-house reporters and produces some original content but is nowhere near the size of ABC News. Under the agreement Yahoo News would carry content from ABC News, and the editorial teams from both organizations would collaborate to create original content. In June 2012 Yahoo news entered into a very similar agreement with CNBC. Under the new agreement CNBC will provide financial reporting and information for Yahoo News. This partnership deal does not include a payment by either company, but the two companies will share advertising revenue.

- The hyperlocal news site Patch, owned by AOL, continued to face criticism that its business model is not viable. In May, 2012 a shareholder in AOL, Starboard Value which owns 5.3% of AOL, released a report sharply criticizing Patch, which included its estimates (AOL does not release earnings for Patch in any regular form) that the local news operation lost $147 million and generated just $13 million in ad revenue in 2011. AOL continues to defend its investment in Patch and in early 2012 revealed a new ad team that it hoped would boost ad sales.

In the days of such metamorphosis in media and communication worldwide academia is also changing its methodology. More individual and independent departments are created, which were once taught under broader discipline of Mass Media and Communication. Departments such as Discourse, Speech Communication, Analogy, Morphology, Corporate Communication, Event Management, Media Management, fashion Communication, Film

Communication, Broadcast Studies, Radio Management and other such departments are created separate to Mass Media and Communication.

More emphasis is given on methodological research which is the backbone of Media and Communication Studies. Keeping all above aspects in mind I decided to do a comprehensive research on various different divisions of Mass Media and Communication by taking global references. The articles which are here before my readers are result of a methodological research done in due course. These articles and papers were either presented or published in international conferences or journals. They are written in a formats that readers can get a clearer idea on what exactly was required to do further studies to explore that area.

The paper which of first chapter"An Analytical Study of 'Sanskrit' and 'Panini' as Foundation of Speech Communication in India and the World" was presented in 3rd International Conference on Language,Culture and Society which was jointly organized by Institute of English Studies,University of London and Russian Academy of Sciences in Senate Hall,University of London,London on July 9-10,2012.The paper was well received by a gathering of 200 academicioans ,researchers and morphologists who debated for two days on structural and morphological importance of different languages and their importance on evolution of society.

I am thankful to Professor Jane Roberts of Institute of English Studies,University of London and event officer Mr Jon Millington who arranged a special facility for me to present my paper by using video conferencing facility from India.

Samskrtam or for short sanskrit or samskrtâ vâk is an ancient sacred language of *bharatavarsha* that is the language of *Hinduism* and the *Vedas* and is the classical literary language of India. The name *Sanskrit* means "refined", "consecrated" and "sanctified". It has always been regarded as the 'high' language and used mainly for religious and scientific discourse. There are still hundreds of millions of people who use Sanskrit in their daily lives, but despite these numbers, its cultural worth is unsurpassed.

There is also a deeply rooted faith among Indians that Sanskrit itself is the language of the *Devas* (Gods), which is why this language was known during the Vedic period (6,000 - 8,000 years ago) as Daivi Vak (the Divine speech). The great grammarian, *Pânini*, structured this language with his grammar in the 7th century BC, and henceforth, it became referred to as Samskritam.

Numerous important works from a cultural, spiritual and scientific standpoint, were written in this ancient language. All of the classic literature of Vedic times was written in Sanskrit too, included the classical texts of yoga, Vedanta and other spiritual and philosophical schools of ancient times, as well as the historical texts in the great sciences of astrology, astronomy, medicine, architecture and the physical sciences.

The language is extremely regular, almost mathematical in its grammar and formulation. It is considered a sacred and mystical language — "the language of the Gods."

The Sanskrit language is the basis for many of modern Indian languages — Hindi, Gujarati, Marathi, Punjabi — as well as the classical Prakrit and the language of Buddhist scripture, Pali and has also helped shape many current languages including French, German, Russian, English and the South East Asian languages such as Malay, Javanese, Cambodia, Vietnam, Thai and the Philippines. It shows many ancient forms of words such as father, through, shampoo, trigonometry, and mouse, while guru, pundit, dharma, bandh, and yoga are among hundreds of Sanskrit words that can now be found in the Oxford dictionary.

Sanskrit is a scientific and systematic language. Its grammar is perfect and has attracted scholars worldwide. Sanskrit has a perfect grammar which has been explained to us by the world's greatest grammarian Panini.

Painci's grammar defines *Classical Sanskrit*, so PâG□ini by definition lived at the end of the *Vedic period*. He notes a few special rules, marked chandasi ("in the hymns") to account for forms in the Vedic scriptures that had fallen out of use in the spoken language of his time. These indicate that *Vedic Sanskrit* was already archaic, but still a comprehensible dialect.

An important hint for the dating of Paini is the occurrence of the word yavanänî (in 4.1.49, either "*Greek* woman", or "*Greek script*"). Some Greeks, such as the Persian admiral *Scylax of Caryanda* were present in Gandhara as co-citizens of the Persian empire, well before the conquests of *Alexander the Great* in the *330s BC*,; the name could also have been transmitted via *Old Persian* yauna, and the administrative languages Elamite or Aramaic, so that the occurrence of yavanânî taken in isolation allows for a *terminus post quem* as early as 519 BC, i.e. the time of *Darius the Great*'s Behistun inscription that includes the Indian province of Gandara (Sanskrit Gandhâra).

It is not certain whether PâG□ini used writing for the composition of his work, though it is generally agreed that he knew of a form of writing, based on references to words such as "script" and "scribe" in his Ashtadhyayi. These must have referred to *Aramaic* or early *Kharosthi* writing. It is believed by some that a work of such complexity would have been difficult to compile without written notes, though others have argued that he might have composed it with the help of a group of students whose memories served him as 'notepads' (as is typical in Vedic learning). Writing first reappears in India in the form of the *Brâhmî script* from c. the 3rd century BC in the *Ashokan* inscriptions.

While Paini's work is purely grammatical and lexicographic, cultural and geographical inferences can be drawn from the vocabulary he uses in examples, and from his references to fellow grammarians, which show he was a northwestern person. New deities referred to in his work include *Vasudeva* (4.3.98). The concept of *dharma* is attested in his example sentence (4.4.41) dharmam carati "he observes the law" (cf. *Taittiriya Upanishad* 1.11).

Paini's work became known in 19th century Europe, where it influenced modern linguistics initially through *Franz Bopp*, who mainly looked at Paini. Subsequently, a wider body of work influenced Sanskrit scholars such as *Ferdinand de Saussure*, *Leonard Bloomfield*, and *Roman Jakobson. Frits Staal* discussed the impact of Indian ideas on language in Europe. After outlining the various aspects of the contact, Staal notes that the idea of formal rules in language, proposed by de *Ferdinand de Saussure* in 1894 and developed by *Noam Chomsky* in 1957 has origins in the European exposure to the formal rules of Painian grammar. In particular, de Saussure, who lectured on Sanskrit for three decades, may have been influenced by Painian and *Bhartrihari*; his idea of the unity of signifier-signified in the *sign* is somewhat similar to the notion of *Sphoma*. More importantly, the very idea that formal rules can be applied to areas outside of logic or mathematics, may itself have been catalyzed by Europe's contact with the work of Sanskrit grammarians.

This paper talks about foundational role of Sanskrit and Panini in speech communiction. Second chapter is dedicated on "Public Accountability and Media :Its Success and Failure in Performing The Role as a Force for Public Accountability".The paper was published in souveniour carried out in International Colloquium of India's apex press body 'Press Council of India' to commemorate 'National Press Day' on November 16,2011. The journal was inaugurated by vice president of India Dr Hamid Ansari. The paper talks about media's both side in performing its role as public watchdog.

Media accountability is a phrase that refers to the general (especially western) belief that *mass media* has to be *accountable* in the public's interest - that is, they are expected to behave in certain ways that contribute to the public good.

The concept is not clearly defined, and often collides with commercial interests of media owners; legal issues, such as the constitutional right to the *freedom of the press* in the U.S.; and governmental concerns about public security and order.

Several *international organizations*, like *International Freedom of Expression Exchange*, *Freedom House*, *International Press Institute*, *World Press Freedom Committee* and the *Inter-American Press Association*, watch over governmental control of the press.

Accountability, one of the most important principles of the media must be ensured in everyday practice of journalism, in times of conflict and turmoil and when transgressions are rife – whether from the state, media owners and vested interests in society or even the public.

Accountability of the media, in all its myriad avatars, is a ticklish issue. The print media has a statutory Press Council, broadcast media has put a regulatory mechanism in place but this is still at an early stage and the Internet is largely unregulated but has not been free from state censorship or from the state. So who will watch the watchdog? The state? The media industry? An ombudsman? Media advocacy groups? Journalist organisations? Or, the public – that amorphous mass of media readers, television and radio audiences, filmgoers, bloggers and internet social networking groups?

In the present scenario, the answer is 'All of the above'! A perfect recipe for chaos and no really effective and foolproof method to ensure media accountability.

Time and again, the state has made attempts to regulate the functioning of the media. Barring the period of the Emergency, the Indian media has vociferously resisted these attempts. Journalists and media owners came together to resist the Bihar Press Bill, the Defamation Bill or even provisions in the infamous TADA and POTA that regulated media coverage. Recently, when a content code was sought to be drafted by the government for the broadcast media, the News Broadcasters Association (NBA) that represents some members of the broadcast media industry, opposed it and drafted their own code.

However, the Press Council has all but disappeared from both media and public consciousness. Earlier, newspapers reported Press Council hearings and orders, even if detrimental to themselves. Not so today. Hardly anyone knows who heads the Press Council today or about its work (For the record, the Press Council is headed by Justice G.N. Ray). Besides, journalists' organisations have long argued that the Press Council needs more teeth and its highest power – that of censure – is hardly deterrent enough.

The third chapter deals with -"Radio in India: The FM Revolution and its Impact on Indian Listeners".It was published in a very reknowned journal of Slovakia,Otazky Zurnalistiky(Question of Journalism) in double issue 1-2,Volume 55,June 2012.The chapter talks about changing trends in Indian radio scenario and its impact on Indian listeners ,particularly after FM revolution.

1.0. Broadcasting began in India with the formation of a private radio service in Madras (presently Chennai) in 1924. In the very same year, British colonial government approved a license to a private company, the Indian Broadcasting Company, to inaugurate Radio stations in Bombay and Kolkata. The company almost went bankrupt in 1930 but the colonial government took away the two transmitters and the Department of Labour and Industries started operating them as the Indian State Broadcasting Corporation. In 1936, this very Corporation was renamed All India Radio (AIR) and was controlled by the Department of Communications. When India became independent in 1947, AIR was made a separate Department under the Ministry of Information and

Broadcasting. FM Radio was first introduced by All India Radio in 1972 at Madras and later in 1992 at Jalandhar.

Phase One: In 1993, the government sold airtime blocks on its FM channels in Madras, Mumbai, Delhi, Kolkata and Goa to private operators, who developed their own programme content.

Indian policy currently laid down that these bids were a One-Time Entry Fee (OTEF), for the entire license period of 10 years. Annual license fee for private players is either 4% of revenue share or 10% of Reserve Price, whichever is higher.

Four years later (1997), after the initial euphoria died out and most of the bidders could not meet their commitments to pay the governments the amounts they had expected and defaulted.

The only non-defaulter was the Times Group which operated its brand, Times FM, till June 1998. The government, therefore, decided not to renew contracts given to private operators.

Fourth chapter deals with"The Politics-Media Equation —Exposing Two Faces of The Old Nexus Through Study of General Elections, Wiki Leaks and Radia Tapes".The paper reveals Politics Media nexus with relevant examples.

The important identity of a responsible media is playing an unbiased role in reporting a matter without giving unnecessary hype to attract the attention of the gullible public with the object of making money and money only.After reporting properly the media can educate the public to form their own opinion in the matters of public interest.The media can highlight the short-comings of the official machinery in its functioning,bringing out the sufferings of the public in general. As political parties start media for themselves and utilise it for their own selfish ends, the role of the media is very much narrowed.During elections ,in democracy the media is an effective tool for getting the public.

The idea that media should serve the society, particularly in the third world, in solving the problems people are facing has already gained momentum. Journalists, politicians and even the general public are talking about the necessity of harnessing the media .

Throughout the centuries, the world has never existed without information and communication, hence the inexhaustible essence of mass media. The government has the power to either make or reject whatever that will exist within its environment. It also determines how free the mass media will be in their dissemination of information to the people.

The question is in what ways has the government influenced the mass media?

The word politics has today acquired many meanings. For an ordinary man in the street, politics is a negative word connoting dubious behavior, scheming and maneuvering to secure an undue advantage over others. But for our purpose here, we shall restrict our consideration of politics to the realm of the state and government wherein it implies that aspect of human activities that deals with distribution of power, influence and authority in the state for the purpose of order and good governance of the state.

The relationship between the mass media and the government institution can best be appreciated if we look at the classical theories of the press. These theories articulate the varying degrees of freedom existing in the media as they operate within any political system. Let us now briefly look at these theories and their basic principles.

Fifth chapter talks about the wikileaks and its revelations in current context"Wiki leaks Revelations in Global Context—The War Between 'Right to Publish' and 'Ethical Code of Conduct".It was Published in International refered Journal,Manthan- Journal of Mass Communication in its Volume-VI, Issue-II, December,2011.

WikiLeaks is an international non-profit organisation that publishes submissions of private, secret, and classified media from anonymous *news sources*, *news leaks*, and *whistleblowers*. Its website, launched in 2006 under The Sunshine Press organisation claimed a database of more than 1.2 million documents within a year of its launch. WikiLeaks describes its founders as a mix of Chinese dissidents, journalists, mathematicians, and start-up company technologists from the United States, Taiwan, Europe, Australia, and South Africa. *Julian Assange*, an Australian *Internet activist*, is generally described as its director. The site was originally launched as a user-editable *wiki*, but has progressively moved towards a more traditional publication model and no longer accepts either user comments or edits.

On 28 November 2010, WikiLeaks and five major newspapers from Spain (*El País*), France (*Le Monde*), Germany (*Der Spiegel*), the United Kingdom (*The Guardian*), and the United States (*The New York Times*) started to simultaneously publish the first 220 of 251,287 leaked confidential—but not top secret—*diplomatic cables* from 274 US embassies around the world, dated from 28 December 1966 to 28 February 2010. WikiLeaks plans to release the entirety of the cables in phases over several months.

The *contents of the diplomatic cables* include numerous unguarded comments and revelations regarding: critiques and praises about the host countries of various US embassies; political manoeuvring regarding *climate change*; discussion and resolutions towards ending ongoing tension in the Middle East; efforts and resistance towards *nuclear disarmament*; actions in the *War on Terror*; assessments of other threats around the world; dealings between various countries; US *intelligence* and *counterintelligence* efforts; and other diplomatic actions. *Reactions to the United States diplomatic cables leak* include stark criticism, anticipation, commendation, and quiescence. Consequent reactions to the US government include sympathy, bewilderment and dismay. On 14 December 2010 the *United States Department of Justice* issued a *subpoena directing Twitter* to provide information for accounts registered to or associated with WikiLeaks. Twitter decided to notify its users. The *overthrow of the presidency in Tunisia* has been attributed in part to reaction against the corruption revealed by leaked cables.

WikiLeaks has been criticized before for revealing sensitive information. For example, the organization published thousands of reports about the Iraq War. Though much of the information was already known in broad terms, many of the specifics were not. WikiLeaks also released classified U.S. military footage from an attack in July 2007 in Baghdad by a U.S. helicopter that killed a dozen people including two journalists. For these leaks and others, many have praised the organization. But what are the ethics behind revealing secrets?

That has been debated in this chapter.Sixth chapter discusses about "Two Faces of Media While Covering Human Right Activities in India. This paper was presented by author in International Colloquium of India's apex press body, Press Council of India on 28-29th April,2011.

The situation of *human rights* in *India* is a complex one, as a result of the country's large size and tremendous diversity, its status as a *developing country* and a *sovereign*, *secular*, *democratic republic*, and its history as a *former colonial territory*. The *Constitution of India* provides for *Fundamental rights*, which include *freedom of religion*. Clauses also provide for *Freedom of Speech*, as well as separation of executive and judiciary and freedom of movement within the country and abroad.

According to the estimates of *Reporters Without Borders*, India ranks 105th worldwide in press freedom index (press freedom index for India is 29.33 for 2009). The *Indian Constitution*, while not mentioning the word "press", provides for "the right to freedom of speech and expression" (Article 19(1) a). However this right is subject to restrictions under subclause (2), whereby this freedom can be restricted for reasons of "*sovereignty* and integrity of India, the security of the State, friendly relations with foreign States, public order, preserving decency, preserving morality, in relation to contempt of court, *defamation*, or incitement to an offence". Laws such as the *Official Secrets Act* and *Prevention of Terrorism Act* (POTA) have been used to limit press freedom. Under POTA, person could be detained for up to six months before the police were required to bring charges on allegations for terrorism-related offenses. POTA was repealed in 2004, but was replaced by amendments to UAPA. The Official Secrets Act 1923 remains in effect.

Seventh chapter talks the Penetration of Social Media in Governance,Political Reforms and Building Public Perception which was published in International refered Journal,Manthan- Journal of Mass Communication carried out by Institute of Management Studies,Noida in its June 2011 issue. Paper discusses how effective social media is in political reforms and building public perception.

Social media are *media* for *social interaction*, using highly accessible and scalable communication techniques. Social media is the use of web-based and mobile technologies to turn communication into interactive dialogue. Andreas Kaplan and Michael Haenlein also define social media as "a group of Internet-based applications that build on the ideological and technological foundations of *Web 2.0*, which allows the creation and exchange of *user-generated content*." *Businesses* also refer to social media as *consumer-generated media* (CGM). A common thread running through all definitions of social media is a blending of technology and social interaction for the co-creation of value.

- Social networking now accounts for 22% of all time spent online in the US.
- A total of 234 million people age 13 and older in the U.S. used mobile devices in December 2009.
- Twitter processed more than one billion tweets in December 2009 and averages almost 40 million tweets per day.
- Over 25% of U.S. internet page views occurred at one of the top social networking sites in December 2009, up from 13.8% a year before.
- Australia has some of the highest social media usage statistics in the world. In terms of Facebook use Australia ranks highest with almost 9 hours per month from over 9 million users.
- The number of social media users age 65 and older grew 100

percent throughout 2010, so that one in four people in that age group are now part of a social networking site.

Over the past few years, many technophiles, activists, and political observers have been lauding the potential of social media platforms such as Facebook, SMS, Twitter, and YouTube to improve governance and foment political change. To date, we possess largely anecdotal data on the impact of new media and technologies on political reform. For example, many argue that Facebook, Twitter, and YouTube have played critical roles in organizing the recent protests in Egypt, Iran, Moldova, and Tunisia. Moreover, anecdotal evidence suggests that cell phone technologies can play an instrumental role in revealing electoral fraud by improving election monitoring and reporting techniques. Yet, in spite of the anecdotal evidence that supports these developments and their use in specific instances, there is a dearth of empirical analysis on the subject. We lack studies that trace the causal impact of these technologies on political reform and improved governance.

Eighth chapter tries to explor the challenges before Traditional Media in the Age of Digital Media,and discusses how to Integrate it with the Digital Media –The Way Ahead.This research paper was presented in International Conference on Digital Media Vs Traditional Media organized by Amity University,Jaipur on 13-14, March 2011.

You may have heard of digital media, but you may have no idea what it is and how it can help you out when it comes to marketing. It's definitely important that you get up to speed so you can use this to benefit your business. Basically digital media refers to any type of electronic media out there. Today media can be accessed in many ways, including with hand held devices like mobile phones, laptops, desktops, mp3 players, and more.

Digital media must be stored in an electronic way, so there is a lot of digital content on the internet today, including text content, pictures, audio content, as well as video content. Through the history of internet, digital media has been developing in various ways. Here's we'll take a look at how it has affected the Internet and ways that it may be integrated moving forwards.

Online media isn't just about content, but relationships and linkages between content. Users want to find relevant information in as few clicks as possible. In order to do that, they will choose a portfolio of sites, some broad and some niche, that suit their interests.

A great way to take advantage of that is by creating new sites with existing content. This can be done by either creating satellite sites for a general product (under a new brand – not a sub brand) or by aggregating related niche sites together into a more general portal.

There are several benefits to doing this. It dovetails very well with integration of social functionality as different content brands initiate different discussions. Also, by linking to the source of the original article, you enjoy SEO benefits on the original site. Finally, you create more inventory to sell.

The problem with most traditional media companies isn't that they're old, but that they're too balkanized. Print people know print, Radio people know Radio, TV people know TV. Business and creative sides have been historically adversarial which makes it hard to build the collaboration needed for digital media.

If all you have is a hammer, every problem looks like a nail. The problem is that very few media people are generalists, which is why they immediately try to solve new media problems using the few tools they know. Unfortunately, digital media knows no bounds and therefore requires greater integration.

To be successful, traditional media needs to not only learn about new media, but about old media as well. Print needs to learn broadcast, creative people need to understand more about business, etc. This approach needs to be absorbed into every facet of the business: strategy, hiring, training, organizational structure, etc.

Ninth chapter discusses the changing pattern in the viewers of Indian TV news channels and Producers.It studies India's number one English news channel CNN-IBN. The title of the paper is" Changing Mutual Perception of Television News Viewers and Program Makers in India— A Case Study of CNN-IBN And Its Unique

Initiative of Citizen Journalism".The paper was published in an cademic journal Pragyan- A journal of Mass Communication, Institute of Management Studies, Dehradun,India in December, 2010.

The Indian television system is one of the most extensive systems in the world. Terrestrial broadcasting, which has been the sole preserve of the government, provides television coverage to over 90% of India's 900 million people. By the end of 1996 nearly 50 million households had television sets. International satellite broadcasting, introduced in 1991, has swept across the country because of the rapid proliferation of small scale cable systems. By the end of 1996, Indians could view dozens of foreign and local channels and the competition for audiences and advertising revenues was one of the hottest in the world. In 1995, the Indian Supreme Court held that the government's monopoly over broadcasting was unconstitutional, setting the stage for India to develop into one of the world's largest and most competitive television environments.

CNN-IBN is a partnership between Global Broadcast News (GBN), a Network18 Company, and Turner International (Turner) inIndia.

The 24-hour, English-language news channel is spearheaded by renowned television journalist Rajdeep Sardesai as the Editor-in-Chief. He is backed in the venture by the strong foundation of Network18's newsgathering experience and infrastructure in India and bolstered byCNN's eminent and extensive global news network.

IBNLive.com is the online arm of GBN with hard news as its core offering and interactivity as its key component. Along with a plethora of mobile- and multimedia-enabled content, IBNLive is a multi-platform offering that, for the first time, provides viewers/users an opportunity to contribute to the news process and interact with editors and reporters. Manned 24x7, IBNlive.com is powered not just by CNN-IBN journalists but also by Network18's team of over 1,000 news professionals.

Citizen journalism is news created by amateur reporters who were previously seen as audiences, viewers or readers. The roots of citizen journalism lie in the self-printed pamphlets that were distributed on the street-side. However, by enabling everyone to report news without the permission of gatekeepers like news organizations or editors, social media has democratized journalism and enriched it by bringing in a diversity of views and voices to it.

Tenth chapter titles as Community Radio—History,Growth,Challenges and Current Status of it with Special Reference to India" discusses evolution an growth of Campus radio worldwide.It gives a special reference to Indian environment and was presented in European Communication Conference an International Conference of ECREA and University of Hamburg held in Hamburg,Germany on 10-15 ,October 2010.

Community radio is a type of *radio* service that caters to the interests of a certain area, broadcasting content that is popular to a local audience but which may often be overlooked by commercial or mass-media broadcasters.

Modern-day community radio stations often serve their listeners by offering a variety of content that is not necessarily provided by the larger commercial radio stations. Community radio outlets may carry *news* and information programming geared toward the local area, particularly *immigrant* or *minority groups* that are poorly served by other major media outlets. More specialized musical shows are also often a feature of many community radio stations. Community stations and pirate stations (where they are tolerated) can be valuable assets for a region. Community radio stations typically avoid content found on commercial outlets, such as *Top 40* music, sports, and "drive-time" personalities.

Eleventh paper looks into media's role in Disaster Management and early warning.It is research paper cum course curriculum. Disaster is a sudden, calamitous event bringing great damage, loss, and destruction and devastation to life and property. The damage caused by disasters is immeasurable and varies with the geographical location, climate and the type of the earth surface/degree of vulnerability. This influences the mental, socio-economic, political and cultural state of the affected area. Emergency Management is one of a number of terms which, since the end of the *Cold War*, have largely replaced Civil defense, whose original focus was protecting civilians from military attack. Modern thinking focuses on a more general intent to protect the civilian population in times of peace as well as in times of war. An academic trend is towards using the term *disaster risk reduction*, particularly for emergency management in a development management context. This focuses on the mitigation and preparedness aspects of the emergency cycle .

While the disaster is on, the media can also play the role of relaying the measures that are being taken and monitoring them, cautioning the affected or to be affected people about the Dos and Don'ts, of scotching rumours and preventing panic and confusion, of establishing contacts, of identifying the needy spots and focusing attention on them, and generally by assisting the authorities, voluntary organizations and volunteers in reaching, informing and assuring the affected ones of the assistance and the measures taken, for their relief. During the onslaught of the disaster, what is of utmost importance is to keep the morale of the people high, to create self-confidence in them, to prevent panic and to maintain order by assuring and making available the necessary help readily and quickly. The media can help, in many ways in ensuring these conditions.

Twelfth chapter is an important aspects in communication .It is discussing the"History Of Communication And Its Application In Multicultural, Multilingual Social System In India Across Ages"I was aprivileged member to present this paper by using video conferencing facility in 5th International conference of Russian Communication Association held in Tver State University,Russia on 9-11 Sept 2010.

The history of communication dates back to the earliest signs of *cavemen.Communication* can range from very subtle processes of exchange, to full *conversations* and *mass communication. Human* communication was revolutionized with *speech* perhaps 200,000 years ago, *Symbols* were developed about 30,000 years ago and *writing* about 7,000. On a much shorter scale, there have been major developments in the field of *telecommunication* in the past few centuries.

Evolution of the *brain* differentiated humans from animals, as among other things it allowed humans to master a very efficient form of communication - speech. A mutation of the *FOXP2 gene*, which occurred in *homo sapiens* about 200,000 years ago, was likely responsible for much of this change.

The imperfection of speech, which nonetheless allowed easier dissemination of *ideas* and stimulated *inventions*, eventually resulted in the creation of new forms of communications, improving both the range at which people could communicate and the longevity of the information. All of those inventions were based on the key concept of the *symbol*: a conventional representation of a *concept.*

India being the largest democracy in the world with a civilization more than five thousand years old boasts of multiple cultural origins. The cultural origins of the Indian subcontinent can be traced back to the Indus Valley Civilizations, the remains of which are cherished even today. Since the late 16th century India was under the influence of the British Empire until 15th August 1947 the day when India gained independence. India is a land of diverse cultures, religions and communities. There is great diversity in our traditions, manners, habits, tastes and customs. Each and every region of the country portrays different customs and traditions. But though we speak different languages yet we are all Indians. 'Unity in Diversity' has been the distinctive feature of our culture.

Thirteenth chapter discusses International Terrorism. The title of chapter is —"International Terrorism—Role, Responsibility and Operation of Media Channels".It was publsished by Pragyan,- A Journal of Mass Communication of Institute of Management Studies, Dehradun in June, 2009.The paper discusses how news channels has responded to the coverage of terrorism.

"Terrorism" is a term that cannot be given a stable defintion. Or rather, it can, but to do so forstalls any attempt to examine the major feature of its relation to television in the contemporary world. As the central public arena for organising ways of picturing and talking about social and political life, TV plays a pivotal role in the contest between competing defintions, accounts and explanations of terrorism.

Television's ability to strike this balance is not just a question for news, current affairs and documentary production however. The images and accounts of terrorism offered by televsion fiction and entertainment are also important in orchestrating the continual contest between the discourse of government and the state, the discourses of legitimated opposition groups, and the discourses of insurgent movements. This struggle is not simply for visibility—to be seen and heard. It is also for credibility—to have one's views discussed seriously and one's case examined with care. The communicative weapons in this battle are unevenly distributed however.

While international media has shown some restraint covering the terror attacks in Mumbai at seven different places,Indian Television channels went up in telling the details about the strength and location of NSG commandos, and marcos involved in operation black Tornado.

If there is a war on terrorism to be won, it will not be on the back of strategies that promote fear, ignorance and intolerance. But the actions of governments in North America and Europe would suggest otherwise. Since September 11 2001 the democracies of Europe and North America have been dangerously ambivalent about their commitment to citizens' rights and press freedom. Their actions have reinforced cynicism in autocratic regimes about western commitment to fundamental rights and, even worse, they have inspired a fresh round of media oppression in countries that routinely victimise and intimidate journalists.

Finally I would like to say one thing that no effort is errorless and errors inspire you to commit fewer errors in next step. The subjects which are picked up here, debated and are discussed may not reflect the opinion of masses but I do hope that these issue will play a point in the days of metamorphosis in the India and the rest of world.

As discussed in first few paragraphs about the changes in U.S. media, the same is applicable about Indian Mass Media and Communication industry and academia. Indian academic and industry is rapidly changing and so is the way we do the research. With this hope that my this effort to discuss these points in this book, will trigger your thought process to contribute in these crucial years of Mass Media and Communication industry as well as academia.

1

An Analytical Study of 'Sanskrit' and 'Panini' as Foundation of Speech Communication in India and the World

Vagarthaviva Sampraktau, Vagartha Pratipattaye/
Jagtah Pitrau Vande, Parvati Parmeshvarau//

–Kalidasa

1. Objective

Sanskrit is the most ancient language known to man. It is believed to be the very origin of language itself; that from which all languages have derived their breath or evolved. The Vedas, the first scriptures of human kind, were written in the Sanskrit language.

The objective of this research paper studies to understand the oldest and finest language in the world as a foundation to human speech communication. The study speaks on basic objectives of Sanskrit grammar and its one of the premier grammarian 'Panini' who constructed more than 3,000 *Sutras* (formulas) of Sanskrit. The objective analyses the language through its oldest form to it is adopted now. The paper further analyses the work and life of 'Panini' who organised foundation to the Sanskrit as a medium of speech communication.

2. Introduction and Description of 'Sanskrit'

Samskrtam, or for short **sanskrit,** or samskrtavak is an ancient sacred language of Bharatavarsha titled as the language of Hinduism and the Vedas and the classical literary language of India. The name Sanskrit means **refined, consecrated** and **sanctified.** Believed to be as the 'high' language and used mainly for religious and scientific discourse, still hundreds of millions of people use Sanskrit in their daily lives. However, despite these numbers, its cultural worth stands unsurpassed.

Deeply rooted belief among Indians holds Sanskrit as the language of the Devas (Gods), hence this language was held during the Vedic period (6,000 - 8,000 years ago) as *Daiviya Vak* (the Divine speech). The great grammarian, Panini, structured this language with his grammar in the 7th century BC, and henceforth, it became referred to as *Samskritam* a new classical form of sanskrit.

Numerous important works on cultural, spiritual and scientific subjects, were written in this ancient language. All of the classic literature of Vedic times written in Sanskrit, included the classical texts of yoga, Vedanta, upanishad and other spiritual and philosophical schools of ancient times, as well as the historical texts on the great sciences of astrology, astronomy, medicine, architecture and the physical sciences.

The language is extremely regular, almost mathematical in its grammar and formulation. It is considered a sacred and mystical language with the script called Devanagari, meaning "used in the cities of the Gods." Words constructed from a number of roots, each considered to have refined quality, embody the meaning themselves, rather than taped arbitrary symbols. Sound considered the subtlest of all five elements, if controlled can help manipulate matter, through the chanting of mantras.

3. Etymology of 'Sanskrit'

The name *samskrtam* is derived from the past participle form *samskrtah* (self-made, self-done) of the verb *sam(s)kar-* 'to make self', where sam- 'with, together, self' and *(s)kar-* 'do, make'. In modern usage, the verbal adjective *samskrta* has come to mean "cultured". The language referred to as *samskrtah vak* "the language of cultured", has by definition always been a high language, used for religious and learned discourse and is contrasted with the languages spoken by the people. It is also called *deva-bhasa*, "Language of the Gods".

3.1. Establishment of 'Sanskrit' as One of the Finest Languages

Being the oldest and fines language in the world, for more than three millennia, Sanskrit was the *lingua franca* of the Indian subcontinent – the language of science, knowledge, spirituality and culture. Sanskrit is the common language of the Hindu Scriptures Vedas, Upanishads, Mahabharata, Ramayana and the Puranas. Sanskrit literature is acknowlewdged the richest in the history of mankind. The word Sanskrit literally means "Perfected Language", or "Language brought to formal perfection". Sc ientificlly proved NASA declared it to be "the only unambiguous language on the planet". Recently linguists and computer-scientists have expressed Sanskrit to be the best of languages for use with computers.

Sanskrit is the basis of many modern Indian languages – Hindi, Gujarati, Marathi, Punjabi – as well as the classical Prakrit and the language of Buddhist scripture, Pali. It has also shaped many alien languages including French, German, Russian, English and the South-East Asian languages such as Malay, Javanese, Cambodia, Vietnam, Thai and the Philippines.

Sanskrit is a scientific and systematic language. Its perfect grammar is perfect and has attracted scholars worldwide; Structured by the world's ever greatest grammarian Panini, who defined it with more than 3000 sutras.

3.2. Writing Pattern in Sanskrit Language

Sanskrit uses the Devanagari alphabet like various other Indian and South-East Asian languages.

Devanagari is a phonetic script of 13 vowels (*svara*) and 34 consonants (*vyanjana*). It is known as a 'syllabic script' – every letter has a unique sound and is a single syllable of each word. The script is written from left to right and does not differentiate as upper or lowercase letters. Most letters have a line across the top, which generally extends across the whole word. There are, however, some cases where an individual letter may break the line.

3.3. History and Origin of 'Sanskrit'

The Vedic tradition informs us that mankind in former ages were physically and intellectually by far able than today. Knowledge was passed on by oral reception. The disciples were able to remember everything by hearingand memorising . Thus, writing was not necessary. But at the dawn of the *kali-yuga*, or "age of quarrel" – mankind gradually lost all good qualities. The duration of life decreased, and with the loss of the keen memory the traditional system of teaching ceased to be applicable. To prevent its decay, the Vedic wisdom had to be conserved in written form, about 5,000 years ago by the divine incarnation Shri Vyasadeva. He compiled the presently existing Vedic literature, namely the four Vedas, the Upanishads, the Puranas and the Mahabharata. Thus, he tried to preserve the original wisdom of mankind for the oncoming ages.

At that time, devanagari was the language of the whole civilised universe earth. But due to lack of training and careless pronunciation, the uneducated people developed numerous dialects. Before, such lingual alienation had been carefully avoided, since the material and spiritual power of the language greatly depends on its purity. Now, however, various dialects came up, after gradually deviating from the original language, which could not be called devanagari anymore. New dialects, called prakrta, came forth.

With the further progress, these prakrta dialects spread more, up to the rank of dominating the original language. Finally, their adoption by the educated circles alarmed the sages and scholars of that time. Together with its language, they foresaw the dying-out of the root of Vedic culture. Thus, they invested enormous intintive time and effort to design a standardised grammar, aimed at preserving Sanskrit in its original purity. Although unnecessary before, this measure seemed to be the only means counter the increasing cultural, intellectual and spiritual demise of the society.

The most successful and ence most prominent amongst these grammarians was Panini. His grammar, surpassing all others' in objective construction and precision, became the standard undisputedly until today. Panini laboured to join the original Sanskrit into an exact framework of rules, thus preserving it for the posterity. Since this revalution, this language is called Sanskrit, "joined together, refined".

According to the Vedic version, Sanskrit did not grow out of the prakrta languages; rather, they have developed from the original Sanskrit, called devanagari. The present Sanskrit is nothing but the successful attempt to conserve the original language and to prevent its further alienation.

3.4. The Dominance of 'Sanskrit' Over Other Languages

Until 1100 A.D., Sanskrit was the official language of the whole of India. Its dominance is scene in the wealth of literature of widely diverse genres including religious, philosophical, fiction (short stories, fables, novels, and plays); scientific (linguistics, mathematics, astronomy, and medicine), as well as law and politics.

During Muslim invasions onwards, Sanskrit gradually became displaced by patronised common languages by the Muslim kings it is seen as a tactic to suppress Indian cultural and religious tradition and supplant it with their own beliefs. But significiantly they could not undo the literary and spiritual/ritual use of Sanskrit. Even today, there is a strong movement to return Sanskrit to the status of "the national language of India."

Sanskrit, being a language derived from simple monosyllabic verbal roots through the addition of appropriate prefixes and suffixes according to precise grammatical laws, is intrinsically incorporated with an infinite capacity to grow, adapt, and expand to the requirements of change in a rapidly evolving world. Even in the last two centuries, due to the rapid advances in technology and science, a literature abundant with new and improvised vocabulary has come into existence. Although such additions are based on the grammatical principles of Sanskrit, and mostly composed of Sanskrit roots, still contributions from Hindi and other national and international languages have been assimilated. For example, the word for television, *duradarshanam*, meaning "that which provides a 'vision' of what is far away" is derived purely from Sanskrit; whereas the word for motorcar, *motaryanam*, borrows from the English.

Furthermore, there are at least a dozen periodicals published in Sanskrit, all-India news broadcast in Sanskrit, television shows and feature movies produced in Sanskrit, one village of 3,000 inhabitants who communicate through Sanskrit alone (not to mention countless smaller intellectual communities throughout India), and schools where Sanskrit is fostered. "Contemporary Sanskrit" is alive and well.

3.5. The Extraordinary Comments About 'Sanskrit'

An extraordinary attribute of Sanskrit is it offers direct accessibility to anyone to the elevation where mathematics and music, brain and heart, analytical and intuitive, scientific and spiritual the differen t constituents unite.

Relevant to this, an astounding discovery made at the NASA research center keeps into a new dimension. The following quote is from an article: *'Sanskrit and Artificial Intelligence'*, which appeared in *AI (Artificial Intelligence)* magazine in spring of 1985, written by NASA researcher Rick Briggs:

> "In the past twenty years, much time, effort, and money has been expended on designing an unambiguous representation of natural languages to make them accessible to computer processing. These efforts have centered around creating schemata designed to parallel logical relations with relations expressed by the syntax and semantics of natural languages, which are clearly cumbersome and ambiguous in their function as vehicles for the transmission of logical data.

> Understandably, there is a widespread belief that natural languages are unsuitable for the transmission of many ideas that artificial languages can render with great precision and mathematical rigour.
>
> But this dichotomy, which has served as a premise underlying much work in the areas of liguistics and artificial intelligence, is a false one. There is at least one language, Sanskrit, which for the duration of almost 1000 years was a living spoken language with a considerable literature of its own. Besides works of literary value, there was a long philosophical and grammatical tradition that has continued to exist with undiminished vigour until the present century. Among the accomplishments of the grammarians can be reckoned a method for paraphrasing Sanskrit in a manner that is identical not only in essence but in form with current work in Artificial Intelligence. This article demonstrates that a natural language can serve as an artificial language also, and that much work in AI has been reinventing a wheel millennia old."

This discovery of monumental significance is mind-boggling to consider the affordance to us a language spoken for at least 5,000 years and in every respect a perfected language for enlightened communication. But the most stunning aspect of the discovery: NASA, the most advanced research center in the world for cutting-edge technology, is that the spiritual language Sanskrit is the only unambiguous spoken language on the planet.

3.6. Sanskrit—A Language of 'Mantra'

Words of power subtly attuned to the unseen harmonies of the matrix of creation, the world is yet unformed. *Vak* (speech) incorporates both the sense of voice and word. It has four forms of expression. The first, *para*, represents cosmic *ideation* which arises from absolute divine presence. The second, *pasyanti* (seeing), is *vak* as subject, the seeing creates the object of *madhyama-vak*, and the third and subtle form of speech manifests as *vaikhari-vak*, the gross production of letters in spoken speech. This implies the possibility of having speech oriented to a direct living truth which transcends individual preoccupation with the limited information available through the senses. Spoken words as such are creative living things of power. They communicateto the essence of what they describe, and mean exactly which reflects the profound inter-relatedness of life.

The unique organisation of the alphabet focuses one's attention on qualities and patterns of articulated sound in a way that occurs in no other language. By paying continuous attention to the point of location, degree of resonance, and effort of breath, one's awareness becomes more and more consumed by the direct experience of articulated sound. This in itself produces an unprecedented clarity of mind and revelry in the joy of language, as every combination of sound follows strict laws which essentially make possible an uninterrupted flow of the most perfect euphonic blending of letters into words and verse.

3.7. Limitation of Sanskrit in English Translations

As Hinduism expands in the West, the emerging forms of this ancient tradition are naturally being reflected through the medium of Western languages, most prominently through English. But the meanings of words are not easily moved from one language to another. The more two distant languages are separated by geography, latitude and climate, etc., the more the meanings of words and ultimately the worldview shift. The differences between the Indian regional languages and Sanskrit are minuscule when compared to the differences between a Western language such as English and Sanskrit.

With this problem in mind, the great difficultly comes in understanding Hinduism in the West, whether from the perspective of conversion, or from a second generation of Hindus, it is not all too easy to approach Hinduism with foreign concepts of religion in mind. It is natural to unknowingly approach Hinduism with Christian, Jewish and Islamic notions of God, soul, heaven, hell and sin in mind. We translate *brahman* as God, *atman* as soul, *pap* as sin, *dharma* as religion. But *brahman* is not the same as God; nor *atman* is equivalent to the soul and *pap* and *dharma* are much more than mere sin and religion. For a true comprehension of sacred writings, such as the Upanishads or the Bhagavad Gita, one must read them on their own terms and not from the perspective of another religious tradition. Because the Hinduism now developing in the West is being reflected through the lens of Christianity, Judaism and Islam, the theological uniqueness of Hinduism is being compromised, or completely lost.

Ideally, anyone attempting to understand Hinduism should have a working knowledge of Sanskrit. Ideally, all Hindu educational institutions and temples should teach Sanskrit, and all Hindu youth should learn Sanskrit.

3.8. Marvel of Sanskrit Language

Indian literature includes everything identical to the word 'literature' in its broadest sense, religious and mundane, epic and lyric, dramatic and didactic poetry, narrative and scientific prose, as well as oral poetry and song. In the Vedas (3,000 BC-1,000 BC), one finds such expressions as "I am standing in water but I am very thirsty", one marvels at the consistant rich heritage which is both modern and traditional. It is, therefore, incorrect to say that ancient Indian literature include only the religious classics of Hinduism, Buddhism and Jainism.

Vedic poets called the rishis envisioned the l;ofty truths of cosmic functioning at all levels of existence. *Devatas* of the vedic poetry reflectthe manifestations of the divine force of the One Supreme. Vedas tend importance to *yajna* (sacrifice). Purusa sukta (Rigveda, 10.90) describes the whole creation as a *yajna* extended by the divine forces of nature. Etymologically, *yajna* means 'the worship of the divine, coordination and giving (sacrifice)'. These three elements together, vision, coordination and giving, provide a basic paradigm for any creative act.

4. Research Methodology

'Sanskrit' and '*Rishis*' who designed the language are beyond the reach of researchers. It is further stressed that the oldest written documents of civilisation–the Vedas are not actually written by any human instead they are procured by 'Brahma'–The creator of this universe. But the scholars of this divine language had tried their best to explore the marvels of 'Sanskrit' and so do I.

I have placed myself best to utilise my little comprehension of the language at foundation level of my study, which helped me apply various methodologies to extract the study as foundation of speech communication. I must express my thankfulness to the teacher shri Shiva Pati Mishra, who taught me the basics of this 'Language of the Gods'.

The researchers through various secondary tools apply four research methodologies to extract the study—Conceptual Research, Historical Research, Analytical Research and Descriptive Research. Along with secondary tools I have interacted with some noblest brains of the language to owe an insight to understand the basic grammar on evolution and growth of this magnificent language as primary mode of communication in ancient India.

The Historical research methodology with its application understands the development of 'Sanskrit' in earlier period. A historical perspective is placed in the beginning of paper on status of Vedic Sanskrit. The methodology narrates the truth of 'Panini's' existence and his life. The conceptual research methodology deals with Panini's marvel book

'Ashtadhyayi'. It helped understand the basic structure of the book, which is foundation in 'Sanskrit' grammar. Analytical research methodology analyses the contents of 'Sanskrit' documents and Panini's grammar. By using analytical research methodology, the researcher understood and presented the brilliance of Sanskrit and Panini's grammar as foundation of speech communication.

Researcher believes that 'Sanskrit' and 'Panini' both have played crucial role in organising Human Speech Communication. By using above mentioned research methodologies the researcher has achieved this conclusion, and these methodologies are the only source in their primary and secondary form to reach on this result.

5. 'Panini' – The Foundation Stone of Sanskrit Grammar

Panini is known for his Sanskrit grammar, particularly for his formulation of the 3,959 rules of Sanskrit morphology, syntax and semantics in Ashtadhyayi, the foundational text of the grammatical branch of the Vedanga, the auxiliary scholarly disciplines of Vedic religion.

5.1. Role of Panini and the Ashtadhyayi as Foundation of Speech Communication

Although Panini refers to previous texts like the Unadisutra, Dhatupatha, and Ganapatha, Ashtadhyayi is the earliest known work on descriptive linguistics. Together with the work of his immediate predecessors (Nirukta, Nighantu, Pratishakyas) it stands at the beginning of the history of linguistics itself. His theory of morphological analysis was more advanced and no any equivalent Western theory was developed until mid 20th century. His analysis of noun compounds still forms the basis of modern linguistic theories of compounding, such as *bahuvrihi* and *dvandva.* Panini's grammar conventionally takes to mark the end of the period of Vedic Sanskrit, introducing Classical Sanskrit.

Panini defines Classical Sanskrit, so it is assumed he lived at the end of the Vedic period. He notes a few special rules, marked *chandasi* ("in the hymns") in the Vedic scriptures; absolete in the spoken language of his time. These predicate substantially that the Vedic Sanskrit was reduced to a comprehensible dialect.

An important hint for the dating of Panini's true is the use of the word *yavanani* (in 4.1.49, either "Greek woman", or "Greek script"). Some Greeks, such as the Persian admiral Scylax of Caryanda, were present in Gandhara as co-citizens of the Persian empire, well before the conquests of Alexander the Great in the 330s BC. The name transmitted via Old Persian *yavana*, and the administrative languages Elamite or Aramaic, so the occurrence of yavanani taken in isolation allows for a terminus post quem as early as 519 BC, i.e., the time of Darius the Great's Behistun inscription that includes the Indian province of Gandara (Sanskrit Gandhara).

There is no certitude whether Panini used writing for the composition of his work, though it is generally agreed upon that he knew of a form of writing, based on references to such words as "script" and "scribe" in his Ashtadhyayi. These must have referred to Aramaic or early Kharosthi writing. It is wisely believed by some that a work of such volume and complexity would have been difficult to compile without written notes, though others have argued that he might have composed it with the help of a group of students whose several memories served him as 'notepads' (as is typical in Vedic learning). Writing first reappears in India in the form of the Brahmi script from the 3rd century BC in the Ashokan inscriptions.

However, Panini's work is purely grammatical and lexicographic, cultural and geographical inferences can be easily drawn from the vocabulary he used in examples, and from his references to fellow grammarians, this particularly show he was a north-western person. New deities referred to in his work include *Vasudeva* (4.3.98). The concept of *dharma* is attested in his example sentence (4.4.41), *dharmam carati* – "he observes the law" (cf. Taittiriya Upanishad 1.11).

The Ashtadhyayi, by far the most complex, is the earliest complete grammar of Classical Sanskrit.its brevity and completeness stands unmatched in any ancient grammar on any language. It taking material from the lexical lists (Dhatupatha, Ganapatha) as input it describes algorithms to be applied to them for the generation of symmetrical words. Highly systematised and technical, Inherent in its approach are the concepts of the phoneme, the morpheme and the root. His rules bear a reputation for perfection – that is, they are claimed to describe Sanskrit morphology fully, without any redundancy. A consequence of his grammar's focus on brevity is its highly unintuitive structure, reminiscent of modern notations such as the "Backus-Naur Form". His sophisticated logical rules and technique have been widely influential in ancient and modern linguistics.

It looks likely that Panini's grammar and the Rig Veda are the only two texts that were passed from one generation to another without any amendments. In the Ashtadhyayi, language is observed in a manner that has no parallel among Greek or Latin grammarians. marks the entry of the non-sacred into Indian speech, which according to Renou and Filliozat, then defines the linguistic expression of that speech.

The thinkers of ancient India being primarily linguists, it is impossible to understand fully the works such as by Shankara, Ramanuja and Madhva without a knowledge of Panini. The Ashtadhyayi is fundamental to the fashionof their thinking. It is not a didactic grammar, for it presupposes a knowledge of Sanskrit. Gradually, mainly after the 10th century CE, some manuals were produced to reorganise the Ashtadhyayi for didactic purposes. These manuals generally were simpler in structures and less ambitious than their source Ashtadhyayi. The Ashtadhyayi consists of 3,959 *sutras* (sutrani) or rules, distributed among eight chapters, each further subdivided into four sections, or *padas* (*padah*).

From examples and the rules, depending on the context of the discourse, additional information pertaining to the geographical, cultural and historical context of Panini can be discerned.

5.2. Shiva Sutras

The Shiva Sutras illustrate a phonemic notational system through the fourteen initial lines preceding the Ashtadhyayi. This introduces different clusters of phonemes that serve special purposes in the morphology of Sanskrit, and are referred to throughout the text. Each cluster, called *pratyhara* ends with a dummy sound called *anubandha* (the so called IT index), which acts as a symbolic reference for the list. Within the main text, these clusters, referred through the *anubandhas*, are related to various grammatical functions.

5.3. Dhatupatha

The *Dhatupatha* inhibits as a lexicon of Sanskrit verbal roots subservient to Ashtadhyayi. This lexicon has the organisation of the ten present classes of Sanskrit, i.e. the roots are grouped by the form of their stem in the present tense.

The ten present classes of Sanskrit are:

1. *bhuadayah* (root-full grade thematic presents)
2. *ad-adayah* (root presents),
3. *ju-ho-ti-adayah* (reduplicated presents),
4. *div-adayah* (ya thematic presents),
5. *su-adayah* (nu presents),
6. *tud-adayah* (root-zero grade thematic presents),
7. *rudh-adayah* (n-infix presents),

8. *tan-adayah* (no presents),
9. *kri-adayah* (ni presents),
10. *cur-adayah* (aya presents, causatives).

These classes are directly inherited from Proto-Indo-European.The small number of class 8 verbs are a secondary group derived from class 5 roots, and class 10 is a special case, in that any verb can form class 10 presents, then assuming causative meaning. The roots specifically listed as belonging to class 10 are those for which any other form has fallen obselete (causative deponents, so to speak).

5.4. Ganapatha

The *Ganapatha* is a list of groups of primitive nominal stems used by the Ashtadhyayi.

Commentary

The *Mahabhasya* ("great commentary") by Patañjali on the Ashtadhyayi is one among the three most commendable works in Sanskrit grammar. With Patañjali Indian linguistic science took its definite form. The system thus established is extremely detailed as to *shiksha* (phonology, including accent) and *vyakarana* (morphology). Syntax is scarcely touched, but *nirukta* (etymology) is amply discussed, to the extent of semantic explanations. Pitaniah is interpreted to be a defence of Panini, who commented on *Sutras* meaningfully. The contributions of Patañjali lies in the way of the principles of grammar are enunciated by him.

5.5. Panini and Bhattikavya

The curriculum of Indian learnin g in late classical times had at its heart a system of grammatical study and linguistic analysis.The core text for this study was the Astadhyayi of Panini, the *sine qua non* of learning. It had been the object of intense study for ten centuries prior to the composition of the *Bhattikavya.* Bhatti's purpose was plainly to provide a study aid to Panini's text and used the examples existing in grammatical commentaries particularly in the context of the gripping and morally improving story of the *Ramayana.* To the dry grammar Bhatti has given juice. The morale behind the poetic presentation was that the author wanted to teach this advanced science through a relatively easy and pleasant medium. In his own words in Bhattikavya (22.33-34).

> "This composition is like a lamp to those who perceive the meaning of words and like a hand mirror for a blind man to those without grammar. This poem, which is to be understood by

means of a commentary, is a joy to those sufficiently learned: through my fondness for the scholar I have here slighted the dullard.

The traditional story accounting for the technical, or *shastric* nature of the poem goes that once Bhatti's class on grammar was one day disturbed by an elephant protruding between him and his pupils. This bestial interruption necessitated an interdict of study for a year as prescribed by the solemn law books. To ensure that no vital study time was lost, poetic form was given to grammar as a mode of teaching without resorting to an actual grammatical text.

5.6. Panini and Modern Linguistics

In 19th century Panini's work became known to Europe. There it influenced modern linguistics initially through Franz Bopp, along with Sanskrit scholars such as Ferdinand de Saussure, Leonard Bloomfield, and Roman Jakobson. The impact of Indian ideas on language in Europe was noticed and discussed by Frits staal. After be outlayed the various aspects of the contact, Staal ascertained, the principle of formal rules in language, propounded by Ferdinand de Saussure in 1894 and developed by Noam Chomsky in 1957, has origin in the European exposure to the formal rules of Paninian grammar. Moreover, de Saussure, influenced by Panini and Bhartrihari lectured on Sanskrit for three decades; his proposition of the unity of signifier-signified in the sign is somewhat similar to the notion of Sphoa. The very idea of formal rules can be conveniently applied to areas outside the logic or mathematics, most likely have been catalysed itself by European contact with the works of Sanskrit grammarians.

5.7. Facts About Existence of 'Panini' and His Work

Panini was born in Shalatula, a town near Attock on the Indus river presently in Pakistan. Experts give assumptions dates for Panini in the 4th, 5th, 6th and 7th century BC and without any agreement among historians on the extent of the work he undertook. What is in little doubt is that, given the period in which he worked, he is one of the most innovative people in the whole development of knowledge. However, it is said a little more below about how historians have gone about trying to pinpoint the date when Panini lived.

The belief goes that he and 'Katyayan' were two among disciples in the same *gurukul.* 'Katyayan' was very intelligent while 'Panini' was not much keen on learning and of criticised by his preceptor and student fellow. To get rid of this demerit, he went in Himalayas and observed the faithful penance to Lord Shiva. It is said the pleased Lord of wisdom, Shiva made fourteen sounds as boons played his musical instrument '*Damroo*' and Panini got himself wise, who later composed first grammar of Sanskrit in which he propounded a *sloka* consisting of fourteen words.

> Aiunrilrik Aiyeyong Aiyvoch, Hayavarat, Lanyamgannam, Yamgannam/
> Khafchatath Chatatva Kapaya Shasar Hal//

The above *sloka* consisting of fourteen sounds of Lord Shiva's *Damroo* became base on which the Sanskrit grammar was founded by Panini. Panini was a constructive grammarian who structured a comprehensive and scientific theory of phonetics, phonology and morphology.

In *Astadhyayi* (or *(Astaka)* Panini distinguishes between the language of sacred texts and the usual language of communication. He gives formal formation rules and definitions to describe Sanskrit grammar. He put about 1700 basic elements like nouns, verbs, vowels, consonants etc. into defined classes. The construction of sentences etc., compound nouns etc. is explained as ordered rules operating on underlying structures in a manner similar to modern theory. In many ways Panini's constructions are similar to the way that a mathematical functions defined today.

Joseph writes that "Sanskrit's potential for scientific use was greatly enhanced as a result of the thorough systemisation of its grammar by Panini. ... On the basis of just under 4,000 sutras [rules expressed as aphorisms], he built virtually the whole structure of the Sanskrit language, whose general 'shape' hardly changed for the next two thousand years. ... An indirect consequence of Panini's efforts to increase the linguistic facility of Sanskrit soon became apparent in the character of scientific and mathematical literature. This may be brought out by comparing the grammar of Sanskrit with the geometry of Euclid – a particularly apposite comparison since, whereas mathematics grew out of philosophy in ancient Greece, it was ... partly an outcome of linguistic developments in India."

Joseph continues on making a convincing argument that the algebraic nature of Indian mathematics can be ascertained as a consequence due to the structure of the Sanskrit language. Categorically he suggests that algebraic reasoning, the Indian way of representing numbers by words, and ultimately the development of modern number systems in India, are linked through the structure of language.

Panini ought to be thought of as the pioneer of the modern formal language theory induced to specify computer languages. The Backus Normal

Form discovered independently by John Backus in 1959, is equivalent in its power to that of Panini's notation and has many similar properties. It is fantastic when one thinks concepts fundamental to today's theoretical computer science should have their origin with an Indian genius around 2500 years ago.

However, certain concepts attributed to Panini by certain historians are disputed by others. B Indraji in 1876 claimed the Brahmi numerals developed out of using letters or syllables. Further, Panini in the eighth century BC was the first to come up with the idea of using letters of the alphabet to represent numbers.

There are a number of pieces of evidence to support Indraji's theory. However it is not totally convincing since, the symbols for 1, 2 and 3 clearly do not come from letters but from one, two and three lines respectively. Panini the originator of this idea would seem to have no more behind it than knowing that Panini was one of the most innovative geniuses that world has known so it is not unreasonable. There are works closely associated with the *Astadhyayi* which some historians attribute to Panini, others attribute to authors before and after Panini.

We also promised to return to a discussion of Panini's dates. The usual way to date such texts would be to examine which authors are referred to and which authors refer to the work.

There are ten scholars mentioned by Panini, all contributed to the study of Sanskrit grammar. This indicates that Panini was not a solitary genius but, like Newton, had "stood on the shoulders of giants". But this is absolutely no help in providing dates since there is absolutely no knowledge of when any of these ten lived.

Panini uses many phrases to illustrate his grammar and these have been examined meticulously to see if anything is contained there to indicate a date. Let us illustrate with two actual examples from the *Astadhyayi* which have been the subject of much study. The first is an attempt to see whether there is evidence of Greek influence. The text had to have been written after the conquests of Alexander the Great? There is a little evidence of Greek influence, but there was Greek influence on this north-east part of the Indian subcontinent before the time of Alexander.

Panini a reference makes to nuns. These must be Buddhist nuns and therefore the work must have been written after Buddha. But there is another argument that there were Jaina nuns before the time of Buddha and Panini's reference could equally well be to them.

However, references by others to Panini would appear that the Panini is a poet. Most historians agree that the linguist and the poet are two different people.

Let us sum up with an evaluation of Panini's contribution made by Cardona:

> Panini's grammar has been evaluated from various points of view. After all these different evaluations, I think that the grammar merits asserting ... that it is one of the greatest monuments of human intelligence.

6. Literature Review

There are number of books written on 'Sanskrit' as one of the oldest language in the world. But study was more focused on role of 'Sanskrit' as foundation of speech communication. 'Panini' had played a very crucial role in developing the grammar of 'Sanskrit'. Two books which caught much attention were – '*Panini*' by Saroja Bhate (1995); it is very fascinating on a small price which clarifies about 'Panini' and his book 'Ashtadhyayi'; the second book was '*Panini' A Survey of Research* by George Cardona, which further signifies role of 'Panini' and his contributions towards the grammar of 'Sanskrit'.

A third book, '*The Wonder That Is Sanskrit–Interesting and Amazing Creations in Sanskrit*' deals with some *shloka* of Sanskrit which is referred as '*Adhamkavya*' having amazing meaning. I have quoted this book in the ending of my paper. Also I have gone through various 'websites' dedicated on 'Sanskrit' and have quoted them.

Since my primary objective was to establish a relation between 'Sanskrit', 'Panini' and their role as foundation of speech communication hence I have gone through number of other papers, journals and organisation which work and publish content on 'Sanskrit'. I have done extensive search through verbal communication with noble brains on Sanskrit to carry out my survey and study.

Finally, I hope that my extensive search gave me result in establishing the relation between Sanskrit's role as foundation of human communication in the world, and Panini had played a remarkable role in designing the foundation of Sanskrit Grammar.

7. The Mercurial Sanskrit–Amazing Creations in Sanskrit

There in Sanskrit is a whole body of literature based on a play with the language. This is but more in nature of linguistic acrobatics. These writings are often obtuse and difficult to understand because they need a complete mastery over all the complex grammatical structures. This is why known as '*Adhamakavyas*', they mean poems of lower quality. However, they demonstrate the amazing possibilities inherent in the language.

Kalidasa, Bhartrihari, Magha and Shriharsha have made use of '*Adhamkavyas*', sometimes in their major works. Instances where entire epic have been written in this style are easy to find. These epics are part of 'Alankarashashtra'.

Here let us look briefly at a few examples to enjoy their flavour and to understand how magnificently these masters have enriched the legacy of 'Sanskrit' to maintain its place as one of the foundation language of human speech communication.

7.1. Varnacitras

The *varnacitras* are *slokas* written with certain constraints on the use of consonants. For example, the following *sloka* have all the 33 consonants in Sanskrit in their natural order:

Kah Khagaughang Chichchauja Jhangyo Tautheedaddhanah/
Tathaodadheen Paafarbabheermayo Rilvashishang Sahah//

"Who is he, the lover of the birds, pure in intelligence, expert in the stealing the strength of others, leader among the destroyer of the enemies, the steadfast, the fearless, the one who filled the ocean? He is the King Maya, the repository of the blessings that can destroy the foes."

And here is *sloka* which uses only three consonants out of 33, Da, Va, and Na:

Devanam Nandano Devo, Nodno Ved Nindinaam/
Divam Dudava Naden Dane Danava Nandinah//

"The God (Vishnu) who causes pleasure to other gods and pain to opponants of Vedas, filled the heaven with loud sound as he killed Hiranyakashyap.

This is a *sloka* which uses only two consonants, Bha and Ra.

Bhuribhir Bharibhir Bheerabhu Bharair Bhirebhire/
Bhereere Bhibhir Bhrabhair Bheerubhir Bhairibha//

"The fearless elephant, who was like a burden to the earth because of its heavy weight, whose sound was like kettle-drum, and who was like a dark cloud, attacked the enemy elephant.

Most amazingly, entire *sloka* have been written using a single consonant-Na.

Na Non Nunno Nunneno Naana Naana nana Nanu/
Nunno Anunno Nanu nneno Naanena Nunn Nunn Nut//

"A man is not a man who is wounded by a low man. Similarly, he is also not a man who wounds a low man. The wounded one is not considered if his master is unwounded. And he who wounds a man who is already wounded, is not a man.

7.2. Sthanacitras and Svaracitras:

The *sthanacitras* are formed either by using the consonants of only one group or avoiding certain groups. This is the *sloka* using only gutturals:

Aga Gaangaang Kaakaak Gaahkaagh Kaakhaa/
Ahaahaank Khagangakag Kangak Gakhag Kaakak//

O you (the traveller of many countries), who bathes in tortous current of rippling Ganga; you have no acquaintance with the sorrowful sound of the suffering world; you have the ability to go till the Meru mountain; you are not under the control of crooked senses. You, being the dispeller of sins, have come on this land.

In the *Svaracitras* the restrictions are on the use of vowels. This *sloka* uses only the vowel 'ee' in the first line and the vowel 'a' in the second line:

Kshiti Sthiti Mitikshipti Vidhivinnidhi Siddhilit/
Mam trayaksh Namdaksh Har Smarhar Smar//

"O Lord Shiva, the possessor of three eyes, the knower of existence, measurer and destroyer of the earth, enjoyer of the eight fold superhuman power and nine treasures of Kubera, you killed Daksha and Kamdeva. O Lord, do remember me.

Next is a *sloka* formed entirely with the vowel 'u':

Urugum Dugurum Yutsu Chakru Shustushtuvuh Puru/
Lulubhuh Pupushur Mutsu Mumumur Hur nu Muhurmuhuh//

"The gods took refuge in Brihaspati, the lord of speech, the perceptor of the gods in heaven, when they went for battle. They prayed so that he would remain happy and strong, and not withdraw into unconsciousness, again and again.

7.3. Amita Compositions

There are many other possibilities in the interplay of consonants, vowels and syllables or the words resulting from them. This *sloka* has an interesting sound effect through the use of 'Ka' and 'La'. This type of composition is called '*Amita*', where the same letter are used frequently.

Bakul Kali Kaal Laamni, Kalkanthi Kal Kalakule Kaale/
Kalya Kalavatoapi Hi Kalyati Kalita Srtam Madanah//

"Madana' the god of love, uses even the spots of the moon as his beautiful weapon at the time when ' Bakula' plant shines with new buds and when the cuckoos and women with melodious voices fill the air with their enchanting sounds.

7.4. Gaticitras

The next category of *chitrakavyas* is the gaticitras. These are variations of what are known as palindromes in English-words or sentences that remain the same even in their mirror images. For example 'noon' and 'eve' are examples of palindromic words. And 'able was I ere I saw Elba' is an example of palindromic sentence.

Here we have a verse in Sanskrit where each line is palindrome; that is, it does not change when read forward or backward. The *sloka* therefore has an axis of symmetry at the centre.

Vaarnaag Gabheera Saa Saaraabheeg Ganarava/
Kaaritaari Vadha Sena Naasedha Vari Taarikaa//

"It is very difficult to face this army which is endowed with elephants as big as mountains. This is a very big army and shouting of frightened people is heard, It has slain its enemies.

Here is an example from a poem where in each *sloka* the first line describes Rama and the second line Krishna. The striking feature is that the second line is always the reverse of the first line.

Tam Bhoosutamuktim Udaarhaasam Vande Yato Bhavya Bhavam Dayashreeh/
Shri Yadavam Bhavyabhatoya Devam Sanharda Muktim Sutasubhutam/

The first line addressed to Rama in prose order is:

Bhoosutamuktim Udaarhaasam Bhavya Bhavam Yato Dayashreeh Tam Vande//

I bow down before krishna, the descendant of Yadava family, who is the lord of sun as well as the moon, who liberated even her (Pootna) who wanted to bring and end to his life, and who is the soul of this entire universe.

7.5. Chitrabandhas

In the *chitrabandhas*, when the sloka is written out, the letters form interesting geomatric pattern. In this example the alternate letters of the first and second '*padas*' and of the third and fourth '*padas*' are the same.

The design is known as '*gomutrika*' or the crisscross pattern formed by urine of moving cow.

Kaangakshan Pulom Tanayastan Peeditaani
Vakshah Sthalo Utthit Rayaanchan Peeditani/
Paayaad Paaya Bhayato Namuchi Prahari
Maayaam Pasya Bhavato Ambumucham Prasari//

"May Indra, who uses thunderbolt as his weapon,who dispereses the clouds in the sky,who desires to embrace and enjoy the pleasures of the bosoms of his consort Sachi,the daughter of demon Puloma, May that Indra, having removed all illusions,protect you from fear of all dangers and misfortunes.

7.6. Samasya

We now come to some other varieties of *chitrakavyas.* There is a variety known as *samasya.* Here the last line or the fourth quarter of *sloka* is given to a poet,but this line does not seem to make sense or appears to be absurd. The challenge for poet is to create the remaining three quarters in a matching meter,giving meaning to last quarter.

For example the last quarter given to a poet is '*Mrigat Sighah Palayate*' meaning 'the lion runs away from deer'. The verse created by poet was:

Tishth Arjunadya Sangrame Tvam Hanishyamyaham Sharaih/
Tishtahmi Karna Kim Mudham Mrigat Singhah Palayate//

"Karan says; O Arjuna, stand(there); I will kill you in battle by my arrows.

"Arjuna replies; Look I am satnding here. Does the lion run away from deer?

The next example is from Kalidasa. He was given as the last quarter just the sounds, *thathan thathan than thatthatthan thathan tha.* Kalidas came out with the *sloka* in '*Indravjra*' meter, which describes a scene in the palace as Ayodhya was getting ready for the coronation of Rama. The verse is:

Ramabhisheke Madvivhlaya Hastachyuto Hemghtas Tarunyah/

Sopanm Saadya Karoti Shabdam thathan thathan thatthathan thathan tha//

"During the coronation ceremony of Rama a golden pot fell on the staircase from the hands of young maidan, excited and happy. While rolling down the steps the golden pot made the sound *Thathan thathan thatthathan thathan tha.*

7.7. Some Interesting Devotional Verses

The devotional movement, in India have projected the rise to different type of poetic expressions. Here we have two verses in praise of Lord Shiva and Goddess Parvati:

Swayam Panchmukhah Putrau Gajanan Shdananu/
Digambarah Katham Jeeved Annpurna Na Chet Gribe//

"He himself has five faces; of his two sons, Ganesha has an elephant face and Kartikeya is of six faces. How then would Lord Shiva live, if Annapurna (another name of Parvati as the giver of food) was not there in house?

Swayam Maheshah Shwashuro Nageshah, Sakha Dhaneshah Tanyo Ganeshah/
Tathapi Bhikshatanmev Shanbhoh Baleeyasee Kevalam Eeshwarechcha//

"He is himself the Lord of gods, his father-in-law, Himalaya, the lord of mountains, his friend Kubera is Lord of wealth, his son Ganesha is the Lord of 'ganas', and yet Lord Shiva begs and lives on alms. Indeed, the will of the supreme is more mighty than all else.

8. Conclusion

Sanskrit is one of the world's oldest and richest languages. It has been as the foundation of human speech communication and an origin point to many other regional languages in India and abroad. It has catered to the need of human civilisation in more grammatical and organised form. The creation of '*Ashtadhyayi*' as a sanskrit grammar has strenthened the foundation of speech.

Science has now also proved Sanskrit to be based on root sounds, or vibrations of the Universe. As Quantum physics now reveals the fact that everything consists of vibration. The primary essence of any object or phenomena, could be thought of as its own unique pattern or composite patterns of vibration.

It is said, the language of Sanskrit itself took evolution from these very root sounds, or vibrations of the Universe. The alphabets that make up Sanskrit words represent these core sounds, as *bijas*. Whilst in state of deep resonance with the cosmos (meditation), the Rishis, the ancient scientists of spirits, could perceive these *bija* sounds. This profound sense of perception recognised the inherent sounds of each and every thing.

A Sanskrit word is not merely an arbitrary word chosen to name something, but an actual reflection of the inherent 'sound' of that object, concept or phenomena. In fact, proper and perfect pronunciation of

Sanskrit words, can replicate the exact nature, or essence of.

If one's mind utterly pure, upon hearing this perfectly pronounced symbols, the Sanskrit words, the images of that object, idea, etc., immediately appear within the mind and the 'field of understanding' of this individual. It culminates even one has never seen or heard of the thing or idea before. Likewise, the perfect pronunciation of a Sanskrit word has the power to manifest and/or influence that particular thing. Thus Sanskrit, for this very reason, is referred to be the 'perfect language'.

This is, sufficiently the essence of the principles behind *mantra* chanting in the vedic tradition. Today there may be very few to possess this precise knowledge and ability of 'perfect enunciation', and fewer still pure enough of mind to be able to receive the innate truths through this language upon hearing it.

Finally, I beg leissure to end up this research paper with an interesting story related to one of the greatest poets of Sanskrit and all times—Kalidasa :

Once it went a serious discussion in the court of King Bhoja, Kalidasa was his court poet. He was absent that day but upon a thought Bhoja pondered over; what would be the version of the verse Kalidasa would compose if the king passes away suddenly. Bhoja was so taken up by the idea that he went with his one of the ministers to the residence of Kalidasa where he stayed hidden behind the door. The minister very sorrowfully informed Kalidasa that king Bhoja had suddenly passed away. Overcome by grief and sorrow he burst forth through the verse:

Adya Dhara Niradhara Niralamba Saraswai/
Panditah Khanditah Sarve Bhoraje Divangate//

"Today Dhara (the kingdom of Bhoja), is without a support, even goddess Saraswati has no support, the poets, the scholars are all overcome with grief with the passing away of Bhoja.

The king so moved walked in. Everybody taken aback wondered what Kalidasa was to do now. Kalidasa immediately with a new verse, echoed the former verse yet with a completely new meaning.

Adya Dhara Sadadhara Sadalamba Saraswat/
Panditah Manditah Sarve Bhojraje Bhuamgate//

"Today Dhara (the kingdom of Bhoja) has gained its support,and also the goddess Sarswati.The poets and scholars are now all adorned with joy with the coming of king Bhoja on this earth.

Bibliography and References

1. History of Sanskrit, Florida Vedic College.
2. Sanskrit alphabet, pronunciation and language.
3. The Importance of Sanskrit to Hinduism.
4. Discover Sanskrit.
5. Sanskrit - Language of Enlightenment by Vyaas Houston.
6. Sanskrit Words, An Introduction to the Ancient Language of Yoga, by Yogacharya, International Yogalayam.
7. Article by: J J O'Connor and E F Robertson.
8. http://www-history.mcs.st-andrews.ac.uk.
9. The Wonder That is Sanskrit - Amazing and Interesting Creations in Sanskrit, (pp. 36-51).
10. "Panini" by Saroja Bhate (1995).
11. "Panini- A Suvey of Research" by George Cardona.

Footnotes

1. Researchers at NASA have been looking at Sanskrit as a possible computer language because of its perfect morphology that leaves very little room for error.
2. Kambodia is veritably the English transliteration of the French name Kambodge implying for Sanskrit Kamboja.
3. Knowledge is very easily transferred through Sanskrit as the language is such that it allows memory to grow sharper - this was proven in ancient days when most of the learning used to happen verbally and none of the student used to forget that was taught, as the language allowed them to bring concepts and words to same space, not allowing much possibility of varied and modified presentations.

External Links

1. Free Devanagari fonts.
2. Learn Sanskrit through self study - The Acharya Web Site disseminates information relating to computing with Indian languages.
3. Ancient Sanskrit Online.
4. Sanskrit Academy.
5. Cologne Digital Sanskrit Lexicon.
6. Sanskrit Library – contains digitised Sanskrit texts and various tools to analyse them.
7. Samskrita Bharati - an organisation established as an experiment in 1981 in Bangalore to bring Sanskrit back into daily life.
8. American Sanskrit Institute
9. Sanskrit Studies

10. Sanskrit Voice – a community of Sanskrit lovers.
11. Download free devanagari fonts and transliteration macros.
12. The six unmatched features of the Sanskrit language.

2

Public Accountability and Media : Its Success and Failure in Performing the Role as a Force for Public Accountability

1. Definition and Classification

Media accountability is the general Western belief that mass media has to be accountable in the public interest – that is, they are expected to behave in certain ways that contribute to the public good. The concept often comes in collition with commercial interests of media owners; legal issues, such as the constitutional right to the freedom of the press in the U.S. and governmental concerns about public security and order. Several international organisations, like International Freedom of Expression Exchange, Freedom House, International Press Institute, World Press Freedom Committee and the Inter-American Press Association, watch over governmental control of the press.

In the media discourse, accountability is used to explain a media behaviour deemed to be questionable. The media is often accused of violating professional norms, and hence, its actions call for certain explanations.

The media plays a vital role in disseminating information to the public to have public well informed. For this purpose, it collects news and presses it on to the public. However, while gathering and disseminating, cautious media may be blamed of performing in unfair and biased manner by violating the professional code of ethics.

In the age of market-driven journalism, the media indulge to maximise profits and commercialism is said to be the motive for such behaviour.

Therefore, society expects the press to be accountable to its constituents and press accountability is central to its behaviour.

2. The Media as a Force for Public Accountability : Excerpts from an Interview

Interviewee: Elizabeth Rubin, 2008-2009, Edward R. Murrow Press Fellow.

September 8, 2009: As part of the Edward R. Murrow 60th Anniversary initiative, current and former fellows discuss the stories of impact and sustaining of serious international journalism. Former fellow Elizabeth Rubin answers why she was blacklisted by the media department of the 101st Airborne Division. She also explores possibilities for the future of international reporting at this time of upheaval.

> *What is one international story or topic (of your own reporting) that you believe had the greatest impact and why? Explain why you chose to report it.*
>
> "The story of mine that has had the most significant impact recently was "Battle Company Is Out There," which was published in February, 2008 in the New York Times Magazine. The military tends to guard its problems, keep them inside the family. But often it is not until the problems are exposed to the general public that the Generals are pushed to make changes.
>
> *Do you have any ideas–whether yours or someone else's–for how the news industry can sustain serious international reporting at a time of great upheaval in the media?*
>
> "The media and the military have always had a complicated relationship. Often the military distrusts journalists' intentions. Yet journalists and the media can be a soldier's best advocate. Take the Washington Post on the appalling conditions for US war wounded at the Walter Reed military hospital. Or NPR's series on the consequences of post-traumatic stress syndrome in active duty soldiers and the military's reluctance to address the problem. In both cases, the conditions and treatment of soldiers were seriously improved because of these in-depth investigations and public reports.
>
> It is the public accountability that lends these reports their weight. If the investigations were internal there'd be much less pressure for the institution to change. Every developing country that is struggling for political freedom or trying to fight government abuses and corruption knows that the media is its most powerful tool.

Foundations, corporations (even if it's against their interests), and philanthropic institutions like the Mac Arthur Foundation, Annenburg Foundation, the Rockefeller Fund, the Pulitzer Center, need to reserve funds that can be used by news organisations to keep international investigations and reporting alive. Without these exposes there is no question our democracy will begin to falter.

3. Public accountability of citizens' media: new theoretical and empirical challenges

For alternative media forms – so called "citizens' media" or "community media" – a self-regulatory process is intrinsically linked to the self-conception. A core condition of citizens' media is that role assignments become more flexible encouraging audience member to become their own content producers and story providers. This more citizen-centered approach of the democratic objectives is directly linked to their understanding of reference groups as some kind of community, defined by social connectedness through common background, habits or interests of a certain kind no matter if it is on a local, cultural, national or trans-national level.

This paper discusses the work-in-progress of a research project elaborating an integrative approach for researching the societal benefits of citizens' media in a comparative perspective. Considering the differences in relation to mainstream media or professional journalistic practices extended analytical requirements for empirical research on this issue become obvious. Therefore this paper will focus on two issues: theoretical efforts in defining the democratic potential and societal obligations of non-mainstream media and empirical challenges considering a mixed-method-design on several levels of media production, presentation and reception of net-based community media.

4. The media, the government and the Citizen: Accountability and Engagement

Reliable information, empowers be impossible for citizens to use their power effectively at election time, nor would they be aware of the problems and issues that need active consideration beyond voting. Since the media are the main source of information and a vital link between the government and citizens they become indispensable precondition for both government and social accountabilities. The media also provides a forum where a broad range of voices – opposition parties, civil society actors, independent experts and ordinary citizens – can express alternative views. Moreover, the media are identified as 'Fourth Estate'. The term locates the media alongside other branches of government who together provide a system of checks and balances to control political officials and misuses of power. The chances for successful watchdog journalism are even more limited in new democracies where the functional interdependence between politicians and journalists is still overimposed by the legacy of censorship list by the old autocratic regime. Political leaders even committed to democratic values was it hard to face an sterm press which pleads for public justification of policy decisions and political conduct.

In fact, the affirmity between democratic governments and the media is characterised by frequent clashes – dubbed as 'media wars' – over the boundaries of government interference into the functioning of the media and its contents at the same time, the codes and ethics of investigative journalism are still vague for reporters. It resulted into the patterns of deference and subservience, labeled as 'attack dog' journalism, this kind of takes on polemicigm and often makes rumours and fabricated accusations rather than engaging in thorough fact checking research.

There are various factors which systematically affect the quality of political information by the media. One concerns news values, or the standards by which journalists select their stories, thereby allocating public attention and setting the agenda. Some most important aspects that guide this selection of news are conflict, impact, deviance, negativity, proximity, high status actors, and timeliness. Eventhough some of these news values might be taken from Westfor example the emphasis on conflict and deviance, the global flow of news and the dominance of international news agencies have brought about a fairly similar pattern of political reporting around the world. The similar importance must be given on the way in which the media present and frame political issues. Reports are structured in a clear narrative on a distinct event and – often stereotyped as to be hero or villain – and is depicted as being responsible for the problem or its solution.

5. Mass Media and Public Accountability in Democratic State: A vicious or a virtuous circle?

The wide gap between normative rules and prevalent media practices raises the question whether media which routinery undermines the ideals of normative media theory can actually meet the social accountability and the development of effective citizenship? Do the democratic media foster, or undermine, the emergence of a political culture, conducive to the of the new democratic order?

Research on media effects in public is a vital area in the field of communication studies. The literature devoted to media on political knowledge, orientations and participation is quantitative. Moreover, the process that links media messages to changes in people's political orientations is extremely complex and dependent on a multitude of individual and social conditions. Most of media effects research has been carried out in established Western democracies, Like U.S.A. which might be fundamentally different from the circumstances of dramatic political and economic change that characterises many emerging democracies. Since the prevelence of the media in modern life is often mistaken as an indicator of their massive enfluences on audiences, it is imperative to look at the factors which restrict the influence of the media.

In a seminal work on campaign communication carried out in the 1940s in a small town of America, Lazarsfeld and his collaborators searched for the impact of the mass media on political orientations and voting behaviour. The authors, wrote, there are three main reasons for the limited power of the media on individual political opinions.

Firstly, people avoid messages that contradict their own convictions, But if, exposure to opposing partical viewpoints in media are anaffair of daily people forget them urgently, or even misperceive them in order to exact them to their own beliefs.

Secondly, voters' electoral preferences are the expression of class, ethnicity and regional identity, which frame distinct set of interests and values. Even if the media contradictly these predispositions they are unlikely to change his or her electoral decision.

Third, and most importantly, political opinions are shaped by social interactions in everyday life. As It was observed, interpersonal communication with people in one's immediate social environment, family members, friends, neighbours or workmates, are more influential than the media. Most social groups are characterised by a high degree of homogeneity, either as the result of social pressure exerted on individual group members who hold deviant views, or because people seek the company of like minded others in the first place.

Hence, the role of the media in public opinion building is primarily, providing the raw material for political or other conversations supplying the events after events, but the evaluation of this information and the conclusions to be drawn from it are largely shaped by te dynamics of social interaction.

Price puts it, it is less important what a person thinks but with whom he or she thinks.

News media play as a forum for diverse of voices which serves an important purpose in exposing citizens to opposite views unlikely to encounter in their own social networks. Research into the consequences of the homogeneity or heterogeneity of people's communication environments begets imperative fats, such as those who event the opportunity to learn about opposing viewpoints through the media are more tolerant toward minority groups and show more respect for political opponents. The effect gets stronger when some members of one's social context hold divergent views, e.g., by supporting a different party. This means that people learn to recognise others they do not agree with as reasonable fellow citizens, instead that people transform their mind of alternative opinions.

6. Just who is the Media accountable to?: Case of India

The most important principles of the media, accountability must be observed in everyday practice of journalism, in times of conflict and transgressions - rife from the state, media owners and vested interests in society or even the public. Inversely proportionate to the phenomenal growth of the media in India over the last decade is the steep decline in media accountability. The Press Council and even within media organisations nowhere accountability near transparency is seen. Thus the result is a further qualitative decline of media freedom and independence as a whole.

Media accountability in all its myriad avatars, is a ticklish issue. The print media and broadcast media has put a schene what regulatory mechanism the Internet is largely unregulated yet free from state carbing. So, the bigger question is: who will watch the watchdog? It is the proper to say : the state? The media industry? An ombudsman? Media advocacy groups? Journalist organisations? Or, the public – that amorphous mass of media readers, television and radio audiences, filmgoers, bloggers and internet social networking groups? At present the answer can be : 'All of the above'! However, there is no really effective and foolproof method to ensure media accountability.

The state has always wished to regulate the functioning of the media, the Indian media has vociferously resisted these attempts. The Bihar Press Bill, the Defamation Bill or even provisions in the infamous TADA and POTA that regulated media coverage. In a recent case, the government instead of draft a content code to regulate thefor the broadcast media, the News Broadcasters Association (NBA) that represents some members of the broadcast media industry, opposed it and drafted their own code. However, the Press Council has disappeared from both media and public consciousness.

Earlier, Press Council hearings and orders, were reported regulartly. But today, hardly anyone knows about the Press Council, or about its work, or by whom Besides, according journalists' the Press Council needs more power of censure – hardly deterrent enough It regulates the print media and it be expanded to a Media council, encompassing all media - such a demand have been extended. But the broadcast media have resisted this move and see it as a means to regulate the media. As a model for accountability, the Press Council can be consolidated with more powers relevance as an enforcement agency.

Media columns in print discuss television coverage, but sad that review of print media coverage never received a from the element media, excepting the significant events, like the Gujarat riots or the killing of Dalits in Khairlanji. The ethical acts of omission and commission requires dedication, persistence and a forum to voice this within the media itself, rather than for private circulation.

The broadcast media's coverage of the November 26 attacks in Mumbai was an interesting example of the face-off between the media, the state and the public – a rare example where all three agencies were in disagreement with one another. The media contended that the government was unprepared and the absence of a central agency to provide with official information resulted in a free-for-all. The government meanwhile sought - curbs on media coverage in instances of terror attacks.

The media, in principle, needs to turn the scanner on itself, but this stands still a long way off to instilitionse such more. Only two media organisations in India so far have appointed Ombudsmen to examine complaints from readers or redress editorial shortcomings. However, these commendable efforts, alas, not been as edifying. In 1988,S.C. (Rtd.) Justice P. N. Bhagwati, was appointed as an wrote long articles on media ethics and a few complaints from readers but the entire process remained unobserved a few years later.

In another example, almost more than 20 years later in 2009, The Hindu appointed K. Narayanan, senior editorial consultant with the paper as an internal ombandsman. The editor-in-chief of the newspaper N. Ram said in a meeting: "Freedom of the press is important. So is its social responsibility, which must begin with interaction with and accountability to readers. For a daily newspaper, this must happen on a daily basis." Well, these are early days yet, so it remains to be seen how this Ombudsman functions. Journalists' organisations, beleagured by rampant contractualisation, voice about ethical issues which is muted by the absence of a forum to voice it within the media. The internet provides a forum of sorts and there are a number of blogs and a few websites that discuss media ethics. While this has managed to break some of the communication deadlock, it is nowhere near critical mass to make a difference.

So why don't media organisations accept the need to put systems in place to ensure media accountability? In today's fractured media environment, where competition to grab the media market is more intense than ever before, ethics are the obstacles in the race.

When media organisations do not respect their counterparts, or even freely discuss or debate criticism, when they refuse self-scrutiny or acknowledge mistakes, when they cannot even agree to disagree, when the spirit of enquiry is all but dead, and the market-savvy cat killed curiosity years ago – how can the media be made accountable?

References

1. http://www.hks.harvard.edu
2. www.unpcdc.org/media
3. english.unak
4. http://www.pjreview.info
5. http://www.karmayog.org
6. bibliotecavirtualut.suagm.edu
7. Project for Excellence in Journalism (PEJ-Weekly Reports)

3

Radio in India–The FM Revolution and its Impact on Indian Listeners

1. Introduction

Most people ask, who invented Radio, and the name Marconi comes to mind. Usually KDKA Pittsburgh is the answer when against the askance about the first Radio station. But are these really Radios firsts? In the interest of curiosity and good journalism, we set out to determine if these were in fact Radios firsts. Was the inventor of Radio the person to discover that electromagnetic waves sent through the air, or the person to send them? Was it the person who sent signals the farthest, or who sent the first with voice? Was the first station the first one to be licensed, or was it the first licensed experimental station?

Within the broader wireless category are many subcategories and industries of which Radio broadcasting is just one, as is wireless telegraph, wireless ship-to-shore communication, etc. To go back to the development of wireless we must first look; into the events which lid up to the discovery of electricity. Though some documentation goes further back.

Electricity as a science was started in 1600 by Dr. William Gilbert, who was Queen Elizabeth's personal physician, who invented the electroscope which detected electromagnetic energy in the body. He coined the word *electricity*. From that point forward many people contributed in the development of electricity: Sir Thomas Browne, Benjamin Franklin, Alessandro Volta and Georg Simon Ohm among others.

2. History of Radio in India

In India broadcasting started with the formation of a private radio service in Madras in 1924. The same year, British government granted a licence to a private company, the Indian Broadcasting Company, to inaugurate Radio stations in Bombay and Kolkata. But the company almost went bankrupt in 1930. The colonial government's Department of Labour and Industries began operating them as the Indian State Broadcasting Corporation. In 1936, this very Corporation was rebaptised as All India Radio (AIR) and was controlled by the Department of Communications. In independent India, AIR was made a separate Department under the Ministry of Information and Broadcasting. Government of India controls the radio broadcasting in India that works under the Directorate General of All India Radio, established in 1936 and since 1957 All India Radio was renamed as *Akashvani*.

There were only six radio stations in India in 1947. All India Radio's network had broadened by the mid-1990s to about 146 AM stations along with a National Channel, the Integrated North-East Service that targeted at reaching out to the tribal groups in north-east India and handles the External Services. There are five regional headquarters for All India Radio, namely, in the North Zone in New Delhi; the East Zone in Kolkata; the North-East Zone in Guwahati, Assam; the West Zone in Mumbai; and the South Zone in Chennai.

The Indian radio broadcasts both national and local programs in Hindi, English, and sixteen regional languages. Commercial Radio services in India started in 1967 by *Vividh Bharati Service* with its headquarters at Mumbai. *Vividh Bharati* earned its revenues from extensive advertisements and broadcast from thirty-one AM and FM stations during the mid-1990s. India has a wide-ranging network of medium wave and short-wave stations.

In 1994, the number rose to eighty-five FM stations and seventy-three short wave stations that connected the entire country. The broadcasting equipment implemented in India is mainly indigenous and reaches special audiences, such as farmers needing agro climatic, plant protection, and other agriculture-related information.

The number of radio receivers were inhanced almost five times between 1970 and 1994. Initially it was around 14 million that rose to nearly 65 million. Radios are almost produced within India.

The foreign broadcast service functions under the External Services Division of All India Radio. In 1994, seventy hours of news, features, and entertainment programs were broadcast routinely in twenty-five languages using thirty-two shortwave transmitters.

The early history of Indian radio broadcasting in independent India set the parameters for the succeeding role of television in the nation.

After Independence, the government followed three major goals: *firstly*, to achieve political integration; *secondly*, to attain economic development; and *finally*, to achieve social modernisation. Indian broadcast medium was hoped to serve important purposes in all three areas. All the national affairs and social changes were informed through the waves of broadcast media and within no time, popularity of radio spread nationwide, proved to be a prime medium of social integration.

Indian radio was promoted by the government for the political objective of nation building. National integration and the development of a "national consciousness" became the primary objective of All India Radio. Broadcasting was organised as the solitary reason of the chief planner of this process of political integration: the State.

It also aided in the development of economic scenario. The use of broadcasting was further considered to be a development process as a consequence to this state-led developmental philosophy. Indian radio had specially designed programmes to contribute to the process of social modernisation, an important pre-requisite of economic development. The main problem was that the old ideas influencing the young minds were hindering the process of social change and modernisation. The role of broadcasting provided an inlet for the flow of modern ideas.

The same reason of static thoughts prevailing in the society; made television came into existence. Television broadcasts started from Delhi in September 1959, again associated with the All India Radio's services. Programs were broadcast twice a week for an hour a day on welfare topics related to community health, citizens duties and rights, and traffic and road sense. In 1961, it was expanded to include a school educational television project. When television was taking birth, radio happened to be a matured medium in India. The oldest radio station of India, All India Radio or Akashvani is one of the largest radio networks in the world.

3. The FM Revolution in India

In the mid-30s, Major Edwin Armstrong, considered a prolific inventor in radio history who had already devised a successful circuit to improve AM radio, came up with a whole new approach to transmitting radio signals. Eventhough, Armstrong was well aware of AM radio's major limitations:

- static interference from household appliances and lighting,

- limited audio quality (frequency response and dynamic range),
- night-time interference between many stations (co-channel interference), because of ionospheric refraction, especially in rural areas.

The Story of FM radio is one of success and tragedy

Armstrong approached with his invention to a friend, David Sarnof, head of RCA, which bought into the patents and supported Armstrong develop an experimental radio station. But, then Sarnof and RCA had much concern to protect their existing AM radio empire and they through a policy avoided the competition from a new and much better form of radio. Years of costly legal battles ensued which Armstrong couldn't afford. RCA closed down the FM station that they had helped Armstrong build. However, dedicated to his invention, Armstrong tried hard to develop FM radio on his own. He sold rights to manufacture FM radios to several companies. By 1941, 50 FM stations were on the air. But the Japanese onslaught on Pearl Harbor diverted resources and froze development.

David Sarnof and RCA, pressured the FCC to change all of the FM radio frequencies – a move to instantly obsolete all of the exiting FM radios. Listeners got upset at having their radios suddenly made useless.

Since radio station owners didn't wish to go to the expense of creating high-fidelity programming just for their FM stations, the FCC allowed them to simultaneously broadcast the same programming on both their AM and FM stations.

However, this didn't show off FM's quality advantages and it did nothing to help the cause of FM.

With the evolution of TV, interest in FM radio further declined and by 1949, many FM stations had shut down.

His continuous endevour to build superior radio system and with RCA years of legal battles. These both sapped his creative energies and drained out his financial resources. On January 31, 1954, Edwin Armstrong stopped his long, over taxing battle against Sarnof and RCA, wrote a note to his wife apologising removed the air conditioner from his 13th storey New York apartment, and jumped and succumbed.

As the graph show below the green line represents the growth of non-commercial and National Public Radio (NPR) stations. FM radio not only climbed out of the cellar of popularity after Armstrong's death, but today it leads AM radio in both number of stations and listeners.

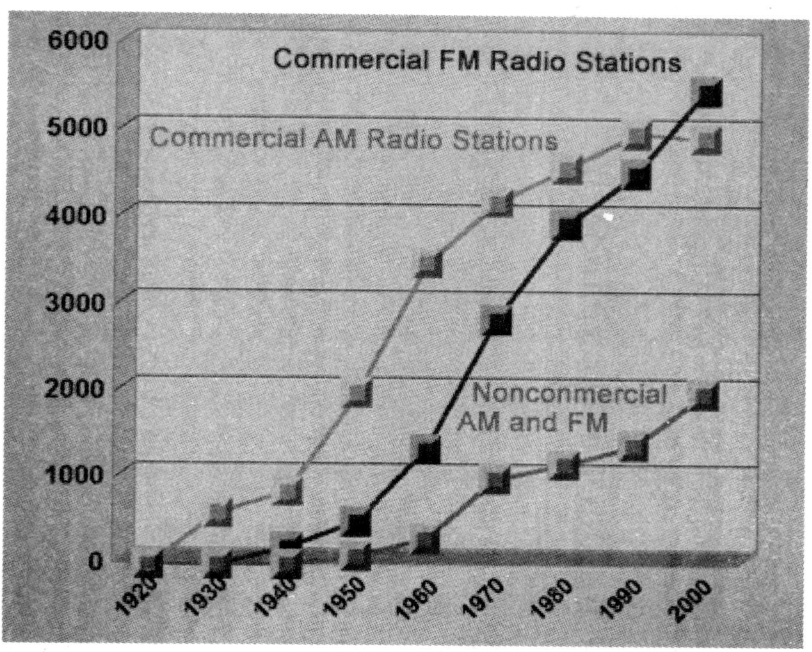

4. HISTORY OF FM IN INDIA

FM Radio was first introduced by All India Radio in 1972 at Madras and later in 1992 at Jalandhar. In 1993, the government sold airtime blocks on its FM channels in Madras, Mumbai, Delhi, Kolkata and Goa to private operators. Later (1997), after the initial euphoria died out and most of the bidders could not meet their commitments to pay the governments the amounts they had expected and defaulted. Indian policy currently laid down that these bids were a One-Time Entry Fee (OTEF), for the entire license period of 10 years. Annual licence fee for private players is either 4% of revenue share or 10% of Reserve Price, which ever is higher.

Only non-defaulter the *Times Group* which operated its brand, *Times FM*, till June 1998. The government, therefore, decided not to renew contracts given to private operators.

4.1. Evolution

The introduction of private broadcasters mainly in Delhi, Mumbai, Kolkata, Goa and Chennai made the entry of private FM slots more possible. These soon followed by stations in Hyderabad, Jaipur and Lucknow. The private broadcasters disappeared from the studios of All India Radio in 1998, as the broadcasting ministry owing to the potential of this medium demanded higher revenues. The Ministry invited bids for FM frequencies in 2001. However, this did not work out as foreseen as most private players bid heavily and most could not meet their commitments to pay the government the amounts they owed which expecting a few stations like *Radio City*, *Radio Mirchi* and *Red FM* which sustained in a poor radio advertising market.

The Phase II of FM licensing happened in 2006, where some 338 frequencies were offered of which about 237 were sold. While the government may go for re-bidding of unsold frequencies, the Phase III of FM licensing sees smaller towns and cities opening up for FM radio. Although they were allowed only 15% of the total allocated frequencies, *Reliance* and *South Asia FM (Sun group)* bid for most of the 91 cities.

4.2. Trends write-up

Indian policy presently offered these broadcasters to be assessed for a One-Time Entry Fee (OTEF) for the entire licence period of 10 years. Under the Indian accounting system, this amount is amortised over the 10 year period at 10% per annum. Annual license fee for private players is either 4% of revenue share or 10% of Reserve Price, whichever is higher. News are not permitted on private FM, although the federal minister says this may be reconsidered in two to three years. India's new private FM channels are said to soon change the advertising scenario. Traditionally, radio accounts for 7% to 8% of advertiser expenditures around the world. Currently in India, it is less than 2%.

5. TIME LINE 1993-2011

1. **1993-Aug 15, 1993:** In India FM broadcasting was opened for private sector on 15 August 1993. After the privatisation of this channel, its quality has improved. FM stands for "Frequency Modulation" and has stereo-phonic sound quality free from disturbance.
2. **1999-Jul 1999:** Distributed Query Optimisation, "Distributed Query Optimisation is more complex du... DEMAT ACCOUNT "DEMAT accounts means Dematerialised account need f... The re-entry of private players-FM Radio.
3. **2001-Oct 2001:** By October 2001, sixteen companies were issued licences to operate private FM radio stations. Some of these were Entertainment Network, India FM Radio, Vertex Broadcasting, Radio Today, Sun TV, Music Broadcast, Millennium Broadcast, Hitz FM Radio.
4. **2004-Apr 13, 2004:** As per the Code for Commercial Advertising on All India Radio dated April 13, 2004, advertisement of political nature was prohibited on All India Radio, which was also applicable to FM radio.
5. **2005-Jul 2005:** The government of India announced in July 2005 that FDI in privately owned FM radio sector was permitted. A public invitation for tender was held to seek for private investors for 330 FM radio stations in 90 cities.
6. **2006-Nov 2006**: According to the Community Radio Policy announced by the Government of India in November 2006, community- based groups and non-governmental organisations can set up and run low-powered FM radio stations. The "Community Radio Revolution" has already begun.
7. **2007-Oct 8, 2007:** Meow FM is a talk-based FM Radio Channel in India currently broadcasting in major cities Delhi and Mumbai and Kolkata from 8 October, 2007. It is an India Today Group venture. Its broadcast frequency is 104.8 MHz FM.

8. **2008-Feb 2008:** This is despite the fact that TRAI's Recommendations on Phase III of FM Radio licensing: issued in February 2008: had already stated that FM Radio broadcasters may be permitted to broadcast news taking content from AIR, Doordarshan (DD).
9. **2009-May 2009:** The initiative got a good response, and by the end of May 2009, 10,000 people are said to have carpooled in the city. Radio Mirchi: Radio Mirchi19 is a nationwide network of private FM radio stations in India.
10. **2010-May 2010:** Upto the end of year 2007, 338 licences were given by the Indian government for FM radio channels in 91 towns and cities of India. In May 2010, government has made a mega expansion plan of FM channels. In this plan, FM channels will be increased to 790.

6. Growth and Developments of Indian Radio

In 1990, V.P. Singh`s National Front government provided financial aid to the Prasar Bharati (Indian Broadcasting) Act. This act provided greater autonomy to Doordarshan and All India Radio. The act allowed the establishment of an autonomous body to control Doordarshan and All India Radio. This unit operated under a board of governors, appointed for policy making and a broadcasting council to redressm the complaints. This was the start of interaction through radio. With time the number of radio stations has increased from about 100 in 1990 to 209 in 1997.

Indian radio now has spread much for and presents the best option for low-cost programming. Listenership of Indian Radio has reached a plateau, risen in certain urban areas due to the recent time allotment to private companies on five FM stations. Film and other popular music constitute the main curriculum of such stations, contributing to an increase in commercial radio time and earned advertising revenues from Rs. 527 million in 1991-92 to Rs. 809 million in 1995-96. The worked development in Indian radio has been due to the proper efforts taken to use radio for social change, like the state-supported radio rural forums for agricultural communication in the 1960s and promotion of adult literacy in the 1980s.

The arrrival of regional radio popularised this medium even more with the Indian masses. More recently NGOs have come together and initiated several broadcast programmes on women and legal rights, emergency contraception, and tele-serials dealing with social issues. In the present decade the functioning of regional radio channels have led to a massive network all across the country.

Some communication experts believe with sound reasons that an inhanced and accelerated commercialisation of radio is to eventually cut down the costs of FM radio sets, thus making local radio even more available to the extreme rural areas. Presently, radio broadcasting is done in 24 languages and 146 dialects all across India and there are 104 million radio households in the country, using approximately 111 million radio sets.

In further aamazing developments the inclusion of FM facility in mobile phones and portable pocket radios have popularised this medium in every nook and corner of urban areas. Although the transmitters have not reached the extreme corners, developments assure quick installation. A recent exhibits shows that Indian radio reaches out to almost 97.3% of the population and 91% of the geographical area. A March 1996 survey, says that there had been around 186 radio-broadcasting centers, 148 medium wave transmitters, 51 short wave transmitters and 94 VHF/ FM transmitters in India.

Indian Radio now has equal status and importance compared to television and print media. The developments of radio in India was steady during the 1960s and 70s, but accelerated during the 1980s and 90s. Radio has now become an intimate form of communication and the FM channels like *Red FM, Radio Mirchi, Power FM* and others have contributed immensely in developing this strong network.

7. Indian Radio Programmes

The Indian radio programmes deal with various kinds of subjects lately. In the previous years, news programmes were presented in a plain manner through news reading. With passage of time, these news programmes on radio have come to be equally interesting and interactive as the ones on Television. *Radio Mirchi* broadcast their news show in each of the cities following the similar pattern, with variation in names to the specific cities, as '*Hi Delhi*' in New Delhi and '*Hi Kolkata*' in Kolkata.

The Indian radio comedy programmes miscellaneous in content aim at entertainment in short durations all through the day. Some Indian radio programmes discuss films and cultural activities of the country. The majority of the Indian radio programmes are music, instrumentals and hit songs, however, the curriculum of such programmes never seem bland, rather come up with surprising twists every time they are presented.

The Indian radio programmes often focus on relationships, personal problems, women activities and charitable activities. Many promoting shows on Indian Radio make the slogans of the local charitable organisations vocal. Such programmes target much higher commerce that just entertainment and Indian radio has sufficed every requirement of the Indians. Whether it is enjoyment, or winning prizes, or debates and even contributing to some social work, the Indian radio programmes have devised enough opportunities for the audiences. Some interesting regional radio programmes come up with respective tradition and culture through discussions with the experts. These Indian radio shows often bring social activists and experts to their studios and discuss about various issues to serve the audience with awakening.

The Indian radio programmes have been believed to be one`s closest and most personal mate that offers numerous options to an individual`s choice and preferences, and an insight to the various problems.

8. Indian Radio Personalities

Lately, the radio organisations include copywriters, producers, comparing executives and most importantly radio jockeys. The radio jockeys (RJs) have been serving the Indian radio competently for almost a century. Earlier known as the radio announcers, news readers or hosts with the advent of FM channels the Radio jockeys play the role of the navigator as well as entertain the listeners and simultaneously provide updated online information. A sweet, mid to heavy voice is considered to be the best one for broadcasting. However, individualistic charm of the Indian radio personalities made them actually famous. To deliver all of it through voice is not that easy task and confidence is the key word to attain success.

One of the most popular radio announcers of Indian Radio, Ameen Sayami presently work for *Red FM*. He attained fame with *Binaca Geetmala* and *Bournvita Quiz Contest* and ruled over the airwaves during 1950s and 1960s. His elder brother Hamid Sayani has also been a radio personality of international fame. The celebrity actor Sunil Dutt started his career in Indian media through Radio. Vijay Kishore Dubey and Shiv Kumar Saroj are also two of the popular radio announcers of Indian Radio. After the popularisation of FM channels, the trend of radio jockeys increased even more.

FM channels broadcast in stereo and produce better sound quality than the other short, medium wave channels. It is why,, the vocal talent of the radio jockeys is truly exploited extensively in these FM channels. Rhicha Vyas and RJ Prateek are the two most popular radio jockeys of contemporary Indian Radio.

The style, expression, delivery, and content have developed in Indian Radio vastly and FM Radio particularly is speedily progressing industry with more and more channels opening up in every city of the world.

RJ Mir is popular in entire eastern India for his popular show *Hi Kolkata* on *Radio Mirchi*, RJ Sree for her show *Khoobsurat*, dealing with women centric affairs. RJ Radhika through *Ananda Junction* entertains with general local affairs. Rakesh and Pragya at *BIG FM* keep their listeners engaged with their witty humor. RJ Jimi in *Red FM* attained great popularity for his heavyset voice. Celebrities like Rupam Islam, Soumitra Chatterjee, Bratati Bandopadhyay sometimes reach out to the audiences through radio, discussing several interesting topics. Apart from these media celebrities, now Indian scenario has crowded with these Media celebrities who in the most particular way contribute to the growth of radio media.

9. FM Radio listening: Past, Presentand Future

In many countries, non-profit radio broadcasters thrive and have become the platforms for the languages, voices and views of citizens and local communities that would otherwise be modernied. There are over 1000 community stations in Latin America and over 2500 non-commercial educational stations in the USA. Post-apartheid South Africa, is currently listening to around 100 community broadcasters.

In 2000, All India Radio was the only major broadcaster of more 200 radio stations in the country. The 21st century saw a handful of commercial entertainment, FM stations being licensed and within years running into a viability crisis, driven in part by high licensing fees. The

Anna University at Chennai is the only recently licensed non-profit broadcaster.

For the common man 'community radio' is not of the same familiarity as 'All India Radio'. This is because the Indian airwaves are not cackling with programs from community supported broadcasters. What really is 'community radio' or CR?

Worldwide, non-commercial broadcasting figures in three sub-categories: educational broadcasters, independent public service (NGO) broadcasters, and community (CR) broadcasters. Mostly CR stations are run by a core group of paid staff that may number 5 to 10 trained individuals, but helped by volunteers, interns, and part-time experts. Grants, memberships and sponsorships are introduced to pay for programming and operating expenses. It is called CR because a critical mass of the listening community participates in the financing, programming and management of the station.

Languishing for want of better radio policy are hundreds of government schemes, development programs and civic coordination tasks that need a low-cost, citizen-driven and local information dissemination medium that working for illiterate and semi-literate people as much as for others. In a resource strapped nation, radio fits that bill. CR policy has seen sincere advocacy in India because of this potential, and in theory at least, New Delhi has acknowledged this.

A UNDP-sponsored meeting between citizens groups and the officials of Ministry of Broadcasting on CR policy created a cacophony of concerns and questions. It further led that government was keen on giving licences for CR. India's telecom regulator looked seriously into a new phase of licensing for commercial and non-commercial FM. In structured manner it asked for public input on non-commercial radio policy which was welcomed. Significant response to TRAI specific consultations on CR itself. The discussion must be in a context organic to the Indian situation, but still leverages the abundance experiences from other countries.

Firstly, licensing policy must take pains to differentiate between non-commercial and commercial stations. Barring Nepal most other countries discriminate the two. For India, the question is how to award radio licences to the organisations, leveraging their current place in the regulatory regime, with additional rules specific to radio.

Secondly, in a country where the NGO sector as well as the tertiary educational system is well-established, licensing eventually attract many takers. Reservations will ensure that as commercial FM grows, a minimum number of FM frequencies remain available for public access in every region. The United States took.

Thirdly, the bureaucracy fears to let community stations air their own news, the insecurity being largely driven by concerns of hijack by terrorists and abuse in remote areas. But such policy will be found illegal in the Courts. The Supreme Court, in the *Union of India* vs. *Cricket Association of Bengal* (1995), affirmed that the fundamental right to telecasting by citizens is subject only to regulation and reasonable restrictions and not outright denial. When news itself is supposedly a public good, a government cannot prevent community broadcasters from airing a news service?

Fourthly, commercial stations ran into crisis due to high licence fees. All cash flows into a community broadcaster may not be 'revenue', because grants, listener membership moneys, and program underwriting are in effect 'contributions' to these organisations classified as donations. Therefore subjecting such money to government revenue shares is ill-advised. Advertisements must be allowed, open to taxation.

Fifthly, a complaints-driven grievance redressal system allows citizens and institutions to pinpoint the objectionable on air and make written representations. Responsive processing of complaints, provision for hearings and dispute settlements, and unavoidable litigation on rare occasion may in effect cost less than policing and work better. Thus community stations need not be abused.

Finally, in the context of rural community radio, low power FM stations must be considered as well. A 100 watts FM broadcast from a 30 metre tall antenna can reach a listening audience within a 5 and 1/2 km. radius, sufficient for most rural communities. LPFM transmitter kits are today available at much lower prices than earlier. There is hope for a community radio station everywhere soon.

The government is also waiting for TRAI's recommendations on reforms for the commercial-FM sector.

Howeveer, the current scenario raises the familiar spectre of the 'two steps forward, three steps back' syndrome that has shackled Indian radio broadcasting for decades. Yet, compelled by civil society, government functionaries did take some bold steps by meeting with citizens groups and experts in May 2012.

10. Evolution of Internet Radio

Internet radio (also web radio, net radio, streaming radio, e-radio) is an audio service transmitted via the Internet. Music streaming on the

Internet is usually termed as webcasting because it is not transmitted broadly through wireless means.

It involves streaming media, presenting listeners with a continuous stream of audio that cannot be paused or replayed, much like traditional broadcast media; in this respect, it is distinct from on-demand file serving.

Internet radio is distinct from podcasting, which involves downloading and not streaming. Many Internet radio services correspond to a traditional terrestrial radio station or network.

Its services one can access from anywhere in the world e.g. one can listen to an Australian station from Europe or America. Some major networks like *CBS Radio* and *Citadel Broadcasting* (USA) and *Chrysalis* (UK) restrict listening to in country because of music licensing and advertising concerns.

Internet radio remains popular among expatriates and listeners for eurodance, progressive rock, ambient music, folk music, classical music, and stand-up comedy). IR services offer news, sports, talk, and various genres of music–every format that is available on traditional radio stations.

10.1 Popularity

By 2006, that figure rose to US$ 500 million. A February 21, 2007, "survey of 3,000 Americans released by consultancy *Bridge Ratings and Research*" had the findings that "as much as 19% of U.S. consumers aged 12 and older listen to Web-based radio stations."

In other words, there were "some 57 million weekly listeners of Internet radio programs. More people listen to online radio than to satellite radio, high-definition radio, podcasts, or cell-phone-based radio combined."

An April 2008, *Arbitron survey* found that, in the US, more than one in seven persons aged 25-54 years old listen to online radio each week. In 2008, 13 percent of the American population listened to the radio online, which stood only 11 percent in 2007.

Internet radio functionality is also built into many dedicated Internet radio devices, which give an FM like receiver user experience.

11. Conclusion

The distribution of audio broadcasts known as "Webcasts" are more than 10,000 available to be streamed and played by a software media player in the computer or in a stand-alone Internet radio, media hub, or media server. An Internet radio with built-in connectivity to a home wireless network, is called a "Wi-Fi radio."

Radio above the general preception as an obsolete medium has its use, people and purpose. The time for Radio is yet not over with the introduction of i-pods and MP3 players, instead, with the introduction of online radio, it is making a come back.

References

1. allindiaradio.org.
2. AIR Manual, Chapter 1: History of All India Radio
3. http://allindiaradio.org
4. http://en.bab.la/dictionary/english-hindi/celestial-announcement
5. http://allindiaradio.org
6. http://india.gov.in
7. http://connect.in.com/fm-broadcasting-in-india

4

The Politics-Media Equation–Exposing Two Faces of the Old Nexus Through Study of General Elections, WikiLeaks and Radia Tapes

1. Introduction

Aresponsible media is reputedly identified when it plays an unbiased social role in reporting a matter sans non-essential sub-attraction of the attention of the gullible public with the sole object of making money. The media can educate the public to frame their own opinion in the matters of interest.The media can, howevere, highlight the short-comings of the official machinery in its functioning, bringing out the sufferings of the public in general. As political parties have media for themselves and utilise it for their own ends, the role of the media in such practical cruciality is very much narrowed. During elections, in democracy the media is an effective tool amply utilised for public attention.

The media ought to serve the society, particularly in the third world to solving the problems beyond human for bearance. It has been treated an essential significan ce of the media in society, owing to its entitlement as the superior fourth estate, moreover, a buffer between at one end of whch stand the public. Journalists, politicians and even the general public are talking about the necessity of harnessing the potential of media in a suitable fashion.

2. The Politics and Media Amalgam–Historical Perspective

With the invbention of civilization and for centuries the world has ever existed with information and communication, that in way the essence of mass media can never be said to be exhaustible. The government has the power to sensor or determine how free the mass media will be in their dissemination of information to the people. The question arises how far the government way influence the media?

The word politics has today acquired many meanings. But purposefully we shall limit the aspect of the politics to the realm of the state and government wherein it implies a particular set of human activities which deals with distribution of organised rights, responsibility and duties for the purpose of order and good governance of the state.

The kinship between the mass media and the government can best be appreciated if the classical theories of the press are wall kept in mind. These theories articulate the varying degrees of freedom existing in media as forms a basic part within any political system. Let us now briefly look at these theories and their basic principles.

Authoritative theory articulates the severe relationship between the press and the authoritarian environment in Europe during the old days of monarchs and emperors. Under this political system, the mass media, are clearly subordinate to the state and are restrained from criticising of the government. Furthermore, it sees the media as only existing for the interest of the government and the elite in the society. To ensure the continuance of such status, a variety of methods is used which include licensing, censorship and legal trial.

This theory dominated over the freedom of the press.

3. The Media and Politics Equation in U.S.A.

The media has remained over in a close relationship with American politics. From the *Gazette of the United States* to the *New York Times*, it has been the linking point between politics and the public. The media is important as there are 4 roles significantly vital attributed to it.

The first of these 4 important roles is identified as that of the *signaler* role. Journalists themselves have principled that part of their job is that once something important political happens, they need to alert the world of the going on. They are ready to cover the story whenever and wherever it takes place. Developments in Washington are especially important. Someone is usually on the scene in the capital when something happens. This may be John Roberts reporting from the White House as Colin Powell speaks out against foreign policy or about Iraq.

Toggling the public attention level is the most vital thing media in a *signaler* role does. Equal coverage of all news across the board puts it on the agenda that the publicmay be well-informed.

The last exclusive role of the media is that of the *public-representative* role. Here media performs as a public spokesperson and advocate. Some argue the journalists do not serve as well a public representative as a politician does of two main arguments the first is the public accountability of journalists and politicians different levels. Journalists are saved from that little thing called elections.

The media works regardless of who is voted to the office or otherwise. Secondly, a journalist in search of a solid news story requires no bias and no views. Moreover, to be successful with public representation, views are essential. In general the media to gets a good news story, may not necessarily good the world with views. The clauses for a pure profit and high ratings/ readership also come into play. In general, the *signaler* role is vital in feeding the public's appetite for political stories, the *common-carrier* role in providing the necessary medicine for politicians to experts so that the public can form their views on them. Watchdogs, in fact are necessary for exposing wrongdoings in Washington. The public-representatives know the clear difference between who makes the true public representative and who is to clearly make profits and get huge ratings/readers.

As far as the media goes today, it does a pretty solid job of getting the news out to the masses. Sure, some news channels and newspapers act biased but it brings viewers and provides a variety. Essentially, media wants as many people paying attention to the news. People may not agree with the way a certain name like *Zee News* or *the Times of India* presents the news. Howevere, the people have independent actions of turning the channel the TV off, or the newspaper to be switch over.

4. Politics, Money and Media–The Effective Triangle

Politics, money and the media are intertwined in the most unlikely situations, especially because of the power of information to fashion reality. Good doctors like to treat the disease rather than its symptoms, nonetheless if it begs in urgent situations the symptoms need be cured to gain time for the treatment.

The expulsion episode taught the MPs to be careful about how they sell their services. Corruption is a fact. The deeper problem as to why MPs are willing to do what they did does not seem to have been properly addressed. The Lok Sabha committee through investigation of the scandal but an extremely poor analysis and report. Headed by Pawan Kumar

Bansal, the committee conclded the investigation in just five days. The television show was broadcast on December 12. The committee started its work on the 14th. On December 18 it interviewed some of the MPs to hear on 19th, it viewed further tapes; and on the 20th it drafted the report to be presented the following in the Lok Sabha. The MPs or their representatives were not given opportunities to hearing as the basic right of the accused in any legal proceedings. If this is to become a precedent detrimental to future actions against MPs, it would be easy for the ruling majority to expel any MP it does not like.

The committee left the finer points beyond examination related to ethics of bribery in lieu of asking a question. What if the money was an election fund contribution? What if the money involved was Rs. 100 rather than Rs. 100,000 ? Moreover should there be proportionality in the punishment? The committee appeared to have followed the precedent of the expulsion of one HD Mudgal on September 24, 1951 whose crime was 'his dealings with a Bombay Bullion Association, which included canvassing support and making propaganda in Parliament on certain problems on behalf of that association, in return for alleged financial and other business advantage.'

In Western democracies, it is practised perfectly appropriate to speak in the legislature in matters even personal interest. However, it is, unethical to legislate on such matters that may give monetary benefit to organisations on a *quid pro quo* basis. Of course, the hustle and bustle of shifting perspectives in the crafting of legislation requires 'canvassing support and making propaganda.' Unlike the West, an MP in India has very little agency. He is not allowed due to his mondatory party affiliations to vote his conscience on issues coming up in Parliament. He asks questions, but approved by the Speaker. The ten MPs accused in 1996 scandalous bribery by the CBI to vote in favour of the P V Narasimha Rao government have still not been punished by the courts or Parliament. This must have been due to belief that to accept money for questions by on MP is alright.

Lok Sabha Rule Book says, 'Voicing the constituents' concerns on the floor of the House is the primary parliamentary duty of an elected representative.' This differs from Western democracies where the primary duty is to enact laws, and the implementation is left to the pleasure of executive and the courts. Meanwhile, more sophisticated MPs are abusing the system in different ways. Brinda Karat's attempt to accuse Swami Ramdev about the adulterated quality of his Ayurvedic medicines is one example. There was a right way, she should have filed a formal complaint with the competent authority in the state against Swami Ramdev's pharmacy. But it looks Ms. Karat slandered him for her political motives, and the Union health ministry did its bit to help her by using dubious samples submitted by her and bypassing the protocol to get them 'tested.' The media should have pointed it out at the start, but it did not. Parliament and the courts must have also locked into this abuse of power.

5. Elections in India and Media

Media performs the main role in ensuring free and fair elections. India is the largest democracy in the world and the massive exercise of conducting free and fair elections.

Out of a total 715 million in the registered electorate, 400 million voters turned out during the general elections to the Lok Sabha in April 2009.

The Election Commission of India has improved the election process by taking up reforming measures introducing codes of conduct for candidates and political parties, and ensuring equal opportunities for all candidates in the election fray. All these while, the media and civil society both have played an important part through the phases of the transformation for free and fair elections in the country. Given the huge electorate, the massive exercise of conducting elections in India involves several phases and a number of ascending processes.

These processes in each phase turn from announcement of election dates and pass through the nomination campaigning, polling and counting of votes before concluding with submission of the list of successful candidates to the executive head of the state or the centre, leading to the formation of a new government. The media of all hues are permitted to access information about all these processes for reporting, including entry into polling stations and counting centres all along the election process to ensure free and fair polls.

The Election Commission work closely with media in de-criminalisation of politics, computerisation of electoral rolls, providing electors with photo identity cards, simplifying the procedure for maintenance of accounts and a variety of measures for strict compliance of the Model Code of Conduct.

5.1. Media – Past and Present

The media in India have a glorious convention of safeguarding the democratic rights and giving exposure to all kinds of injustices and inequities as a watchdog. When democratic elections are a relatively new phenomenon in the world, the free media in India have been educating and informing voters in an objective non-partisan manner and contributing to the opinion formation of the electorate. The aim full media performs objective during campaigning, providing information to the electorate about the political parties, their programmes and candidates.

Besides, media inform about the constituencies and various human development indice and offer chances for people to comment on their elected representatives at the same time providing feedbacks to the candidate. Emerging as a potentially powerful force, electronic media have also been playing a similar role to that of print media in conducting free and fair elections. Though no specific laws or regulations governing media activities during elections especially during campaigning, the Election Commission of India has been issuing guidelines from time to time to prevent the media. Political parties and candidates tend to find the media, visual more important for campaigning and seek much media exposure. Since, television channels are widely regarded as the most important instrument for campaigning and communication to the voters due to its audience size and widespread coverage.

5.2. Public Media – Duty for Equal Opportunity

The government-owned public broadcasters, All India Radio and Doordarshan have been pledged with a special duty to broadcast election statements in a balanced manner. It is a general perception that accepted that these the public owned media stations have ordained with an obligation to distribute equal time frame to various parties to communicate directly to the electorate, unlike the private media which tends to publish or broadcast statements of the parties and candidates accoroding to their own preferences. Here, the scope of misusing media will appear as no specific regulations are in force to curb misuse. Newspapers and the majority of television channels may provide their space and airtime the specific candidates of their choice.

Known as AIR Code (All India Radio Code), it incorporates the directives issued by the Election Commission from time to time, and provides guidance to journalists during elections. The AIR Code has become a reference document whenever media regulation is discussed by the authorities, and also when fresh guidelines are to be issued to media on any issue including elections.

It is crucial to ensure all parties, national or regional, and their candidates that they enjoy access to the media, in particular radio and television, as even the illiterate voters can learn about political parties and their candidates. It means that a media is not entitled to influence public opinion by different treatment of one or the other candidate or party. But it is often the media in the case of newspapers and private television channels, which decides who will feature in special stories or debates and discussion programmes. In the absence of clear regulations, manipulation often takes place during the planning for news reports and discussion programmes, or even for non-news programmes such as entertainment shows and movies.

By now the media has revolutionary changes. New phenomena such as growing use of new technology and new styles of presentation of news and opinions have started begun reduce the difference between editorial and commercial space. Space is being sold to individuals' reports or interviews under the garb of news, paving way for a new media phenomenon of "paid news". The gradual emergence of this unfair practice is causing concern nationwide among the institutions of democracy, professional bodies of media and the polity, as it is eroding the basic ethos of democracy as well as media principles.

5.3. Code of Conduct for media in Connection with Elections

The significance of television and radio in the coverage of elections is well reorganised. Their reach is widespread and impact substantial. The EC recognises that electronics media properly can be an important source of providing the widest first hand education for voters on political parties, their symbols, various leaders and different issues in the election.

It seemede essential therefore to establish a model code of conduct for electronic media both misuse as well as to ensure their use in the best interest of democracy.

6. Political Corruption and Media

There is an overpowering sense of anger, despondency and depressive pessimism as one is forced to be in the position of a helpless spectator to the all pervading political corruption that has engulfed the Indian Republic due to acts of omission or commission at the highest political levels of leadership and governance. Yet all is not lost, the Indian Republic is still moving and progressing despite high level political corruption. Despite the sordidness of India's political firmament, the Indian Republic is fortunate to have many shining stars in the form of the Higher Judiciary, the Indian Armed Forces, and India's Central Police Forces, to name a few besides vigilant media. Admittedly these fraternities, too, have corrupt aberrations infected by the all pervasive political corruption, yet these organisations contrast to India's polity.

India's Higher Judiciary have prevented India's political leaders from a wholesale trampling of constitutional niceties and the major provisions of the Indian Constitution. Today where even the Prime Minister is dumb in calling into account those involved in unprecedented corruption, the Higher Judiciary has boldly stepped in. The high-level corruption cases have been probed and by the CBI under Supreme Court to offset interference, and scuttling by the political masters. It gives a little hope to right thinking Indians for redemption of the Indian Republic from the dirty clutches of its unscrupulous and dirtier political leadership.

India's political leadership is expected to set exemplary standards of honesty, integrity and probity to match the sterling qualities of patriotism, selfless service and dedication to the ideals of the Indian Republic, day in and day out, as displayed over the last sixty three years by the Indian Armed Forces. They have over the years unflinchingly sacrificed their lives to protect the Indian Republic.

The Indian Armed Forces have on a different and higher plane epitomised the highest virtues. In marked contrast to the nobility of the Indian Armed Forces, India is pensive of the ignoble deeds of her shameless politicians living off India's riches and skimming it for personal enrichment.

Nevertheless, we must not forget some sections of the media who rather than acting as the handmaidens of politicians, highlight the corruption and shenanigans of the ruling establishment and the cases of social injustice.

So breaking through the dark clouds of despair, there are still shining hope on India's firmament who continue to provide comparatively to the sordidness political establishment, shining rays of hope that in the end good in India will prevail and the muck of the Indian political establishment will be swept into the gutter by the anger of the citizens someday in the short future.

7. WikiLeak Cables – Exposing the Rotten Eggs

Five days before the Manmohan Singh government faced a crucial vote of confidence on the Indo-U.S. nuclear deal in 2008, a political aide to Congress leader Satish Sharma showed a U.S. Embassy employee "two chests containing cash" he said was part of a bigger fund of Rs. 50 crore to Rs. 60 crore (about $250 million) that the party had assembled to purchase the support of MPs: The Hindu.

WikiLeaks exposed corruption more massive in the Indian political system, dominating the Indian media scene as people elsewhere were more focused on the earthquake in Japan and air strikes by US-led coalition forces in Libya.

Documents released online alleged that the ruling Congress Party paid millions of dollars to oppositions Members of Parliament of the to vote the government in July 2008.

"Five days before the Manmohan Singh government faced a crucial vote of confidence on the Indo-U.S. nuclear deal in 2008, a political aide to Congress leader Satish Sharma showed a U.S. Embassy employee 'two chests containing cash' he said was part of a bigger fund of Rs. 50 crore to Rs. 60 crore (about $250 million) that the party had assembled to purchase the support of MPs." The Hindu reported on March 17.

In fact, the Hindu has an exclusive arrangement with Wikileaks to publish the leaked diplomatic communication widely known as a cable in India. In total there were 5,100 U.S. Embassy cables of relevance to India. The range of subjects, issues and persons covered were extraordinary. In a July 17, 2008, cable the then-U.S. Charge d'Affaires Steven White wrote about a visit the embassy's political counselor paid to Sharma, who told him how the Congress party was working hard to ensure the government won the confidence vote on July 22. Dr. Manmohan Singh the government was reduced to minority after one in coalition partners drew differences on the India-U.S. civilian nuclear deal.

"Sharma's political aide Nachiketa Kapur mentioned to an embassy staff member in an aside on July 16 that Ajit Singh's RLD had been paid Rupees 10 crore (about $2.5 million) for each of their four MPs to support the government. Kapur mentioned that money was not an issue at all, but the crucial thing was to ensure that those who took the money would vote for the government," White wrote.

Manmohan Singh said the government "cannot confirm the veracity, contents or even the existence of such communication." The Opposition disrupted parliamentary proceedings and demanded an investigation into the cash-for-vote scam which the government entrightly rejected.

"There is no doubt that these are bona fide reports sent by an American ambassador back to Washington, and these should be seen in that context. That does not mean every fact in them is correct: you have to look at their sources and how they gave this information," WikiLeaks founder Julian Assange told Indian television network NDTV in an interview. "There is no doubt whatsoever that the cables are authentic,". Wikileaks Twittered, that it would shortly release the third instalment of classified US documents being the first instalment of 77,000 documents related to the American military campaign in Afghanistan the second instalment of 400,000 documents related to the American military presence in Iraq. It further Twittered, its third instalmentwould contain a much larger number of documents.

Wikileaks never revealed what the third instalment of their release would cover. However, a Reuters despatch from Washington DC hinted, the classified US diplomatic cables would report on corruption allegations against foreign governments and leaders are expected to feature in the official documents. It added: "Three sources familiar with the US State Department cables held by Wikileaks say the corruption allegations in them are major enough to cause serious embarrassment for foreign governments and politicians named in them. The detailed, candid reports by US diplomats also may create foreign policy complications for the administration of US President Barack Obama. Among the countries are Russia, Afghanistan and former Soviet republics in Central Asia.

State Department spokesman Philip J. Crowley said Washington was assessing the implications of what Wikileaks may reveal and was notifying foreign governments about the possible release. "We wish that this would not happen, but we are obviously prepared for the possibility that it will," he said. The media have reported that the US warned India and other key governments across the world about the expected release. Among other governments cautioned were those of Israel, Russia, Turkey, Canada, UK.

When Wikileaks reportedly developed electronic access to the data bases of the US State Department and the Pentagon and the US military formations in Afghanistan and Iraq, the US authorities tightened document security to prevent further leaks. Wikileaks, documents also covered US Embassy reporting on other subjects. Previously, Pakistan's relations with the US were the focus of Wikileaks. It now focused on India's relations with the US, too. It were likely in addition to corruption involving Indian personalities, the documents about India relate to India's policies on Afghanistan, Iraq and Iran. Among the various events relating to Afghanistan, Iraq and Iran in which India figured during this period, four could be sensitive from India's point of view.

Firstly, the pressure exerted on the Atal Behari Vajpayee government by the George Bush administration to send Indian troops to Iraq. By July' 2003, the Vajpayee government had decided to deny Washington DC, even there was a lot of voices in Delhi in favour US. Secondly, the papers captured by the US intelligence after the occupation of Iraq from the Iraqi government departments showing or corroborating the alleged involvement of Indian politicians with the Saddam Hussein government to acquiring preferential quotas for the import of oil from Iraq (the oil for food scandal).

Thirdly, the pressure by the Bush Administration on the Manmohan Singh Government for voting against Iran in the International Atomic Energy Agency in Vienna . India succumbed to this pressure as a quid pro quo for the Indo-US civil nuclear co-operation agreement of July, 2005. Fourthly, the analysis made in the State Department and the Pentagon regarding Pakistani allegations of Indian involvement in Balochistan.

Wikileaks might have also got hold of diplomatic cables between exchanged the US Embassy in New Delhi and Washinton DC on Indian political leaders, bureaucrats and policy-making? Messages sent by the US Embassy in New Delhi to Washington DC about the escape of Major Rabinder Singh, to the US in 2004 and about the detection by the Indian counter-intelligence of a US mole in the sensitive National Security Council Secretariat in 2006? Wikileaks need to be carefully scrutinised.

8. Radia Tapes–The Nexus Between Media and Politics

The controversy related to the taped and released telephonic conversations between Niira Radia and politicians, corporate icons, industrialists, bureaucrats, aides and journalists taped by the Indian Income Tax Department in 2008-09]. Niira Radia runs a public relations firm named Vaishnavi Corporate Communications, and also operates through subsidiaries such as Neucom, Noesis Strategic Consulting Services and Vitcom Consulting whose clients among others, includes Tata Group, Mukesh Ambani's Reliance Industries and Prannoy Roy's NDTV.

8.1. The Radia Tapes

Radia started her consultancy career first in the field of Aviation, Infrastructure and Telecommunications Projects. She proved to be one of the few professionals in the country, with such wide depth of understanding and domain expertise Strategic Business Communications and the business environment in general. she identified India as an important business destination and over the years, she admirably executed one of her most well known business consulting mandates, as an advisor to the Singapore Airlines – Tata Consortium on the Air India divestment process.

In early December 2010, the Department of Income Tax and the Central Government of India – in a joint affidavit submitted to the Supreme Court of India revealed the tapping was ordered eight months after the office of the Union Finance Minister received a complaint against Niira Radia on Nov 16, 2007. One Gaurav Wahi, Vice-President of corporate communications at Reliance Communications, wrote the letter of complaint with Rashmi Naik, an ex-employee (Director) of the Radia owned Vaishnavi Corporate Communications. Directorate General of Income Tax (Investigation) ordered the surveillance of Radia's phones in August 2008, On 17 December, 2010, a spokesperson of Radia's Vaishnavi Corporate Communications issued a statement we do not believe that any existing or former employee complained to the government or any investigating agencies on the operations of our chairperson."

Journalist J. Gopikrishnan filed the first report in mainstream media about Niira Radia's phone recordings and her involvement in the 2G spectrum scam along with A. Raja. This report "Tapped and Trapped" published in The Pioneer on April 28, 2010, goodedNiira Radia respond with a legal notice demanding The Pioneer to issue "a full and unequivocal public retraction and apology... to publish the same in an appropriately prominent position in the next Edition... A Hindi web portal Bhadas took up this story in May. In November 2010, OPEN magazine reported transcripts of some of the telephone conversations of Niira Radia with senior journalists, politicians, and corporate houses. The Central Bureau of Investigation had 5,851 recordings of phone conversations by Radia in 2G spectrum scam.

On November 29, 2010, the Outlook magazine published transcripts of the Radia tapes with : "India, the republic, is now on sale. Participating in the auction is a group of powerful individuals, corporate houses, lobbyists, bureaucrats and journalists...Radia's conversations show how even cabinet berths can be decided by this select oligarchy....The tapes also paint a dismal picture of how everything–from cabinet berths to natural resources–is now available for the right price. The now controversial 2G allocation was just one of the many manipulations orchestrated by players in high places."

Revelations shocked the ; of India. Supreme Court: "We have been talking about pollution of the sacred rivers like the Ganga. This pollution is quite mindboggling." Centre for Public Interest Litigation (CPIL), through counsel Prashant Bhushan, said, the chance publication of the Radia tapes showed "subversion of government decisions, policy, even discussions and law making in Parliament, the reportage of stories in media and even Cabinet formation by powerful corporates in their commercial interest being successfully achieved by paid lobbyists/brokers/fixers".

8.2. Political lobbying

According to the transcripts of the tapes, Radia lobbied against the reappointment of Dayanidhi Maran to the post of Union IT and Communications minister.

Radia spoke with Ms. Barkha Dutt at 0948 IST

Dutt: 'The stalemate (between Congress and DMK) continues, ya'

Radia: 'My honest advice is that you tell them (Congress) that they need to tell him (Karunanidhi) directly...'

Dutt: 'OK, let me talk to them'.

Later at 1047 IST, Dutt says that it (conveying the message to Congress) was 'not a problem' and that she would talk to Ghulam (Nabi Azad).

Radia, in a later with Ranjan Bhattacharya exchanged 'I made Barkha call up Congress, and get a statement from Congress whether the Prime Minister has actually said that he does not want Baalu, which she carried that he had never said it your friend Sunil Mittal, has been lobbying against Raja (for Maran).'

On January 17, 2011, the Public Accounts Committee (PAC) of the Indian Parliament examined journalists recorded in the tapes. With Aaj Tak, PAC chairman Murli Manohar Joshi said, journalists incriminated themselves in the 2G scam tapes will be summoned by the PAC."

8.3. Public Accounts Committee (Parliament of India)

Since 1993 to provide for greater scrutiny of government functioning by the Indian Parliament, The Public Accounts Committee (PAC) is constituted every year with duty to ascertain the distribution of the budget by the government. The PAC scrutinises the accounts of the Government of India on the basis of Comptroller and Auditor General of India (CAG) reports. The composition and functions of the committee governed by parliamentary procedures, The PAC consists of 15 to 22 members, not more than 15 members from Lok Sabha, and from the Rajya Sabha 7 members. Besides minister cannot be a member of the PAC.

On February 15, and March 10, 2011, CBI appeared before the Public Accounts Committee regarding the A. Raja-Radia scam investigations. On March 08, 2011, journalist J. Gopikrishnan before the Public Accounts Committee to record evidence. By March 2011, the PAC sought depositions of the Prime Ministers Principal Secretary T K A Nair, Cabinet Secretary

K M Chandrasekhar and Director of Enforcement Arun Mathur and declared summon Radia and some journalists (Vir Sanghvi, Barkha Dutt) figured in the tape.

On March 14, 2011, editors, Vinod Mehta of Outlook and Manu Joseph of Open submitted to their journalistic duty as to publish the transcripts of tapped conversations between Radia and others implicated the 2G spectrum allocation scandal.

8.4. Alleged media blackout and reactions in social media

The news gained prominence following sustained pressure on social networking sites Twitter and Facebook against an attempted blackout orchestrated by many prominent Indian TV channels and newspapers. The barkhagate began trending as number one on Twitter in India for several days after the breakout of the news. Washington Post, said "Twitter has played an important role in launching what has become an international conversation on the issue, with the Indian diaspora weighing in".

Initially, The Hindu, The Deccan Herald, The New Indian Express in The Daily News and Analysis (DNA) what about the tapes. HT Media, Mint and NDTV said "the authenticity of these transcripts cannot be ascertained". CNN-IBN's discussed with a panel of experts, if the corporate lobbying is undermining democracy, on the Face the Nation, but avoided the crux and chose not to take names. The Radia tapes is seen to have also made a dent in the image of the media in the country.

"The complete leak out of the tapes by the entire broadcast media and most of the major English newspapers paints a truer picture of corruption in the country," wrote G. Sampath, the deputy editor of the Daily News and Analysis (DNA) newspaper. After it became an international news, more and more media houses covered the story. Karan Thapar's show on CNN-IBN, "The Last Word" (November 27, 2010) was the first show in mainstream Indian television to address the Radia tapes and the involvement of Barkha Dutt and Vir Sanghvi in malpractices, thus ending the TV news channel blackout of the story. The Deccan Chronicle commented, "The 'Radia tapes' may have torn the veil off the nexus between information hungry journalists, lobbyists and industrialists, and opened everyone's eyes to what has long been suspected – the ability of a small but powerful group to use their connections to influence policy." The Times of India commented on November 25, 2010, "The people are showing who the boss is. The weapon in their hands is the internet, ... has seen frantic activism against "power brokering" by journalists in collusion with corporate groups and top government politicians..."

On November 30, 2010, NDTV India Barkha Dutt was questioned by a panel of journalists - Dileep Padgaonkar, Sanjaya Baru, Swapan Dasgupta and editor of OPEN magazine Manu Joseph. Analysis of the show by Tripti Lahiri and Shailaja Bajpai termed Barkha as too argumentative to allow any meaningful discussion. Manu Joseph expressed dissatisfaction with Barkha's answers. On December 2, 2010, Headlines Today Vir Sanghvi and Prabhu Chawla were questioned about their conduct by Rahul Kanwal, Executive Editor of Headlines Today. Though Vir Sanghvi he apologised for "massaging a source".

8.5. Protests and developments

Niira Radia had served a legal notice on The Pioneer which asserted that The Pioneer's report regarding corruption and manipulation in the allotment of 2G spectrum to telecom operators, in so far as it referred to Radia's connections with Telecom Minister A. Raja, are "absolutely false, baseless and malicious and constitute gross defamation".

Open Magazine maintained the conversations as they appeared in the recordings. Dutt commented through her Twitter account: "Struck by the bizarre irony of being accused of favouring a man i have never met (raja) and have always attacked in print and on TV. Gnite!"

New Delhi Television Limited posted a strong rebuttal that Barkha lobbied for A. Raja as "unsubstantiated, baseless and defamatory" and threatened action against Open Magazine. Hindustan Times cited Sanghvi's clarifications and stated the authenticity of these transcripts would be found. On 26 November, 2010, Barkha Dutt, addressed questions raised by the tapes, which she claims were edited.

On 27 November, 2010, Vir Sanghvi, clarified his role in the controversy. On 30 November, 2010, NDTV, she discussed the allegations against her with a panel of newspaper and magazine editors.

On 19 December, 2010, Tarun Das, denied any wrongdoing in Karan Thapar's "Devil's Advocate" on CNN-IBN.

The original Radia tapes were annexured in a Supreme Court petition seeking A. Raja's prosecution. The Opposition demanded a Joint Parliamentary Committee (JPC) probe into the 2G spectrum scam, and into the Radia tapes to ascertain the media's role in the controversy. The complete shutdown of parliamentary proceedings, over the Opposition demand of a Joint Parliamentary Committee (JPC) probe, was the longest ever for 22 working days in independent India.

The CBI in its affidavit submitted to the Supreme Court, on Nov. 22, 2010, stated Radia to be approached for investigation at an appropriate time, and the probe to be completed latest by March 2011. On 24 November, 2010, Radia was questioned by the Enforcement Directorate (ED) and recorded her statements.

Home Minister P. Chidambaram found himself against investigations but felt "some of it is inevitable. In November 2010, Ratan Tata urged the Supreme Court of India to issue direction to the government to probe into the tapes containing his private conversations with Radia, and stop further publication of the same. Outlook and OPEN, challenged the maintainability of the petition moved by Ratan Tata in the Supreme Court, arguing it was private interest litigation cloaked in the form of public interest litigation.

On 14 December, 2010, the NGO – Centre for Public Interest Litigation (CPIL) filed a petition in the Supreme Court through counsel Prashant Bhushan "to seek the active intervention of SC (Supreme Court) to lift forever the officially protected cloak of secrecy that conceals from public gaze, any revelation of the backdoor manipulation of government and active subversion of government decisions and policy for private commercial interest".

The South Asian Media Commission had observed with shock and anguish the contents of the conversations of high-profile lobbyists seeking to manipulate media coverage to serve the interests of the corporate sector and asked journalists figuring in the tapes to express their regrets. "Particularly disturbing were the moves to use media persons for help to influence decisions by the government and leadership of the ruling dispensation on crucial issues like the composition of the Union Cabinet," the Indian chapter of the commission said in a statement.

Ratan Tatas writ petition filed in December 2010 was not merely to block publication of his conversations with Radia, but to redress "wholesale violation of the constitutional rights of a large number of persons" by the "indiscriminate publication" of wiretap material. His affidavit filed on 8 January, 2011, stated that big corporate houses own substantial stakes in media groups and therefore a "potential conflict" had arisen. Reliance Capital, owned 10% of the TV Today Networks, which belonged to the India Today Group. RPG and the Mumbai-based Rajan Raheja Group owned OPEN and Outlook, which published extensive excerpts from the Radia tapes.

In a fallout from the leakage of the Radia tapes, the Tata group had asked executives in its companies to avoid cooperating in news stories of several major Indian publications and television channels, Sunit Arora, Outlook's business editor, tweeted on 11 January, 2011: "The Tata group has banned story-related contact with four news organisations: The Economic Times, India Today, Headlines Today and Outlook."

In another fallout a committee headed by the cabinet secretary showed two recommendations in early March 2011: (1) the Indian Central Board of Direct Taxes (CBDT) be taken off the list of agencies authorised to request for wiretaps; (2) for agencies, like the Indian Enforcement Directorate (ED) and the Directorate of Revenue Intelligence (DRI), had to go through higher level of scrutiny within the Indian finance ministry before it goes for approval to the home secretary.

8.6. The Investigations and Arrest in Radiagate

The CBI told the Supreme Court of India in November 2010 the role of Niira Radia in the 2G spectrum controversy to be thoroughly investigated as the irregularities were of "enormous magnitude" having international ramifications. That investigation by March 2011, and that it was examining transcripts relating to Niira Radia's 5,851 phone calls and 82,665 pages of documents.

The Enforcement Directorate (ED), questioned Radia for more than eight hours on the 24th of November, 2010, Radia's first interrogation by an investigating agency. She had excused herself from earlier summons by the ED on health grounds in another investigation CBI revealed Radia brokered a mining deal between former (convicted) Jharkhand Chief Minister Madhu Koda wherein Koda allegedly sought a pay-off of Rs. 180 crore in return for extending the mining lease of a prominent corporate house.

On December 8, 2010, the CBI conducted raids in Delhi and Chennai, Tamil Nadu, 14 residences connected to A.Raja, his relatives and aides, as part of the investigation.

On December 15, 2010, it again raided various premises in Delhi and Chennai, the homes and offices of lobbyist Niira Radia, former telecom regulatory (TRAI) chief Pradip Baijal and relatives of former telecom minister A. Raja. The A. Raja's auditors and Kamaraj, a journalist known to be close to A. Raja's.

On December 16, 2010, the Supreme Court announced to monitor the investigations and asked the CBI, the ED and the Income Tax Department to file their investigation status before February 10, 2011.

The Centre for Public Interest Litigation had moved a petition to the Supreme Court, in mid-2010, asking it to supervise the investigation. On December 20, 2010, the CBI issued notices to A. Raja and Radia under Section 160 of the Indian Criminal Procedure Code asking them to appear for interrogation it further interrogated Pradip Baijal the same day. A. Raja sought additional time on health grounds, but on December 21, 2010, the CBI interrogated Niira Radia at her residence in Delhi. On December 24 and December 25, 2010, the CBI interrogated A. Raja at the CBI headquarters in Delhi. The CBI revealed, Niira Radia, to be instrumental in getting 2G spectrum and licences for "at least four companies" by using her "proximity to the former minister (A. Raja) during his stints as telecom minister".

The Indian Department of Income Tax special cell probed the trail of money transfers made to Radia's firms and to individuals and corporates. Hence on 25 January, 2011, the CBI questioned Radia for nearly four hours to understand the functioning of her firm and her alleged involvement in getting the telecom portfolio for A. Raja. On 27 January, 2011, the CBI again questioned Radia for several hours. On 14 February, 2011, the CBI summoned Unitech chairman-cum-managing director Sanjay Chandra in connection with the 2G spectrum allocation scam. Unitech was mentioned in the Radia tapes. On 16 February, 2011, Anil Ambani, was interrogated by the CBI, jointly with the arrested A Raja and the Swan Telecom promoter Shahid Usman Balwa at the CBI headquarters for over an hour as investigators tried to reconcile their individual claims about Swan Telecom, one of the biggest beneficiaries of the 2G specturm scam.

On 17 February, 2011, the CBI interrogated Essar group CEO Prashant Ruia for the alleged role of the company in conniving with Loop Telecom to get licences in an manner.

On 24 February, 2011, the CBI interrogated Ratan Tata's right hand man, R K Krishna Kumar, for nearly six hours. Kumar is the Chairman of Tata Realty and Infrastructure Ltd. He was mentioned in the released Radia tapes and Niira Radia is heard in conversation with Cecilia, Kumar's personal assistant.The CBI gathered evidence of A. Raja using his wife's bank accounts in Mauritius and Seychelles to deposit part of the INR 3,000 crore (USD 669,493,397) bribe.

In March 2011, the Enforcement Directorate (ED) tracked down three Malaysian nationals –Vijaykumar Ratnavelu, Gunasegaran Thiagarajan and Rajesh Ishwarbhai Bhatt – suspected to be involved in laundering money that the arrested former telecom minister A. Raja allegedly gained from the sale of 2G spectrum licences. Vijaykumar and Gunasegaran are linked to M/s Wellcom Communications India Pvt. Ltd. while Rajesh Ishwarbhai Bhatt is connected to M/s Starnet Communications (formerly Ampoules (India) Pvt. Ltd.).

On 11 March, 2011, the CBI interrogated key A.Raja supporter, Rajya Sabha Member (of Parliament) Kanimozhi and her step-mother Dayalu Ammal along with the Managing Director of DMK owned Kalaignar TV, Sharad Kumar, in Chennai. Kanimozhi was heard in conversation with Niira Radia in the released Radia tapes.

Arrests

On February 2, 2011, the CBI arrested former Telecommuni-cations Union Minister A.Raja, R.K. Chandolia, Raja's personal aide, and Siddharth Behura, the former Telecom Secretary. On February 8, 2011, the CBI arrested Dynamix Balwas (DB) group managing director Shahid Usman Balwa in connection with the 2G spectrum allocation scam. The CBI has evidence from the Income Tax department that Shahid Usman Balwa, considered close to A. Raja, was instrumental in channelling the kickbacks allegedly received by the former telecom minister.

That is how the nexus of media and politics was redefined in a obvious way through Radiagate issue.

Anubha Bhonsle, and Sr. Editor at CNN-IBN, rightly said, "Everything is exposed before people. There is nothing hidden about the nexus between bad faces of Media and Politics".

9. Conclusion

Throughout the centuries, the world has ever existed with information and communication, hence the inexhaustible essence of mass media. The government either makes or reject whatever exists within its environment, and determines the quantum of freedom to the mass media government influenced the mass media?

The 'politics' has today acquired many meanings. For an ordinary man in the street, politics is a negative word for dubious behaviour, scheming and maneuvering to secure an undue advantage over others. But implicit our consideration of politics remained to the realm of the state and government, a particular aspect of human activities that deals with distribution of power, influence and authority in the state for the purpose of order and good governance.

Money is the mother's milk of politics, but now information is no less. Politics, money and the media are intertwined in the most unlikely situations, especially because of the power of information to fashion reality.

References

1. "The spotlight is on the media now : The Niira Radia episode raises questions about the boundary between legitimate news gathering, lobbying and influence peddling", *Indian Express*, November 24, 2010. http://www.indianexpress.com
2. "Radia tapes featuring senior scribes create stir", *The Indian Express, Express Buzz*, 20 Nov., 2010, http://www.indianexpress.com/news/media-introspection-needed/729365/. Retrieved 23 November 2010.
3. November 23, 2010, "Indian media's mighty stand exposed on wrong side of 2G spectrum scam". *International Business Times*, http://www.mediacrooks.com
4. "2G: 'Lobbyist' Niira Radia under ED scanner", Central Chronical. November 24, 2010, http://www.centralchronicle.com
5. "Queen of connections : First a quiz, What connects Ratan Tata, Mukesh Ambani and Sunil Mittal? Niira Radia", E Jayakrishnan, India Syndicate, *Indian Express India*, 22 November 2010, http://www.indianexpress.com
6. "Does media follow unethical, biased journalism?". Oneindia.in. November 21, 2010, http://news.oneindia.in, Retrieved 23 November 2010.
7. "'Radia lobbied to get Raja telecom ministry'", *Indian Express*, http://www.indianexpress.com, Retrieved 23 November 2010.
8. On "Govt places in SC complaint leading to tapping of Radia's cell", *Business Standard*, 2 February, 2011, http://www.indianexpress.com on, Retrieved 13 February, 2011.

5

WikiLeaks–The Harmony Between 'Right to Publish' and 'Ethical Code of Conduct'

1. Introduction

WikiLeaks is an internation humanifarian non-profit media organisation it leaks the submissions of private, secret, and classified media from anonymous news sources, and whistle-blowers. Launched in 2006 under The Sunshine Press a database of more than 1.2 million documents within a year of its launch. WikiLeaks describes its founders as a mix of Chinese dissidents, journalists, mathematicians, and start-up company technologists from the United States, Taiwan, Europe, Australia, and South Africa. Julian Assange, an Australian Internet activist, is introduced as its director.

The site was originally formed as a user-editable wiki, but progress a more traditional publication mode and no longer accepts either user comments or edits.

In April 2010, it released gunsight footages from the 12 July, 2007 Baghdad airstrike in which showed Iraqi civilians and journalists indiscriminately killed by an Apache helicopter, as the Collateral Murder video. In July 2010Afghan War Diary, more than 76,900 documents about the War in Afghanistan for the first time made available to public review.

In October 2010, it further released almost 400,000 Iraq War Logs with major commercial media houses. This covered every death in Iraq, and across the border in Iran,

In November 2010, itreleasing U.S. State department diplomatic cables.

1.1. Founding

The wikileaks.org was registered on 4 October, 2006. released its first document in December 2006. The founders, however, have not been formally identified. It has been pushed in public since January 2007 by Julian Assange wife describes himself as a member of WikiLeaks' advisory board. The Australian have called Assange the "founder of WikiLeaks".

Wired magazine reported once on, a volunteer is instance said that Assange partrayed himself in a private conversation as "the heart and soul of this organisation, its founder, philosopher, spokesperson, original coder, organiser, financier, and all the rest". By June 2009, the site had over 1,200 registered volunteers and an advisory board comprising Assange and eight other people.

1.2. Purpose

WikiLeaks asserts as its "primary interest in exposing oppressive regimes in Asia, the former Soviet bloc, Sub-Saharan Africa and the Middle East, but we also expect to be of assistance to people of all regions who wish to reveal unethical behaviour in their governments and corporations."

Once said:

One of the WikiLeaks activists owned a server that was being used as a node for the Tor network. Millions of secret transmissions passed through it. The activist noticed that hackers from China were using the network to gather foreign governments' information, and began to record this traffic. Only a small fraction has ever been posted on WikiLeaks, but the initial tranche served as the site's foundation, and Assange was able to say, "[w]e have received over one million documents from thirteen countries."

It aims to protect the whistle-blowers and journalists Who must not be given jails for e-mailing classified documents, as happened to Chinese journalist Shi Tao, who was sentenced to 10 imprisonment years in 2005 after publicising an email from Chinese officials about the anniversary of the Tiananmen Square massacre.

It drew comparisons to Daniel Ellsberg's leaking of the Pentagon Papers in 1971. In the United States, the leaking of some documents can be legally protected. The U.S. Supreme Court has ruled that the Constitution guarantees anonymity, at least in the area of political discourse.

Author and journalist Whitley Strieber has expressedabout the benefits of the WikiLeaks project, noting that "Leaking a government document can mean jail, but jail sentences for this can be fairly short. However, there are many places where it means long incarceration or even death, such as China and parts of Africa and the Middle East."

1.3. Operational challenges

On 17 July, Jacob Appelbaum represented WikiLeaks at the 2010 Hackers on Planet Earth conference in New York City, and announced, the WikiLeaks submission system was again up and running, after temporarily suspenion. Assange made a surprise presence a TED conference 2010, 19 July, in Oxford, and confirmed the site accept submissions again.

On 29 July 2010, Appelbaum was detained for three hours at the airport by US agents. He was returning from Netherlands. told Cnet reported Appelbaum's bag was searched, receipts from his bag were photocopied and his laptop was inspected, and ppelbaum reportedly refused to answer questions without a lawyer present, and was not allowed to use his phones reportedly seized. On 31 July, at a Defcon conference he mentioned about his being "seized". That day, too, he was by two FBI agents questioned.

On 25 September, 2010, after being suspended for "disloyalty, insubordination and destabilisation", Daniel Domscheit-Berg, the German spokesman for WikiLeaks, saying, "WikiLeaks has a structural problem. I no longer want to take responsibility for it, and that's why I am leaving the project".

Assange accused Berg of leaking information to Newsweek claiming the WikiLeaks team was unhappy with Assange's leadership and handling of the Afghan war document releases. Domscheit-Berg resigned with a small group started OpenLeaks.com, with a different management and distribution philosophy. Herbert Snorrason, Iceland MP Birgitta Jonsdottir also from WikiLeaks on non transparency, non-structured, and non communication in the organisation. The Independent, at least a dozen key supporters of WikiLeaks in 2010.

1.4. Administration

A January 2010 interview, disclosed, the WikiLeaks team composed of five pronomenent iffucuak along with about 800 were non compensated. WikiLeaks has no official headquarters. The expenses met per year are about €200,000, mainly for servers and bureaucracy, it is assumed, it can the works done by them.shot up to €600,000 if volunteers are paid for. WikiLeaks does not pay for lawyers, as hundreds of thousands of dollars in legal support have been donated by media organisations such as the Associated Press, Los Angeles Times, and the National Newspaper Publishers Association.

Its only revenue stream is donations, but WikiLeaks has planned to add an auction model to sell early access to documents. The Wau Holland Foundation processes donations to WikiLeaks. In July 2010, the Foundation stated that WikiLeaks was receiving no money for personnel costs, only for hardware, travelling and bandwidth.

1.4.1. Financing

WikiLeaks dependents on public donations,through conventional bank transfers and online payment systems. Wau Holland Foundation, disclosed that it received more than €900,000 (US$ 1.2 million) in public donations between October 2009 and December 2010, and passed €370,000 on to WikiLeaks. Hendrik Fulda, vice president of the Foundation, mentioned that the Foundation had been receiving twice as many donations through PayPal as through other banks, however, PayPal's decided later on to suspend WikiLeaks' account. It is also recorded through the Foundation that every new WikiLeaks publication brought "a wave of support", and that donations flowed liberally in the weeks after publishing of leaked diplomatic cables by WikiLeaks.

1.4.2. Name and policies

"WikiLeaks", is no longer wiki-based as of May 2010. WikiLeaks and Wikipedia have no affiliation with each other Wikia, a for-profit corporation loosely affiliated with the Wikimedia Foundation, however, purchased several WikiLeaks-related domain names wikileaks.com and wikileaks.net) as a "protective brand measure" in 2007.

The "about" page originally reads

> To the user, WikiLeaks will look very much like Wikipedia. Anybody can post to it, anybody can edit it. No technical knowledge is required. Leakers can post documents anonymously and untraceably. Users can publicly discuss documents and analyse their credibility and veracity. Users can discuss interpretations and context and collaboratively formulate collective publications. Users can read and write explanatory articles on leaks along with background material and context. The political relevance of documents and their verisimilitude will be revealed by a cast of thousands.

However, WikiLeaks editorial policy accepted only documents "of political, diplomatic, historical or ethical interest" and excluded "material that is already publicly available". It is no longer possible for anybody to post to it or edit it, as the original FAQ promised. Instead, submissions are regulated by an internal review process and some are published, while documents not fitting the editorial criteria are rejected by anonymous WikiLeaks reviewers.

By 2008, the revised FAQ stated that "anybody can post comments to it. [...] Users can publicly discuss documents and analyse their credibility and veracity." After the 2010 relaunch, posting new comments to Leaks was no longer possible.

1.4.3. Verification of submissions

WikiLeaks never released a misattributed document. About the possibility of misleading or fraudulent leaks, WikiLeaks has ensured that misleading leaks "are already well-placed in the mainstream media. WikiLeaks is of no additional assistance."

The FAQ states that "the simplest and most effective counter-measure is a worldwide community of informed users and editors who can scrutinise and discuss leaked documents."

Assange in 2010 stated that the submitted documents are assessed by a group of five reviewers, with expertise in different fields, who also investigate the background of the leaker. In that group, Assange has the final decision about the assessment of a document.

1.5.Legal status

The legal status of WikiLeaks is complex. WikiLeaks is a whistle-blower protection intermediary. Leaking directly to the press, and fearing exposure and retribution, whistle-blowers leaks to WikiLeaks. Its servers are located throughout Europe and are accessible from any uncensored web connection. Its headquarters operates in Sweden because it has one of the world's strongest shield laws to protect confidential source-journalist relationships. Assange used his speech during the Hack In The Box conference in Malaysia to ask the crowd of hackers and security researchers to help find documents on its "Most Wanted Leaks of 2009" list.

1.6. Leaks

1.6.1. 2006-08

WikiLeaks posted its first document in December 2006, a decision to assassinate government officials signed by Sheikh Hassan Dahir Aweys.

In August 2007, The Guardian published a story about corruption by the family of the former Kenyan leader Daniel arap Moi based on information provided via WikiLeaks.

In November 2007, a March 2003 copy of Standard Operating Procedures for Camp Delta detailing the protocol of the U.S. Army at the Guantanamo Bay detention camp was released. The document that some prisoners were off-limits to the International Committee of the Red Cross, which the U.S. military had in the past repeatedly denied.

In February 2008, WikiLeaks released allegations of illegal activities at the Cayman Islands branch of the Swiss Bank Julius Baer which led to the bank suing WikiLeaks and obtaining an injunction a movement temporarily to shut down WikiLeaks.org. The was instantly organised by supporters. Later that month the judge upset his previous decision citing First Amendment concerns and questions about legal jurisdiction.

In March 2008, WikiLeaks released "the collected secret 'bibles' of Scientology," and within days received letters of threatening to sue them for breach of copyright.

In September 2008, during the 2008 United States presidential election campaigns, the contents of a Yahoo account belonging to Sarah Palin (the running mate of Republican presidential nominee John McCain) were posted on WikiLeaks after being hacked into by members of Anonymous.

In November 2008, the membership list of the far-right British National Party was posted to WikiLeaks, after briefly appearing on a blog. A year later, on October 2009, another list of BNP members was leaked.

1.6.2. 2009

In January 2009, WikiLeaks released 86 telephone intercept recordings of Peruvian politicians and businessmen involved in the 2008 Peru oil scandal.

In February, WikiLeaks released 6,780 Congressional Research Service reports followed in March, by a list of contributors to the Norm Coleman senatorial campaign and a set of documents belonging to Barclays Bank that had been ordered removed from the website of The Guardian.

In July, they released a report relating to a serious nuclear accident that had occurred at the Iranian Natanz nuclear facility in 2009. Later media reports have suggested that the accident was related to the Stuxnet computer worm. In September, internal documents from Kaupthing Bank were leaked, from shortly before the collapse of Iceland's banking sector, which led to the 2008-2010 Icelandic financial crisis. The document shows that suspiciously large sums of money were loaned to various owners of the bank, and large debts written off.

In October, Joint Services Protocol 440, a British document advising the security services on how to avoid documents being leaked was published by WikiLeaks.

Later that month, they announced that a super-injunction was being used by the commodities company, Trafigura to gag The Guardian newspaper from reporting on a leaked internal document regarding a toxic dumping incident in the Ivory Coast.

In November, they hosted copies of e-mail correspondence between climate scientists, although they were not originally leaked to WikiLeaks. They also released 570,000 intercepts of pager messages sent on the day of the 11 September attacks.

During 2008 and 2009, WikiLeaks published the alleged lists of forbidden or illegal web addresses for Australia, Denmark and Thailand. These were originally created to prevent access to child pornography and terrorism, but the leaks revealed that other sites covering unrelated subjects were also listed.

1.6.3. 2010

In March 2010, WikiLeaks released a secret 32-page U.S. Department of Defense Counter-intelligence Analysis Report written in March 2008 discussing the leaking of material by WikiLeaks and how it could be deterred.

In April, a classified video of the 12 July, 2007 Baghdad airstrike was released, showing two Reuters employees being fired at, after the pilots mistakenly thought the men were carrying weapons, which were in fact cameras.

In the week following the release, "WikiLeaks" was the search term with the most significant growth worldwide in the last seven days as measured by Google Insights.

In January 2010, WikiLeaks received the first test cable A 22-year-old US Army intelligence analyst, PFC (formerly SPC) Bradley Manning, a US embassy cable relating about IceSave, thereafter referred as "Reykjavik 13".

In June 2010, he was arrested after alleged chat logs were turned into the authorities by former hacker Adrian Lamo, in whom he had confided. Manning reportedly told Lamo he had leaked the "Collateral

Murder" video, in addition to a video of the Granai airstrike and around 260,000 diplomatic cables, to WikiLeaks.

In July, WikiLeaks released 92,000 documents related to the war in Afghanistan between 2004 and the end of 2009 to The Guardian, The New York Times and Der Spiegel. The documents detail individual incidents including friendly fire and civilian casualties.

At the end of July, a 1.4 GB "insurance file" was added to the Afghan War Diary page, whose decryption details would be released if WikiLeaks or Assange were harmed. About 15,000 of the 92,000 documents have not yet been released on WikiLeaks, as the group is currently reviewing the documents to remove some of the sources of the information. WikiLeaks asked the Pentagon and human-rights groups to help remove names from the documents to reduce the potential harm caused by their release, but did not receive assistance. Following the Love Parade stampede in Duisburg, Germany on 24 July, 2010, a local published internal documents of the city administration regarding the planning of Love Parade. The city government reacted by acquiring a court order on 16 August forcing the removal of the documents from the site on which it was hosted.

On 20 August WikiLeaks released a publication titled Love Parade 2010 Duisburg planning documents, 2007-2010, which comprised 43 internal documents regarding the Love Parade 2010. Following on from the leak of information from the Afghan War, in October 2010, around 400,000 documents relating to the Iraq War were released in October. The BBC quoted The Pentagon referring to the Iraq War Logs as "the largest leak of classified documents in its history." Media coverage of the leaked documents focused on claims that the U.S. government had ignored reports of torture by the Iraqi authorities during the period after the 2003 war.

1.6.4. Diplomatic cables release

On 28 November, 2010, WikiLeaks and five major newspapers from Spain (El País), France (Le Monde), Germany (Der Spiegel), the United Kingdom (The Guardian), and the United States (The New York Times) simultaneously began publishing the first 220 of 251,287 leaked confidential-diplomatic cables from 274 US embassies around the world, dated from 28 December 1966 to 28 February, 2010.

The diplomatic cables include numerous unguarded comments and revelations regarding: critiques and praises about the host countries of various US embassies; political manoeuvring regarding climate change;

discussion and resolutions towards ending ongoing tension in the Middle East; efforts and resistance towards nuclear disarmament; actions in the War on Terror; assessments of other threats around the world; dealings between various countries; US intelligence and counter-intelligence efforts; and other diplomatic actions.

Reactions to the United States diplomatic cables leak include stark criticism, anticipation, commendation, and quiescence. Consequent reactions to the US government include sympathy, bewilderment and dismay.

On 14 December, 2010 the United States Department of Justice issued a subpoena directing Twitter to provide information for accounts associated with WikiLeaks. Twitter decided to notify its users. The overthrow of the presidency in Tunisia has been attributed in part to reaction against the corruption revealed by leaked cables.

1.6.5. Upcoming leaks

In May 2010, WikiLeaks received video footages of a massacre of civilians in Afghanistan by the US military which meant to release.

On 19 July, 2010, in an interview with Chris Anderson Assange a document on an Albanian oil well blowout, and had material from inside BP, and enormous quantity of whistle-blower disclosures of a very high calibre" WikiLeaks had not been able to verify and release due to non-avalability enough volunteer journalists.

In October 2010, Assange told a leading Moscow newspaper that "The Kremlin had better brace itself for a coming wave of WikiLeaks disclosures about Russia." Assange later clarified, "We have material on many businesses and governments, including in Russia. It's not right to say there's going to be a particular focus on Russia".

In a 2009 Computer World interview, Assange claimed to be in possession of "5 GB from Bank of America".

In 2010 he told Forbes WikiLeaks was planning another "mega leak" early in 2011, from inside the private sector, involving "a big U.S. bank" and revealing an "ecosystem of corruption". Bank of America's stock price fell by 3% as a result of this announcement. Assange commented on the possible impact of the release that "it could take down a bank or two."

In December 2010, Assange's lawyer, Mark Stephens, told The Andrew Marr Show on the BBC, that WikiLeaks had information it considers to be a "thermo-nuclear device" which it would release if the organisation needs to defend itself.

In January 2011, Rudolf Elmer, a former Swiss banker, passed on data containing account details of 2,000 prominent people to Assange, who stated that the information will be assessed before being made publicly available at a later date.

1.7. Backlash and pressure

1.7.1. Governments

1.7.1.1. Germany

The house of Theodor Reppe, registrant of the German WikiLeaks domain name, wikileaks.de, was raided on 24 March, 2009 after WikiLeaks posted the Australian Communications and Media Authority (ACMA) censorship blacklist. The site was not affected.

1.7.1.2. People's Republic of China

The WikiLeaks shares the government of the People's Republic of China has attempted to block all traffic to web sites with "wikileaks" in the URL since 2007, but that this can be bypassed through encrypted connections or by using one of WikiLeaks' many covert URLs.

1.7.1.3. Australia

On 16 March, 2009, the Australian Communications and Media Authority added WikiLeaks to their proposed blacklist of sites that will be blocked for all Australians if the necessary internet filtering censorship scheme is executed as per The blacklisting was removed on 30 November, 2010.

1.7.1.4. Thailand

The Centre for the Resolution of the Emergency Situation (CRES) is currently censoring the website WikiLeaks in Thailand and more than 40,000 other webpages because of the emergency decree in Thailand imposed as a result of political instabilities (Emergency decree declared beginning of April 2010).

1.7.1.4. United States

Access to WikiLeaks is currently blocked in the United States Library of Congress. On 3 December, 2010, the White House Office of Management and Budget sent a memo forbidding all unauthorised federal government employees and contractors from accessing classified documents publicly available on WikiLeaks and other websites.

The U.S. Army, the Federal Bureau of Investigation and the Justice Department are considering criminally prosecuting WikiLeaks and Assange "on grounds they encouraged the theft of government property", although former prosecutors say doing so would be difficult. According to a report on the Daily Beast the Obama administration asked Britain, Germany and Australia among others to also consider bringing criminal charges against Assange for the Afghan war leaks and to help limit Assange's travels across international borders.

Columbia University students are warned by their Office of Career Services that the U.S. State Department contacted the office in an e-mail saying the diplomatic cables which were released by WikiLeaks were "still considered classified" and that "online discourse about the documents would call into question your ability to deal with confidential information."

All U.S. federal government staff are blocked from WikiLeaks. Some Department of Homeland Security staff accessing ban on accessing WikiLeaks on government computers and other government devices as hampering their work; "More damage will be done by keeping the federal workforce largely in the dark about what other interested parties worldwide are going to be reading and analysing." The ban apparently covers personal computers, too.

Although Hillary Clinton refused to comment on specific reports, she claimed the leaks "put people's lives in danger" and "threatens national security." On the other hand, Robert Gates, a former CIA chief and Deputy National Security Adviser under George H.W. Bush, argued, "Is this embarrassing? Yes. Is it awkward? yes. Consequences for U.S. foreign policy? I think fairly modest."

1.7.1.5. Iceland

After the posting of the 2007 airstrikes video and preparation to release film of the Granai airstrike, Julian Assange along with his group of volunteers came under intense surveillance. In an interview and Twitter posts Assange said a restaurant in Reykjavík where his volunteers usually had meetings came under surveillance in March; there was "covert following and hidden photography" by police and foreign intelligence services; that an apparent British intelligence agent made thinly threats in a Luxembourg car park; and that one of the volunteers was detained by police for 21 hours. Another volunteer complained of sezure of computers saying "If anything happens to us, you know why ... and you know who is responsible." According to the Columbia Journalism Review, "the

Icelandic press took a look at Assange's charges of being surveilled in Iceland and, at best, have found nothing to substantiate them."

1.7.2. Organisations and companies

1.7.2.1. Facebook

WikiLeaksinformed in April 2010 that Facebook removed their fan page, which had 30,000 fans. However, by of 7 December, 2010, the group's Facebook fan page was available and had grown by 100,000 fans daily since 1 December, to more than 1.5 million fans. The largest growth of the week. About existance of the of WikiLeaks on Facebook, Andrew Noyes, the company's D.C. based Manager of Public Policy Communications has stated. "The WikiLeaks Facebook Page does not violate our content standards nor have we encountered any material posted on the page that violates our policies."

1.7.2.2. Moneybookers

In October 2010, there came a report that Moneybookers, after collecting donations for WikiLeaks, had ended its repport with the site. Moneybookers stated about decision "to comply with money laundering or other investigations conducted by government authorities, agencies or commissions."

1.7.3. U.S. diplomatic cables leak responses

The Times, incessent reported, WikiLeaks and its members have complained about harassment and surveillance by law enforcement and intelligence organisations, including extended detention, seizure of computers, veiled threats, "covert following and hidden photography." The lawyers for WikiLeaks in the The Guardian they had belief being watched by the security services after the U.S. cables leak.

Moreover, several companies severed ties with WikiLeaks. After providing 24-hour notification, American-owned EveryDNS dropped WikiLeaks from its entries on 2 December 2010, citing DDoS attacks that "threatened the stability of its infrastructure". The site's 'info' DNS lookup continued to be operational at alternative addresses for direct access respectively to the WikiLeaks and Cablegate websites.

On the same day, Amazon.com severed its ties with WikiLeaks, to which it was providing infrastructure services, after an intervention by an aide of U.S. Senator Joe Lieberman. Citing indirect pressure from the U.S. Government, Tableau Software also dropped WikiLeaks' data from its site for people to use for data visualisation.

In the coming days, hundreds of mirrors of the WikiLeaks site appeared, and the Anonymous group of Internet activists called on supporters to attack the websites of companies which opposed WikiLeaks, under the banner of Operation Payback, previously aimed at anti-piracy organisations. AFP reported that attempts to shut down the WikiLeaks.org address had led to the site surviving via the so-called Streisand effect, whereby efforts to censor news online leads to it being replicated in many places.

2. WikiLeaks Raises New Ethical Issues (Taken from concordmonitor.com)

By now, most people know that like the London alleys Sherlock Holmes prowled, the internet is heavily burdened not just by good guys but also by cutthroats, thieves, perverts and spies. during every hour of every day, a great cyber-war rages as governments, attempt to critical information about allies and enemies alike.

WikiLeaks.org, a clandestine non profit organisation devote pselt to publish secret information governments and corporations. efforts are global, ethical code its own, and defences against lawsuits excellent. WikiLeaks make put a transparancy on the workings of the powerful and for this, provided information to tip off by extension, the law enforcement agencies to wrongdoing.

The group's unhesitated hope is to ruin wrongdoing of all sorts, by making the truth come out. But the release of some of the information that appears on the group's website could lead to harm. A sensational stery posted on site toward the ethical dilemmas about the source. In April, sensitive 17-minute video of an attack by an American Apache helicopter crew on a group of Iraqis civilians and two Reuters journalists was posted on YouTube and other internet sites with the title "Collateral Murder." It, and the accompanying purloined Army code governing the rules of engagement, has been viewed by more than 5 million people and drawn an angry response from U.S. military officials. A news confirmed the arrest of Army Specialist Bradley Manning of Potomac, MD, on charges he leaked the video and other materials to WikiLeaks. He sai badly, he stoled and secreted 260,000 cable messages about foreign leaders and diplomatic affairs from government computers and was ready to make them public.

Journalists typically have developes a habit of want the maximum possible release of government information. But Publishing stolen information that can destroy international relations and compromise national security is a kind of treason.

The New Yorker Columnist writer Raffi Khatchadourian many members of the organisation are unknown to each other and to Assange. These unpaid members scale great lengths to keep the anonymity of informators to the group for posting. This description of WikiLeaks' secret computer server from The New Yorker by Steig Larsson is as:

"These machines are maintained by exceptionally secretive engineers, the high priesthood of WikiLeaks. . . The entire pipeline, along with the submissions moving through it, is encrypted, and the traffic is kept anonymous by means of a modified version of the Tor network, which sends internet traffic through 'virtual tunnels' that are extremely private. Moreover, at any given time, WikiLeaks computers are feeding hundreds of thousands of fake submissions through these tunnels, obscuring the real documents."

In such open circumstance and cruiatily of operating under different standards, it is difficult to determine the truth of the information posted by WikiLeaks for good or ill.

3. The Cause of Embarrassment, Disappointment and Anxiety

The Absence of Ethical Code of Conduct in WikiLeaks has raised a greater concern for Americans and the Western alliance overcoming Julian Assange far he brings to light 250,000 sensitive documents regarding national security.

Shock, embarrassment, disappointment and anxiety have overwhelmed the planet in recent days.

WikiLeaks raises a number of ethical issues to contemplate.Firstly, to what extent the public has the right to know in a democracy ?

Abraham Lincoln, who knew democracy a bit betters actually made the groundwork for government security measures during the Civil War as he proclaimed authority to covert military action, information surveillance and secret negotiations with allies.

We must remind of the crunial circumstances that deserve secrety to accesive a result. Such circumstance are many as technical support, military resources, plans and strategies, treaty negotiations, human rights issues and security for leaders are on . But a time comes when a democratic government its accountable for of its action know the accountability. The people can use the Right to Information Act to know the accountability.

WikiLeaks material clearly portray a sordid picture of influence brokerage, and misdirected attempts at espionage using high-level government servant it.

Figure out why taxpayer funding is used to collect credit card information and frequent flier numbers for foreign diplomats. why is the U.S. Secretary of State orchestrating such activities?

This is also an ethical offen to demean prominent diplomats and leaders.

4. WikiLeaks, knowledge, and abuse of power

By Lyombeeko – Guest Opinion , September 20, 2010, 7:20 AM

An old proverb states that "there is nothing hidden under the Sun." Sooner or later, even the most tightly guarded secrets become public knowledge. That "time will tell" logic was not good enough for WikiLeaks, a website founded by an idealistic group of self-styled "whistle-blowers, activists, and journalists."

WikiLeaks was conceptualised as a whistle-blower's Wikipedia, an open repository for purloined governmental, corporate, and private information. From its servers located somewhere between Australia and Sweden, WikiLeaks went drip, drip, drip – leaking "sensitive" information from corrupt, dictatorial regimes as well as from democracies that did not live up to their values.

In 2008, Index on Censorship awarded WikiLeaks its Freedom of Expression Award for leaking information about the alleged illegal offshore activities of a Swiss investment bank and successfully fighting off a permanent injunction issued by an American court against publication of that information.

In 2009, WikiLeaks and its enigmatic frontman, Julian Assange, won Amnesty International's UK Media Award in the New Media category. WikiLeaks had been accepted into the ever-expanding, "media" fraternity.

In July, WikiLeaks published the fruits of what is probably the biggest leak in U.S. military history – 91,000 classified field reports on the war in Afghanistan. The so-called "Afghan War Diaries" contains data on Afghan civilian casualties, as well as the names of Afghans who collaborated with American and NATO troops. It also contains information about the allegedly duplicitous role of Pakistan. WikiLeaks has threatened to release 15,000 more reports from the leaked archive.

The Obama administration was not amused. It denounced the leaks, but played down their impact. It was an empty gesture of helplessness.

Amnesty International, the Afghanistan Independent Human Rights Commission, and other human-rights organisations joined the United States in condemning the leaks. These organisations claimed that by dumping the secret documents on the Internet without adequately redacting the names of Afghans who worked with American and NATO forces, the international media, and human-rights groups, WikiLeaks had endangered lives.

The activities of WikiLeaks raise several ethical issues.

Publication of stolen, confidential documents, many of which do not deal with matters of public interest, is problematic. In order to burnish its "media" credentials, WikiLeaks collaborated with The Guardian (UK), Der Spiegel (Germany) and the New York Times when it decided to leak the "Afghan Diaries." The question is whether WikiLeaks should be held to the same legal and ethical standards as the "traditional media."

Anne Garrels, veteran foreign correspondent for National Public Radio, discussed the WikiLeaks affair in a keynote address at the annual conference of the Association for Education in Journalism and Mass Communication. Garrels told her audience of educators and administrators from around the world that when she was based in Iraq, her driver/ interpreter was abducted, raped, and held for ransom. She said she went to extraordinary lengths to have him released and spirited out of Iraq. Garrels deplored the fact that WikiLeaks had published the names of Afghans who worked with Westerners.

"You don't want blood on your hands," she said in reference to Taliban threats to kill all Afghans who worked with foreigners in Afghanistan.

Whistle-blowers are often driven by the highest ethical ideals. They ought to know that information is power, but that too much information can be an abuse of power. WikiLeaks has done the world a great service by exposing human-rights abuses, governmental and corporate corruption, and other predatory activities that diminish the humanity of the weak and defenseless. However, transparency must not come at the expense of human life, individual privacy, and reputation.

5. Discussing The Two Sides–The Ethics and Right to Publish

Let us thin k over the ethical evaluation of the questions: Is whistle-blowing motivated by resentment and an attitude to harm its target is ethical? And is WikiLeaks' facilitation of whistle-blowing ethical, even if it might put at risk innocent people? The deontologist, that telling the truth virtue is an absolute appreciate whistle-blowing as the right thing to do, independent of the reasons behind it. The consequentialist may support WikiLeaks as a means to maximise the welfare of the largest number of people, by censuring sensitive information.

However, confidential communication operates amongst the – sender, receiver and referent – in which sender and receiver trust each other. The receiver, trusts and holds responsible the sender for the truth of what is communicated about the referent. The referent may know about such communication and may even easily guess its contents, but there is confidentiality only if the receiver, has access to the information exchanged. Accountability is present and connects sender and receiver.

Whistle-blowing such a three-player game. In the new profile of the game, the sender is the whistle-blower through WikiLeaks, the whole world is the potential receiver, and the referents are the players in the previously confidential communication. The relation of confidentiality of the original game is shattered: the new referents are also among the new world-receiver, which now holds the old sender responsible for what is communicated, not only for its truth

The metagame reinstates, somewhat hypocritically, the same rules it criticises: WikiLeaks, quite rightly but inconsistently, protects the anonymity and confidentiality of its sources, which are likely to make an exception about the information transparency of their own identity, frowning upon Meta WikiLeaks, with leaks on leaks.

Finally, the relation of accountability is missing in the metagame, the whistle-blower and WikiLeaks might be good-willed and well-intentioned but are not obligated by professional codes of conduct or legalessentials. So the receiver, which is also the referent, is at the mercy of the sender. WikiLeaks knows this and that is why it "whitemails" the world, i.e., it blackmails it by threatening to disclose even more damaging information through its "insurance file", should anything happens to WikiLeaks or its spokesman Julian Assange.

WikiLeaks itself clamours that a , without confidential communication, there is not possibility of a communication at all. The argument in favour of WikiLeaks, that most of the information was already public or suspected misses the point, it means that WikiLeaks may undermine the possibility of future frank communication. After the initial embarrassment, the whole system would come to a standstill.

Finally, "information liberation" arguments are of limited scope. The new WikiLeaks' About file holds that "publishing improves transparency, and this transparency creates a better society for all people". Yet this is naïve at best because the value of information is not absolute, but relative to its use. Judas' kiss tells the truth about the identity of the kissed, but it scarely makes a better society. Further for the value of the use of information is relative to the goals and the sort of possible world about. Thus, the personal details about religious and sexual orientations must be untouched some. Information "act as a necessary condition for discrimination.

Thus, facilitating whistle-blowing is morally good only if the whistle-blowing itself is morally good; and only if the specific cause morallyu good it fosters. "Our primary interest is in exposing oppressive regimes in Asia, the former Soviet bloc, Sub-Saharan Africa and the Middle East, but we also expect to be of assistance to people of all regions who wish to reveal unethical behaviour in their governments and corporations. We aim for maximum political impact." Unfortunately, this strong and explicit ethical statement has disappeared Luckily, so far WikiLeaks has picked up causes judged by most morally good.

Support for WikiLeaks if the leaks a cause defend use of accountability should themselves be accountable. Moreover, who will blow the whistle on the whistle-blowers, if their behaviour become unethical?

6. WikiLeaks: The Ethics of Revealing Secrets

WikiLeaks published thousands of reports about the Iraq War. Though much of the information was already known if further, released attack in July 2007 in Baghdad by a U.S. helicopter that dozen people and two journalists. For such leaksit has received welcoming nots

But the ethics behind revealing secrets have received multiple questions. Despite what conspiracy theorists may think, secrecy is not an inherently bad thing; in fact, it usually keeps us safe. For revealing may put one' stakes at risk. People keep personal information away from other people, not to deceive but simply because it's a tone of vigil. Similarly, revealing state secrets may put national security at risk, or may fall into the category of "too much information." But under what circumstances is revealing secrets ethical?

Sissela Bok submits that the ethics of revealing secrets lies in the nature of what is being exposed: "Whistle-blowing and leaks may be starkly inappropriate when used in malice or in error... the judgment expressed by whistle-blowers concerns a problem that should matter to the public. Certain outrages are so blatant, and certain dangers so great, that all who are in a position to warn of them have a prima facie obligation to do so. Conversely, other problems are so minor that to blow the whistle would be a disproportionate response." Thus some of what WikiLeaks does is ethical, and some is not. But much of the material that WikiLeaks has published has had little to do with revealing "unethical behaviour" in governments and corporations. While many consider Scientology to be a science-fiction-based cult, for example, divulging its teachings (though secret) hardly qualifies as exposing corruption or "murderous leadership."

The New York Times sourced buy W.K. Leaks's "reveals for the first time that the United States believes that Iran obtained advanced missiles from North Korea." This information potentially concerns to national security, but it does not expose any unethical behaviour. Nor do the dozens of references to analysts' assessments of foreign leaders and governments; State Department employees' opinions that Zimbabwe president Robert Mugabe "will not wake up one morning a changed man, resolved to set right all he has wrought," or that Libyan leader Muammar el-Qaddafi's "long-time Ukrainian nurse.... has been described as a 'voluptuous blonde" have no unethical behaviour on the part of any government.

These cases, clear by purpose not to expose any wrongdoing or grave dangers, but instead to merely embarrass government officials and complicate diplomacy. WikiLeaks astrays from its organisation's mission and weilds into unethical behaviour.

The website states: "Our primary interest in exposing oppressive regimes in Asia, the former Soviet bloc, Sub-Saharan Africa and the Middle East, but we also expect to be of assistance to people of all regions who wish to reveal unethical behaviour in their governments and corporations. Our goal is to bring important news and information to the public."

Revelations, are certainly serious. But the fact that WikiLeaks is unable (or unwilling) to make a distinction between important information (e.g., genocide) and gossip (e.g., Qaddafi's arm candy) attenuates its credibility.

7. Journalism Ethicist Calls for WikiLeaks Code of Ethics –by Sydney Smith, StinkyJournalism.org

Stephen J.A. Ward called for WikiLeaks and other "whistle-blower" sites to establish some form of ethics code. He explained his concerns and call in the article, "How to Reveal Secrets," published on The Canadian Journalism Project Aug. 24.

Ward is a journalism ethics professor at the University of Wisconsin-Madison, the founding chair of the Canadian Association of Journalists' ethics advisory committee and the director of the Center for Journalism Ethics.

Noting that WikiLeaks's publication of secret Afghan War documents "sparked an ethics firestorm," Ward wrote that WikiLeaks is a blend of old and new media. In fact, it's such a blend that when the Afghan documents were published, many in the media and public didn't know how to treat WikiLeaks – is it a source or a news agency?

A further case in point: analyses of the Afghan War documents were published concurrently by major newspapers The New York Times, Der Spiegel, and The Guardian through the collaboration of new media (WikiLeaks) with old media (the newspapers).

"The technology of mixed media creates an online world where hybrid sites exercise political and moral power," Ward wrote.

Because WikiLeaks is operated in numerous countries and has established safeguards to prevent a government from shutting it down or censoring it, Ward concluded that WikiLeaks has political power.

Morally, however, WikiLeaks has an ethical problem, according to Ward. The site holds moral power, yet Ward can't discern how the site weighs moral decisions. Where many journalists voluntarily abide by a code of ethics (whether it be the U.S. Society of Professional Journalists', the UK National Union of Journalists' or so on), WikiLeaks and whistle-blower sites are seemingly without such ethical guidelines.

"WikiLeaks is seen by many as an Internet cowboy on a white horse, fighting the dark forces of censorship, corruption, and military secrecy," Ward explained. "It celebrates the Internet's love of free voices and combines it with a journalist's hatred of secrecy." But, what are WikiLeaks' ethics and standards?

In order to determine what some of WikiLeaks' ethics may be, Ward listed numerous questions he has for WikiLeaks, including:

- What wouldn't the site publish and why?
- Are there legitimate reasons for secrecy, and what?
- Would WikiLeaks publish NATO codes for protection against nuclear attack? Would it publish the security plans of energy installations or airports against terrorist attack? Would it publish information that would place in danger individuals, informants, or soldiers?
- What is WikiLeaks' editorial process?
- How does WikiLeaks decide what to publish?
- Does WikiLeaks attempt to be accurate, complete, and fair?
- Does WikiLeaks consider any government "an oppressive regime?
- Will the advocates of the site publish secrets from all countries equally, or will they favour reports that support their favoured causes or do damage to countries they dislike?
- What does the public do when the site errs? How does WikiLeaks handle complaints?

Further, Ward clarified he's not necessarily against WikiLeaks, but that he sees the need for "open and responsible ethical policies." Likewise, in the media, he wrote, "We need a serious debate on the ethics of secrecy." How does the media report secret information and what codes or rules guide those reporting decisions?

He wrote that while it's important for newsrooms to decide their ethical policies when it comes to the publication of secret documents, it's more important to "critically challenge these sites about their ethics."

Ward also wondered how newsrooms can work with sites like WikiLeaks. He wrote that "rules of collaboration should be no different from the rules for using data from any external source."

For example, newsrooms should be certain to independently verify data and have editorial freedoms. Journalists should "balance truth telling and minimising harm" when dealing with data like the Afghan documents.

8. WikiLeaks Revelation About U.S. Diplomacy–The Need of Journalistic Ethics

WikiLeaks' systematic release of classified United States' diplomatic cables raises questions, is whether or not WikiLeaks endeavour towards "crack[ing] the world open" is ethical. There are no easy answers to the ethical questions posed by WikiLeaks. According to Merriam-Webster, ethics are "the principles of conduct governing an individual or a group." Many organisations have a "Code of Ethics" to act as a compass when the organisation is presented with an ethical quandary. The standard of journalistic ethics comes from the Society of Professional Journalists (SPJ).

SPJ's Code of Ethics rests on four pillars (a) Seek the truth and report it, (b) minimise harm, (c)act independently, and (d) be accountable. WikiLeaks is seeking the truth or acting independently; the real questions enclude whether WikiLeaks minimises potential harm asan accountable organisation. Indeed, many have decried WikiLeaks for "data-dumping" without restraint or thought of the consequences. Others argue WikiLeaks continuing without being held ccountable by someone or something. While the WikiLeaks' controversy has brought censorship to the forefront, it is not new to the United States or journalism. Indeed, Benjamin Franklin's brother, James, was once forced to publish beyond the reach of censors. Today, reporters will often not publish material for fear of receiving flak from official sources. This leads to (and always has to some degree) self-censorship. This, however, is not always bad.

"Self-censorship... is based on context, careful calibration of circumstances with the public's right to know always paramount," Clifford Christians, Professor Emeritus at the University of Illinois, said, "There is always accountability of whom and why the decisions were being made."

Thus, there are at least two ethical battles: between too much and too little, and between carelessness and prudence.

Professor Lisa Lynch best explained the friction between traditional journalism, governed by rules attempting to resolve the questions above, and WikiLeaks, which is largely free from those rules.

"In a moment when investigative journalism is recognisably in crisis, WikiLeaks has emerged as something of a strange bedfellow to a beleaguered industry, one that holds itself up as a champion of principles many journalists hold dear freedom of information and the sanctity of the source yet embeds these principles in a framework of cyberlibertarianism that is frequently at odds with the institutional ethics of journalists and editors," Lynch wrote.

Tom Blanton, Director of the National Security Archives, said at a congressional hearing. "So far, with only a few mistakes to date, the treatment of the cables by the media and by WikiLeaks has been very responsible, incorporating governmental feedback on potential damage, redacting names of sources, and even withholding whole documents at the government's request,"

WikiLeaks has only released 2,000-3,000 cables out of the reported more than 250,000. WikiLeaks is at least attempting to take care in releasing the documents. Indeed, CNN WikiLeaks, has more information than the Pentagon has. WikiLeaks has the potential to radically better transform the way the public views the world it lives in. WikiLeaks must be as transparent as it wishes the rest of the world to be It must also make attempts to work with the organisations that it reports on to minimise potential harms from its disclosures.

9. How India Was Shaken by WikiLeaks?

File photo of Prime Minister Manmohan Singh speaking to the media after his government won a vote of confidence in parliament in New Delhi, July 22, 2008. REUTERS

The secret U.S. state department cable obtained by WikiLeaks and published by The Hindu newspaper detailed a conversation between a senior Congress party member and a U.S. Embassy official surrounding the payment of almost $9 million by a government going to face a crucial confidence vote to members of a regional political party to secure their support.

Leader of the Opposition Sushma Swaraj, led a scathing attack government for failing to tackle corruption, posted on Twitter: "The wikileaks details in today's Hindu about payoffs to MPs are shocking. I will raise this issue in Parliament today."

Both houses of parliament were adjourned after 30 minutes after uproar over the cable's contents.

The cable detailed that four MPs belonging to the Rashtriya Lok Dal (RLD) party had been paid 100 million rupees ($2.2 million) each in a tight confidence vote over the Congress party's support of a nuclear deal between India and the U.S. White, who authored the secret cable, described how Embassy staff were shown two chests containing 500-600 million rupees ($11-13 million) that had been earmarked for "use as pay-offs".

The RLD party MPs, three, not four as specified in the cable, stood against the government in the vote, which Singh's Congress party won with 275 in favour and 256 against in the lower house of parliament.

"I have three and not four MPs so the facts in WikiLeaks are wrong. I had decided a long time back to go along with the Left, and not to vote for the UPA. So the question of negotiating with money doesn't arise. There was no question of influence on me to change my stand," Ajit Singh, RLD party president, told CNN-IBN. Prior to the July 2008 vote, Bharatiya Janata Party opposition MPs brandished wads of cash at ruling party officials accusing them of paying for MPs to support the government.

The cable is likely to increase pressure on parliament to reconsider the allegations against Prime Minister Singh's party,and the faith in the morality of India's political elite – both on the streets of New Delhi and in foreign ministries overseas – after a season of corruption scams, looks set to fall further.

10. The Bombardment of Wiki Bombs Over India

WikiLeaks triggered eight bombs on India.

Wikibomb 1: Congress bought MPs for 2008 trust vote.

Wikibomb 2: P. Chidambaram's son and Azhagiri bribed voters.

US cable made claims that DMK's Azhagiri paid Rs 5000 per voter in Thirumangalam. Karti Chidambaram was quoted as saying it impossible when the villages are spread so far apart in 2009 LS polls.

Wikibomb 3: The Afzal Guru dilemma.

US cable sent on Oct. 20, 2006 highlighted Congress' fear of losing Muslim votes in UP if Parliament attack convict Afzal Guru was hanged.

Wikibomb 4: India, US face-off on sharing 26/11 info with Pak.

Wikibomb 5: PM isolated on Pakistan.

Wikibomb 6: Pro-US tilt in cabinet shuffle.

US cables sent by David Mulford claimed the 2006 cabinet reshuffle observed a pro-US tilt.

Wikibomb 7: West Asia policy hostage to Muslim vote.

US cables stated the UPA's policy towards West Asia is dictated by its anxiety to keep Muslims in good humour.

Wikibomb 8: Elitist Congress unwilling to engage with masses

Another US cables released on March 15 claim Congress top brass is unwilling to go into the Hindi belt to address the masses.

11. How WikiLeaks Founder Links 'War on Corruption' in India with WikiLeaks

LONDON: In London WikiLeaks founder Julian Assange has said the "tremendous" anti-corruption movement "building up" in India is a result of the publication of "cablegate" revelations by The Hindu in recent weeks.

Citing the campaign, led by Anna Hazare, as an example of the impact of WikiLeaks cables, he said what was happening in India was "something that has not happened since the time of Gandhi."

He noted: "Just yesterday [on Saturday], the Editor of The Hindu, the most respected paper in India, brought over 21 front pages from the past six weeks that were based on cablegate material. Indian Parliament walked out four times and there's now a tremendous anti-corruption movement that has been building up in that country – something that has not happened since the time of Gandhi."

Making a difference

Mr. Assange, said the WikiLeaks cables were making a difference and referred to the developments in India following The Hindu's reporting of WikiLeaks documents. A 900-strong audience in the packed Kensington Town Hall in central London defended the need for anonymous whistle-blowing, arguing that it made the world a safer place.

Dynamic feedback

Challenged over transparency, he said: "We are directly supported on a week-to-week basis by you. You vote with your wallets every week if you believe that our work is worthwhile or not. If you believe we have erred, you do not support us. If you believe we need to be protected in our work, you keep us strong. That dynamic feedback, I say, is more responsive than a government that is elected after sourcing money from big business every four years."

12. Conclusion–The War Ahead

WikiLeaks, many believe has crossed the journalistic code of conduct and more firmly buy this opinion that it's not a journalism, but WikiLeaks has done something which traditional journalism has not been able to do so far.

The question now is whether to go ahead with these revelation trusting on the cables and then to realise the dirt in media and politics or just avoid the thought by saying that its unethical and what WikiLeaks has done so far may be punished in the name of national security. The debate is on.

References

1. http://www.concordmonitor.com
2. http://www.ethicsdaily.com
3. http://www.dailyiowan.com
4. http://thephilosophyofinformation.com
5. http://www.news.discovery.com
6. http://www.stinkyjournalism.org
7. http://indiatoday.intoday.in
8. blogs.reuters.com/india
9. www.thehindu.com

6

The Two Faces of Media While Covering Human Right Activities in India

1. Human Rights Status in Inda

Human rights in India is in a complex situation one, of the country's large size and tremendous diversity, her status as a developing country and a sovereign, secular, democratic republic, with her recey former colonial history. The Constitution of India provides for Fundamental rights, as well as separation of executive and judiciary and freedom of movement within the country and abroad. In a report made on human rights in India during 2010, Human Rights Watch found India with "significant human rights problems". It identified in accountable for security forces and impunity for abusive policing including "police brutality, extrajudicial killings, and torture" as major problems.

An United Nations expert in 2011 expressed concern she found human rights workers and their families killed, tortured, ill-treated, disappeared, threatened, arbitrarily arrested and detained, falsely implicated and under surveillance

2. Chronology of Events Regarding Human Rights in India

- 1829 : The practice of sati abolished by Governor General William Bentick it took years of campaigning by Hindu reform movements prominent among them being as the Brahmo Samaj of Ram Mohan Roy. Hey opposed this orthodox Hindu funeral custom of self-immolation of widows after the death of their husbands.
- 1929: Child Marriage Restraint Act, prohibited marriage of minors under 14 years of age.

- 1947: India achieves political independence from the British Raj.
- 1950: The Constitution of India established her a sovereign democratic republic with universal adult franchise. Part 3 of the Constitution contained a Bill of Fundamental Rights enforceable by the Supreme Court and the High Courts, and provided for reservations for previously disadvantaged sections in education, employment and political representation.
- 1952: Criminal Tribes Acts repealed by government, former "criminal tribes" categorised as "denotified" and Habitual Offenders Act (1952) enacted.
- 1955: Reform of family law concerning Hindus gives more rights to Hindu women.
- 1958: Armed Forces (Special Powers) Act, 1958.
- 1973: Supreme Court of India in Kesavananda Bharati case recognised the basic structure of the Constitution beyond constitutional amendment.
- 1978: SC in Menaka Gandhi v. Union of India held the right to life under Article 21 of the Constitution not to be suspended even in an emergency.
- 1978: Jammu and Kashmir Public Safety Act, 1978.
- 1984: Operation Blue Star and the subsequent 1984 Anti-Sikh riots.
- 1985-86: In the Shah Bano case, the Supreme Court recognised the Muslim woman's right to maintenance upon divorce, sparked protests from Muslim clergy. To nullify the decision of the Supreme Court, the Rajiv Gandhi government enacted The Muslim Women (Protection of Rights on Divorce) Act, 1986.
- 1989: Scheduled Caste and Scheduled Tribe (Prevention of Atrocities) Act, 1989 Is passed.
- 1989: Present Kashmiri insurgency sees ethnic cleansing of Kashmiri Pandits, desecrating Hindu temples, killing of Hindus and Sikhs, and abductions of foreign tourists and government functionaries.
- 1992: A constitutional amendment establishes Local Self-Government (Panchayati Raj) as a third tier of governance at the village level, with one-third of the seats reserved for women. Reservations were provided for scheduled castes and tribes as well.
- 1992: Babri Masjid demolished by Hindu mobs, resulting in riots across the country.

- 1993: National Human Rights Commission is established under the Protection of Human Rights Act.
- 2001: Supreme Court passes extensive orders to implement the right to food.
- 2002: Violence in Gujarat, chiefly targeting its Muslim minority, claims many lives.
- 2005: A powerful Right to Information Act is passed to give citizen's access to information held by public authorities.
- 2005: National Rural Employment Guarantee Act (NREGA) guarantees universal right to employment.
- 2006: Supreme Court ordered police reforms in response to the poor human rights record of Indian police.
- 2009: Delhi High Court delcared that Section 377 of the Indian Penal Code, which outlaws a range of unspecified "unnatural" sex not acts, is unconstitutional when applied to homosexual acts between private consenting individuals, effectively decriminalising homosexual relationships in India.

3. Custodial Deaths

Despite statutory prohibitions against torture and custodial misconduct, is widespread in India which is a major reason behind custodian deaths. The police often torture innocent people until aapplied 'confession' is obtained to save influential and wealthy offenders. The prisoners either are compelled to opt to0 self death or succumb to applied death consprised by the profilez low police in coluzion with the politicians. G.P. Joshi, the programme coordinator of the Commonwealth Human Rights Initiative Indian in New Delhi says that the main issue at hand concerning police violence is a lack of accountability of the police. About 800 people die in Indian prisons each year. In 2006, the Supreme Court of India in Prakash Singh vs. Union of India ordered central and state governments with seven directives meant to process the police reforme. The main two told objectives of this set of directives were to, provide tenure to the appointment/transfer processes of policemen, and to increased the accountability of the police.

3.1. India Administerd Kashmir

In a recent press release the OHCHR spokesmen said, "The Office of the High Commissioner for Human Rights is concerned about the recent violent protests in India-administered Kashmir that have reportedly led to civilian casualties as well as restrictions to the right to freedom of assembly and expression."

A 1996 Human Rights Watch report accused the Indian military and paramilitaries of "committing serious and widespread human rights violations in Kashmir." One such alleged massacre occurred on January 6, 1993 in the town of Sopore. TIME Magazine presented the incident as such: "In retaliation for the killing of one soldier, paramilitary forces rampaged through Sopore's market setting buildings ablaze and shooting bystanders. The Indian government pronounced the event 'unfortunate' and claimed that an ammunition dump had been hit by gunfire, setting off fires that killed most of the victims."

In addition, there have been claims of disappearances organised by the police or the army in Kashmir by several human rights organisations. Many human rights organisations such as Amnesty International and the Human Rights Watch (HRW) have condemned human rights abuses in Kashmir by Indians such as "extra-judicial executions", "disappearances", and torture; the "Armed Forces Special Powers Act", which "provides impunity for human rights abuses and fuels cycles of violence. The Armed Forces Special Powers Act (AFSPA) grants the military wide powers of arrest, to shoot and to occupy or destroy property in counter-insurgency operations. Indian officials opine that army need such powers because the army is only deployed when national security is at serious risk from armed militants.. Such circumstances, call for extraordinary measures."

Human rights organisations have regularly asked Indian government to repeal the Public Safety Act, since "a detainee may be held in administrative detention for a maximum of two years without a court order." A 2008 report by the United Nations High Commissioner for Refugees determined that India Administered Kashmir, was 'partly Free', (whereas Pakistan administered Kashmir was determined 'Not Free').

3.2. Religious Violence

Communal conflicts between religious groups are prevalent in India since independence struggle from British Rule. Among the oldest incidences of communal violence in India was the Moplah rebellion, when Militant Islamists massacred Hindus in Kerala. Communal riots are the brazen truths during the partition of India between Hindus/Sikhs and Muslims where numbers of people in large-scale violence.

The 1984 Anti-Sikh Riot was a four-day mega massacre during which Sikhs were 2000 brutally massacred by members of the secular-Congress

Party of India; Hashimpura massacre during communal riots in Meerut, 1992 Bombay Riots and the 2002 Gujarat violence are the major violent events - in the latter, more than 1,000 Muslims were killed it had followed in Islamist attackd a train full of Hindu pilgrims Known as the Godhra Train Burning, where more than 58 Hindus were burnt alive.

Lesser incidents plague many towns and villages; of five people were killed in Mau, Uttar Pradesh during Hindu-Muslim rioting, triggered during the celebration of a Hindu festival. The 2002 Marad massacre, carried out during Islamist group National Development Front, as well as communal riots in Tamil Nadu executed by the Islamist Tamil Nadu Muslim Munnetra Kazagham against Hindus.

The Graham Staines and his children murder and the various istances of minority christians along with burning of christian churches in Orissa and in other states in India only multiply the cases of religious violence in India.

3.3. Other Violence

Sometime Violence has the ethics sechional class, caste, riverly nature. All that can be recommended through the hunted cooperation and a tending to the democratic providence in a more civilized and culturally Eophisticated Civilization and Citizenship. Conflicts such as Anti-Bihari sentiment have sometimes escalated to violence.

Invasive methods like 'narcoanalysis' (controlled anesthesia) is now commonly accepted by Indian courts for crime investigation. Even though according to Indian constitution "nobody may be made a witness against himself", courts have recently ruled that even a permission from court is not necessary for conducting this analysis. It is now widely used to circumvent the lack of skill and infrastructure for conducting scientific methods of crime investigation, as against medical ethics.

More than half of the prisoners of the country are detained without adequate evidence. Unlike in other democratic countries, the investigation in India generally go with the apprehension handsome arrest of the accused. As the judicial system is sluggish, it is common to find innocent civilians languishing in jail for many years. For instance, the Bombay high court in September 2009 ordered the Maharashtra government to pay a sum of Rs. 1 lakh as compensation to a 40-year-old man who was kept in prison for over 10 years for a crime he didn't commit.

4. Human Right and Press Freedom

Reporters Without Borders, ranks India as 105th worldwide in press freedom index (press freedom index for India is 29.33 for 2009). The Indian Constitution, while not mentioning the word "press", provides for "the right to freedom of speech and expression" [Article 19(1) (a)], subject to restrictions under subclause (2), whereby this freedom can be restricted for reasons of "sovereignty and integrity of India, the security of the State, friendly relations with foreign States, public order, preserving decency, preserving morality, in relation to contempt of court, defamation, or incitement to an offence".

Laws such as the Official Secrets Act 1923 and Prevention of Terrorism Act (POTA) have been used to limit press freedom. Under POTA, person could be detained for up to six months before the police were required to bring charges on allegations for terrorism-related offenses. POTA was repealed in 2004, but was replaced by amendments to UAPA.

Earlier, media control by the state was the major constraint on press freedom. Indira Gandhi 1975 stated in that All India Radio is "a Government organ, it is going to remain a Government organ..." But the advert of liberalisation in the 1990s, private control of media has Organisations like Tehelka and NDTV influentialy brought about the resignation of powerful Haryana minister Venod Sharma. In addition, laws like Prasar Bharati Act contribute significantly to reduced the control of the government on press.

5. The Responsibilities and Challenges before Media While Covering Human Rights Issues (Reference from K. Nageshwar Rao's Speech)

Human rights ranging from personal to social and political rights, several international treaties, conventions and the constitutional and legal measures recognise the human rights. Right to education, health, life, privacy, free speech, fair trial, right against abuse, right to form an association, right against illegal detention, right of movement, right to information, etc., form a wide spectrum of human rights that need to be zealously protected.

Today free media is acknowledged a powerful instrument against abuse and violation of human rights. In an illustrious work edited by Amartya Sen the Nobel prize winning economist presents comparison between post-independent China and India. The facts that these two countries took independentce almost at the same time. But, China made rapid progress in many spheres of social and economic development. However, in one area India could surpass Chinese experience. Post-independent India could conquer famines, due to multi-party system and free media. The free media fore warn of impending crisis. Right to food life is an important human right and hunger a significant deprivation. Therefore the free media can work with human rights groups effectively for protection of human rights. The media can come to the rescue of citizens who are denied fair trial by powerful interests.

Everywhere the purpose surved by media in the protection of human rights has a wide scope increase manifold in the coming days as media reach is going to multiply. The studies done by *World Association of newspapers* noticed the declining popularity of media in the Western world due to the onslaught of internet. However, in India. In India, all forms of mass media are expanding. This main expansion of mass media will continue for many more decades in India. The multiplicity of media and its pluralism can be useful to inhance the human rights coverage in the media.

However, the homogenisation of content despite pluralism is an impediment in this struggle for improving the human rights coverage. Media being a reflection of society, respond to violation of human rights. The media percept of human rights has a leaving toward change if the human rights movements are taken seriously.

The media suffers from yet an another serious structural deficiency. It fails in covering the process that leads to an event.. When a farmer commits suicide, media covers it from all possible angles, but, a farmer suicide or a starvation death does not take place in reasoned. The suffering goes unnoticed by the media. The media has to demonstrate creativity to unravel the suffering that causes death. This is possible only if the media has direct exposure to primary classes in society.

Unfortunately freedom of press has proved to be the freedom for the rich. Philosopher once said: the class which owns the material means of production owns the production and dissemination of ideas. This is precisely why the ideas that represent the poor and under-privileged largely goes unrepresented in most of the media. The conspiracy of silence on the issues of the poor results from an ideological disposition against poor and systematic malfunctioning of the structure of the media houses. The media also suffers from a deep elitist bias, which blatantly is disappeared when the human rights of the rich and the middle class are questioned. The rights of the under-privileged should get the same attention if not greater.

Noted economist Jayati Ghosh referred to the media coverage of Dengue outbreak in Delhi. Media clamour made even the court intervened and pulled up the government. But the English media didn't show similar attention to the rights of the poor to health. Many more people including the children die of malaria, cholera, diahoera, etc. But, the media did not recognise this problem unless there are sensational number of deaths. The media appeared much concerned because the Dengue fly breeds in the luxuries of the rich and the middle class like the refrigerators, air coolers, water filters while the malaria mosquitoes breed on the dirty environs of poorer localities. The human rights violation of the poor are covered as a daily reality. The violation of human rights of the rich attract the huge attention of the media. The class bias in reporting the issue of human rights need to be eliminated.

Moreover, the media view the human rights violation as sporadic and isolated happenings. Thus fail to connect them with the social, political and economic policies implicated in ssuch events. This weakness comes clear in reporting starvation deaths of handloom weavers or atrocities on migrant labourers or the tribal unrest. The brazen commercialisation of media, the trivialisation of the content, sensationalism etc., create a great disconnect between the media and the people. Thus, the mass media are supposed devoid of mass reality. The media is obsessed with the reality shows, personal and private lives of celebrities and ignores the real lives of millions of people.

The civil society may perform as a watch dog. It further requires a media literacy movement. A critical evaluation of media should form part of academic curriculum of schools and colleges. A grass root's social pressure would only provide a human rights perspective for the media.

6. Why Media Should 'Not' Intervene in Sensitive Issues : The Other Side

Does a nobody shouldering a video camera, have the freedom to videograph promulgate your activities and as part of media freedom? Whose freedom is more important here, individual's freedom or the freedom of individual media house? Our visual media have done much damage to the such individuals involved in some kind of offence. Why are these media making such beeline wherever there is (not-so) worthy reporting? Is it their social commitment or their avarice for their own media space in the market place?

To answer these questions very seriously is a big concern. It disturbs to know about the behaviour of todays 24×7 news media. The so-called professionalism, social commitment and media attitude commonly seen in today's media domain which have enough proofs to establish one simple fact that they are doing a sizable portion of their job by simply spoiling the dignity, reputation and fortunes of countless individuals.These media bipeds have no idea what they in haste and in their own personal whims are doing. They uplink anyone to the rest of the world.

This media crew has the least comprehension of such gross violation of basic human rights to photograph one without individual permission, and support such footages with premature speculative comments and commercially motivated commentaries. Do these people know that a free individual has all the right to keep his face intact, and nobody has the freedom to tarnish it saying that it is part of his/her job? In such media gl;are, perhaps one prudently opine that there is none mkissing to be uncovered, still the scope remains for the media to observe its termitations. The accountability factor in today's visual media is obviously much limited under the impression of their boastful supremacy over anyone's life and fortune. This is callous violation of basic individual rights.

However, there are certain areas where video cameras can be used, criminal cases must be informed to keep the public aware of the same as a democratic responsibility of the media. However, this 'democratic' loophole is being blatantly misused to be called anti-democratic and asocial. A good number of their stories instance of making hay when it suns. They simply go scot-free. Media which is supposed to safeguard the basic rights of the individual, stands succumbed to the exponential growth of this media mania.

Therefore, to save it stakes it is time our democracy takes time off to look into the possibility of establishing a more accountable media regime very urgently.

- For a suspect or an accused no media should be allowed to blaze on his/her face and person. The media beyond this limitation.
- The media should be made accountable for the loss of face by paying compensation and corrigendum, if an innocent individual gets wrontly portrayed and this repute assasinated. If the media fail to show the same kind of interest, that they had shown to portray the individual so, to use their platform to make the people understand the story otherwise, there should be legal proceedings like defamation suits and libels.
- The strict constitutional provisions are required to check the nexus between police officers and media. When an accused is taken to the police station, the responsibility of the police must be to save him or her from media unless demands so. In the same vein, they

have the responsibility to cover and air all incidents irrespective of their political, communal and commercial implications.

- The same way, if the media channel is found to be reluctant to cover certain footages and give them due importance, there needs to be provision to demand explanation as to why it was so.
- Today media must be made accountable and all their activities confirming to human norms and their implications.
- A marring media can never be allowed to mar the lives and reputation of any individual. It is criminal and chronic violation of basic human rights, thus illegal.

The media persons do not make the world know that they erred in reporting these cases where media victimise the individuals. The victims are left in the lurch and vanquished. It is needed a constitutional body in the country to monitor this specific side of the media, to make the visual side of the media more humane and ethical.

We belong to a civilised order and need to be honoured by other civilised orders elsewhere, we have to urgently manage our media in very decent terms. The indecent and roguish media cannot work at the cost of someones life and fortune. The media must not be allowed to videograph an individual without some genuine reason to do so. Mindless media can be a menace to any society.

7. United Nation's Press Release- Statement of the Special Rapporteur on the Situation of Human Rights Defenders by Margaret Sekaggya

NEW DELHI, 21 January 2011

"From 10 to 21 January, 2011, I carried out a fact-finding mission to assess the situation of human rights defenders in India, and traveled to New Delhi, Bhubaneshwar (Orissa), Kolkata (West Bengal), Guwahati (Assam), Ahmedabad (Gujarat), Jammu and Srinagar (Jammu and Kashmir).

"I met with the Foreign Secretary; the Union Home Secretary; the Additional Secretary (International Organisations and Environment Diplomacy); the Joint Secretary (Human Rights), Ministry for Home Affairs; the State Chief Secretary, State Home Secretary and Director-General of Police in states visited; the Chairperson of the National Human Rights Commission; Members of the Statutory Full Commission; Chairpersons and Members of State Human Rights Commissions; and Judges from the High Court in Delhi. However, I regret I was unable to meet the Prime Minister, or the members of the Parliament.

"I thank very much the Government of India for extending an invitation to me and for its exemplary cooperation throughout the mission. I further want to thank all human rights defenders with whom I had meetings, some of whom had to travel long distances to meet me. Finally, I want to express my appreciation to the Office of the United Nations Resident Coordinator in India for its invaluable support in preparation of and during the mission.

"While I must now take some time to review and analyse the considerable amount of information I have received, and to follow up on further exchanges of information with the Government, human rights defenders and other stakeholders, I would like to provide a few preliminary observations and recommendations.

"I further commend the Government for enabling me to visit five States, which assisted me in gaining a clear understanding of the local specificities in which human rights defenders work. Given the duration of the mission and the size of the country, I regret I could not access all parts of the country, but I invite those who wish to do so to provide me with information now or in the near future.

"I note with satisfaction that India has a comprehensive and progressive legal framework which guarantees human rights and fundamental freedoms, as enshrined, inter alia, in the Constitution, the Protection of Human Rights Act, the Scheduled Castes and Scheduled Tribes (Prevention of Atrocities) Act, and the Right to Information Act. I welcome the commitment expressed by Indian authorities to uphold human rights.

"Throughout my mission, I heard numerous testimonies about male and female human rights defenders, and their families, who have been killed, tortured, ill-treated, disappeared, threatened, arbitrarily arrested and detained, falsely charged, under surveillance, forcibly displaced, or their offices raided and files stolen, because of their legitimate work in upholding human rights and fundamental freedoms. These violations are commonly attributed to law enforcement authorities; however, they have reportedly also shown collusion and/or complaisance with abuses committed by private actors against defenders. Armed groups have also harassed human rights defenders in some instances.

"I am particularly concerned at the plight of human rights defenders working for the rights of marginalised people, i.e. Dalits, Adavasis (tribals), religious minorities and sexual minorities, who face particular risks and ostracism because of their activities. Collectivities striving for their rights have in fact been victimised. Women human rights defenders, who are often at the forefront of the promotion and protection of human rights, are also at particular risk of persecution. Right To Information (RTI) activists, who may be ordinary citizens, have increasingly been targeted for, among others, exposing human rights violations and poor governance, including corruption of officials.

"While I acknowledge the security challenges faced by the country, I am deeply concerned about the arbitrary application of security laws at the national and state levels (in Jammu and Kashmir and in the North-East of India), most notably the Public Security Act and the Armed Forces Special Powers Act, the Jammu and Kashmir Public Safety Act and the Unlawful Activities Prevention Act, which direly affects the work of human rights defenders.

"The National Human Rights Commission and the existing State Human Rights Commissions is an important additional avenue where human rights defenders can seek redress. However, all the defenders I met during the mission voiced their disappointment and mistrust in the current functioning of these institutions.

The following preliminary recommendations:

7.1. To the Central and State Governments

The Prime Minister and the Chief Secretaries should publicly acknowledge the importance and legitimacy of the work of human rights defenders, i.e. anyone who "individually and in association with others, promote[s] and strive[s] for the protection and realisation of human rights and fundamental freedoms at the national and international levels " (article 1 of the Declaration on Human Rights Defenders, A/RES/53/144).

In the same vain, security forces should be clearly in and to respect the work and the rights and fundamental freedoms of human rights defenders. Sensitisation training to security forces on the role and activities of human rights protectors should be organised with technical advice and assistance from relevant UN entities, non-governmental and other organisations.

Prompt and impartial investigations on violence committed against human rights defenders should be observed.

The Supreme Court directives on police reform should be implemented in line with international standards, in particular at the State level.

A law particular on the protection of human rights with civil society and UN entities should be enacted. *The Foreign Contribution Regulation Act* should be reviewed. The Bill on Prevention Against Torture should be passed without further delay.

The Optional Protocol to the Convention on the Elimination of all forms of Discrimination Against Women should be ratified. This would provide women human rights defenders an optional forum and procedure to redress any violations of rights under the Convention.

The Armed Forces Special Powers Act and the *Public Security Act* should be repealed and application of other security laws which adversely affect the work and safety of human rights defenders should be reviewed.

National Human Rights Commission should be reviewed and strengthened by broadening the selection criteria for the appointment of the Chairperson; diversifying the composition of the Commission; extending the one-year limitation clause; establishing an independent committee in charge of investigating complaints filed; elevating the status of the human rights defenders focal point by appointing a Commissioner. *The Protection of Human Rights Act* should be amended in consultation with civil society. State Human Rights Commissions should be established in states without further delay. Central and State Governments should collaborate with *Special Procedures of the Human Rights Council.*

The Human Rights commissions should take initiatives to safeguard human rights workers by *inter alia* conducting regular regional visits; meeting human rights workers at risk; and undertaking trial observations of cases of human rights workers wherever appropriate. The public profile of the commissions should be ensured through regular and proactive engagement with civil society and the media.

A toll-free 24-hour emergency hotline for human rights workers must be established.

The commissions should monitor the implementation of recommendations chartered by UN human rights mechanisms, including *Special Procedures mandate-holders, Treaty Bodies*, and the *Universal Periodic Review.*

7.2. To the judiciary

In the absence of a witnesses and victims protection Act, the judiciary should take measures to ensure the protection of human rights workers at risk, witnesses and victims. Moreover the judiciary should *suo motu* juridiction in cases of violence against human rights workers.

In the vibrant functioning of the judiciary the role of such workers (better to term them as Human Rights leaders) ought to be taken in complete acknowledge.

7.3. To human rights leaders

The human rights leaders should comply to the United Nations Special Procedures and other international human rights mechanisms on human rights violations, when they lead a struggle.

7.4. To the international community and donors

The European Union Guidelines on Human Rights Defenders and local strategies on India should be implemented. The situation of human rights defenders, should be continually monitored, and support for their work should be expressed through, inter alia, interventions before central and state institutions. Efforts should be intensified in empowering civil society.

7.6. To all stakeholders

The Declaration on Human Rights Defenders should be disseminated widely through regional and local dialects. Efforts should be continued to raise civic awareness among the general public, and the spirit of dialogue and cooperation in society fostered.

7

Social Media in Governance, Political Reform and Building Public Perception

1. Introduction

Andreas Kaplan and Michael Haenlein define social media as "a group of Internet-based applications that build on the ideological and technological foundations of Web 2.0, which allows the creation and exchange of user-generated content."

Business refers to social media as consumer-generated media (CGM). Social media is a blending of technology and social interaction for the co-creation of value.

1.1. Social Media and Traditional Media

Social media are different from industrial or traditional media, such as newspapers, television, and film; relatively inexpensive and accessible to enable anyone to publish or access information, compared to industrial media, which require significant resources to publish information. Both social and industrial media have the capability to reach small or large audiences; one characteristic shared by both.

The differences between social media and industrial media can be discribed on the basis of reach, accessibility usability, immeditary and permanenance.

Both industrial and social media technologies scale and are capable of reaching a global audience. Industrial media, use a centralised framework for functioning, whereas social media are by their very nature more decentralised, less hierarchical, and distinguished by multiple points of production and utility.

The means of production for industrial media are government and/ or privately owned; social media tools are generally available to the public at little or no cost.

Industrial media production typically requires specialised skills and training, whereas social media does not require specialised skills and training. In theory, anyone with access can operate the means of social media production.

Communications produced by industrial media can be long compared to social media capable of instantaneous responses. However, because the industrial media start adopting aspects of production normally associated with social media tools, this feature may not prove distinctive over time.

Industrial media, once created, cannot be altered, whereas social media almost instantaneously by comments or editing.

In *The Wealth of Networks: How Social Production Transforms Markets and Freedom*, (2006) Yochai Benkler analysed many of these distinctions and their implications in terms of both economics and political liberty. Benkler, used the neologism network economy or "network information economy" to illustrate the underlying economic, social, and technological characteristics of "social media".

Andrew Keen criticised social media in *The Cult of the Amateur*, "Out of this anarchy, it suddenly became clear that what was governing the infinite monkeys now inputting away on the Internet was the law of digital Darwinism, the survival of the loudest and most opinionated. Under these rules, the only way to intellectually prevail is by infinite filibustering."

Account for social media usage and effectiveness for individuals worldwide the most recent statistics are as follows:

Social networking now accounts for 22% of all time spent online in the US. A total of 234 million people aged 13 and older in the U.S. used mobile devices in December 2009. Twitter processed more than one billion tweets in December 2009 and averages almost 40 million tweets per day.

Over 25% of U.S. internet page views occurred at one of the top social networking sites in December 2009, up from 13.8% a year before. In terms of Facebook use, Australia ranks highest with almost 9 hours per month from over 9 million users.

Social media users aged 65 and older grew 100 percent throughout 2010, that is, one in four people in that age group are now part of a social networking site.

1.3. Examples of Social Media

The Dutch man Ramon Stoppelenburg created his own necessary network online which offered accomodations to stay. This made Stoppelenburg one of the first people online who used the online media on a social and effective manner. Social media culminate into many different forms, including Internet forums, weblogs, social blogs, microblogging, wikis, podcasts, photographs or pictures, video, rating and social bookmarking.

According to Kaplan and Haenlein there are six different types of social media: collaborative projects, blogs and microblogs, content communities, social networking sites, virtual game worlds, and virtual communities. Technologies include: blogs, picture-sharing, vlogs, wall-postings, e-mail, instant messaging, music-sharing, crowd-sourcing, and voice over IP, to name a few.

2. Social Media, Government, Public and Politics

For few years, many technophiles, activists, and political observers have been lauding the power of social media platforms such as Facebook, SMS, Twitter, and YouTube to enhance governance and foment political change. Today, we have largely anecdotal data on the impact of new media and technologies on political reform. Facebook, Twitter, and YouTube have played critical roles in promoting the recent protests in Egypt, Iran, Moldova, and Tunisia.

Moreover, cell phone technologies can play an instrumental role in fracing electoral fraud by enhancing election monitoring and reporting techniques. Yet, in spite of the anecdotal evidence that approves of these developments and their use in specific instances, there is a want of empirical analysis on the subject. We lack studies that trace the causal impact of these technologies on political reform and improved governance. Some areas that mandate more serious inquiry are the following:

Evidence of Political Change

Social media can impart an important role in publicising political activities such as protests. But we have not much evidence that such actions have led to substantive political change. Is there any possibilityh to develop a set of indicators to more effectively gauge the impact of new technologies and media on questions of political change?

Technology and Governance

Is there any evidence that these technologies can help to improve day-to-day governance and improve political accountability? Further as a transparency instrument how citizens can be persuaded to adopt such technology. What incentives do citizens contribute in mobile governance, and how can new technologies be deployed to advocacy efforts already underway?

Questioning Access and the Digital Divide

Since the countries with the worst governance are the poorest ones as well, how much affordable are these advanced technologies to the people living in the countries with the worst forms of governance?

Dictators versus Demonstrators

How quickly are regimes opposed to the spread of these technologies to suppress political dissent more effectively? U.S. policy in this area works in contradictory manners; while the U.S. State Department has evolved as strong advocate for Internet freedom, the U.S. Department of Defense is building more effective programmes to supervise the use of the Internet.

Substitute versus Complement

Is social media complementary to political action, or a substitute for it? How does it offer problems to the nature of direct political action today?

Are people to take direct action, for example participating in a protest, or are virtual procession, becoming substitutes for actual ones?

3. Social Media and Good Governance

Thailand has embraced the idea of good governance has been a key concept for democratic development in many countries around the world during the past few decades.

The 'good governance' was not understood at its inception, not people, at the grass root level, understood what it meant. However, attempts were made to explain this concept to the public by community leaders and scholars with the hope it easier to understand.

One of various explanations widely accepted, focuses on the ability of the state to perform its key functions in the needs of its citizens, and to be accountable for its doings. Emphasis has been placed on the needs of the people, public interest, transparency, accountability and responsibility of the policy-makers; central to establishing sustainable development. The public, or even the government officials in possession of information, could adequately comprehend the need of information dissemination. To perform the monitoring duty as a mirror of the society, the media have been playing an important role in educating the people about good governance.

The news and investigative reports on state performances need insightful information. Whether such classification of information was correct had rarely been questioned in the past. Accurate and sufficient information makes the people better enjoy their freedom of speech, attributing to rational decisions and right course of action beneficial to them.

The Print, Television and Radio media consider it a top priority to report corruption cases in their news. *"India @ 9"* broadcast on *CNN-IBN* has broadcasted many bulletins featuring news on corruption cases and related issues. Copies of this daily news programme are often procured by the government agencies themselves for further investigation. Rajdeep Sardesai, Editor-in-Chief, this kind of information to promote good governance making it more responsive to the audience.

CNN-IBN relays a weekly Citizen Journalism on core problems of public in an emphatic way. The host of the show and Sr. Editor at *CNN-IBN*, Anubha Bhonsle foundb her show allow people to come up in camera with their own problems. *CNN-IBN* distributes awards among its Citizen Journalists in an encouraging award function.

In the UK, a *Survey of Policy Opinion on Governance and the Media* published by *BBC* (2009) finds that although the emphasis on good governance in the development agenda is questionable, "there seems to be increasing recognition of the media's role in governance in the development community. There are also some indicators that media are being more recognised by the policy-makers as having a central role in development. Good governance needs the understanding and participation of every member of the society. The media are assessed powerful enough to turn this achievement into a reality. The work of the media should not divide the citizens into the information-rich and information-poor. In other words, channels must promote the right to know of the people and the interest of the public, without any control of the state or commercial entities. In particular, content must be informative and useful – turnable into knowledge and wisdom to eliminate poverty and hardship, and enhance quality of life in the 21st century society.

4. Social Media and Political Reforms

Civil unrest in the African countries of Tunisia and Egypt began with citizens publicly lighting themselves on fire to display their displeasure towards the corrupt leaders.

The first protester to sacrifice was a gremgrocer by occupation, Mohamed Bouazizi. His economic woes made him publicly fuel massive protests in the country of Tunisia. Bouazizi's example has been followed by dozens of protesters in nearby Egypt, who have also immolated themselves to motivate others to take action against high food prices and acute unemployment rates.

The betterment and fame of social networking sites make them centre for various types of communication. The question remains, is there too much freedom on Facebook and other sites? If ordinary citizens can organise a rally and protest on these sites, it is hard to cheak it because of the right to assemble and the right of free speech.

4.1. Egyptian Transformation

The most recent transformation of Egypt's secular government was viewed possible through traditional media and computer social networks such as Facebook and Twitter. Further this latest political transformation in Egypt was possible due to cultural change in the country. The younger population escaped the hand of autocracy and through social networks organised a revolution.

Egypt prmised to form a new government, following the startling success of the rather bloodless Egyptian Revolution of February 2011 which boasted a united goal.

Other nations have also planned following the amazing sudden revolt and sudden sweeping changes seen in Egypt's ruling structure of President Hosni Mubarak.

4.2. Facebook and Egypt's Reform

The *Huffington Post* (February 14, 2011) reported that Wael Ghonim, gave thanks to *Facebook* for assistance in the unseen background of the people's uprising. Ghonim, a marketing manager at *Google* helped stage the January 25 demonstrations in Egypt asking for the immediate resignation of Hosni Mubarak on power for the past 30 years after the rule of King Farouk, Gamal Abdal Nasser and Anwar al-Sadat.

Wael Ghonim was imprisoned in Egypt for 12 days. After his release, Ghonim continued to motivate social change from his computer keyboard and through the power of social networking gathered hundreds of thousands of supporters globally. Huge numbers responded to his and other posts on the social networks planning the demonstrations which demanded the immediate removal of Mubarak.

Thousands demonstrated in loud but peaceful protests that resulted in the toppling down of the Mubarak regime in a moment. The sounds of this rapid revolution were heard by other nearby countries resulting in similar plans for movements and political change, particularly with the ongoing influence of the internet.

4.3. Social Media and Democracy

(Reuters) : Saudi Islamists and opposition activists have launched a political party in a rare challenge to the absolute monarchy, asking King Abdullah for a voice in the Gulf Arab state's governance, its organizers said Thursday.

The move was apparently prompted by popular revolts in the Arab world that toppled Tunisia's president last month and have loosened the grip of Egypt's autocratic leader.

But it was more an act of protest than an effective start-up of a political party since Saudi Arabia has no elected parliament and parties and public dissent are banned by the Al-Saud monarchy, which rules the world's No. 1 oil exporting country in alliance with Sunni Muslim clerics.

There have been other attempts to form parties but analysts said the new "Islamic Umma" group appeared to be the first to be revealed publicly. They said members included Islamist intellectuals and lecturers, human rights activists and lawyers.

"You know well what big political development and improvement of freedom and human rights is currently happening in the Islamic world," the group of ten activists said in a letter to King Abdullah, obtained by Reuters and also posted on their website.

"It's time to bring this development to the kingdom," they told the king, who is about 87 and now recuperating in Morocco after medical treatment in the United States.

Islamists and liberals both seek more political freedoms in Saudi Arabia and, while differing on details such as the rights of women, say that reform is their overriding goal.

4.4. Saudis Key to Regional Stability

Any instability at the helm of Saudi Arabia, the strategic U.S. policy in the Middle East, can ripple across the Arab Gulf region and beyond. Anti-government protests swept Tunisian President Zine al-Abidine Ben Ali out of power, igmitting a revolt in Egypt that has unraveled the autocracy of President Hosni Mubarak and paralysed the country for two weeks. Diplomats did not expect such massive unrest to spread to Saudi Arabia, which can easily wash out social tensions over high youth unemployment with funding out of massive oil wealth.

But in social media such as *Facebook* or *Twitter*, liberal Saudis have demanded political reforms and more freedom.

5. Social Media and Political Reforms in Middle East and North Africa

After the Tunisia's *Twitter* revolution and the social media–fueled protests in Egypt, the social media revolution penetrated to other areas of North Africa and the Middle East. Who could have imagined the speed and depth of the popular uprisings ignited by anti-government sentiment with timbers of anger piled sky high because of authoritarian repression, economic stagnation and loss of hope?

Middle East unrest

Country	Unrest Index*	Corruption	Poverty %	Age**	Literacy
Yemen	86.9	146	41.8	17.9	61
Libya	71	146	n/a	24.2	88
Egypt	67.6	98	16.7	24	66
Syria	67.3	127	n/a	21.5	n/a
Saudi Arabia	52.8	50	n/a	24.9	n/a
Algeria	51.3	105	22.6	27.1	73
Jordan	50.3	50	14.2	21.8	92
Tunisia	49.4	59	7.6	29.7	78
Morocco	48.2	85	19	26.5	56
Bahrain	37.7	48	n/a	30.4	91
Iran	n/a	146	n/a	26.3	82

SOURCES: *SHOE-THROWER'S INDEX FROM THE ECONOMIST, TRANSPARENCY INTERNATIONAL 2010 CORRUPTION INDEX (HIGHER NUMBER = GREATER CORRUPTION), WORLD BANK, CIA WORLD FACTBOOK, UN (** MEDIAN AGE)

Iran's leaders ironically appreciated the demonstrators in Tahrir Square in Cairo, but tried to terminate its own protestors and have put leaders of the government's opposition under house arrest. Protest featured words on *Facebook*, *Twitter* and *YouTube* are more powerful in mobilising the masses, building worldwide support and forcing old men to step down. Tunisia's and Egypt's uprisings spread to at least 10 countries in which Facebook posts and tweets are organising protestors across North Africa and the Middle East.

Those protestors received a big boost in political support from U.S. Secretary of State Hillary Clinton.

"We believe that governments who have erected barriers to Internet freedom – whether they're technical filters or censorship regimes or attacks on those who exercise their rights to expression and assemble online – will eventually find themselves boxed in," Clinton said.

During Tunisia's *Jasmine revolution* or *Twitter revolution*, bloggers identified the power of a *Facebook* page to ignite largely peaceful demonstrations that ousted Egyptian President Hosni Mumbarak.

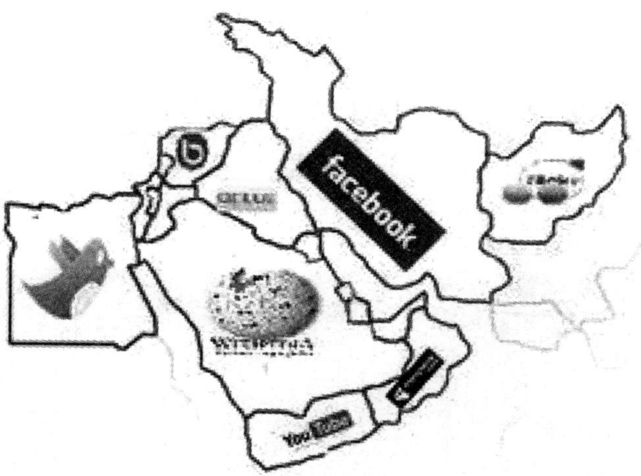

Here is an interesting "corruption index" compiled by the Economist Intelligence Unit as reported by the London-based BBC News.

Yemen

Yemen's President Ali Abdullah Saleh announced he would not seek another term in office, after three decades in power. He told parliament he would not hand over power to his son, saying: "No extension, no inheritance, no resetting the clock." But the opposition regained infact with people taking to the streets in the cities of Sanaa, Aden and Taiz. Anti-government protesters demanded political reforms clashed with pro-government loyalists Police struck up the demonstrations. Yemen is the Arab world's most-impoverished nation and nearly half of the population lives on less than $2 a day.

Libya

Hundreds of people took to streets of the Libyan city of Benghazi. Protests are prohibited in Libya, but the latest unrest had its fuel from the arrest of a lawyer, outspoken critic of the government. Colonel Gaddafi was the most autocraticlongest serving ruler in Africa and the Middle East.

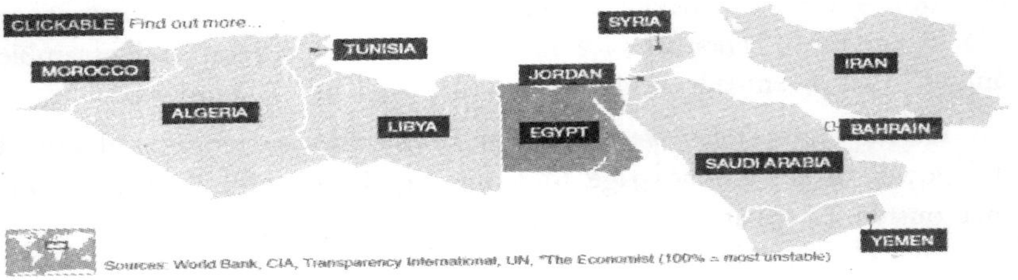

Egypt

President Hosni Mubarak announced he was stepping down on Feb. 11 after 18 days of protests. Aged 82, he was in power since 1981. Egypt known as a centre of stability in a volatile region, masked problems which erupted in popular demonstrations against the 30-year rule of President Mubarak on Jan. 25, 2012.

The main factors driving the unrest were poverty, rising prices, social exclusion, corruption and personal enrichment among of political elite, and acute unemployment. Egypt's Armed Forces Supreme Council ruled the country until elections are conducted. Islamist fracternity was expected to do well in any free and fair elections, but concerns about a lurch towards Islamist rule was the main worry for Western powers and Israel.

Syria

President Bashar al-Assad promised political reforms after succeeding his father, Hafez, in 2000, a three decade authoritarian rule. The country was ruled under emergency provisions since 1963. Syria had a degree of relaxation and hundreds of political prisoners were released after the death of Hafez-al-Assad. But the real political freedoms and reforms ikn the state-dominated economy have to be materialised.

Saudi Arabia

Saudi Arabia has become one of the wealthiest nations in the region, due to its vast oil resources. It has always been in the ruling Al-Saud family's interests to preserve stability in the region and to clamp down on extremist elements. Regionally, the country is regarded important with King Abdullah Bin-Abd-al-Aziz Al-Saud in the Arab world as a supporter of Arab interests. It was in Saudi Arabia that Tunisia's ousted leader, Zine al-Abidine Ben Ali, took refuge.

Algeria

Sporadic protests continued with demonstrators demanding the resignation of President Abdelaziz Bouteflika. The United opposition included small trade unions and minor political parties. The factor for the unrest was mainly economic – sharp increases in the price goods.

President Bouteflika promised to lift the country's state of emergency since 1992 – in the "near future". The government piles wealth from its rich oil and gas exports and can address social and economic complaints with a huge public spending program.

Jordan

Jordanians took to streets demanding better employment prospects and cuts in foods and fuel costs. King Abdullah II dismissed Prime Minister Samir Rifai over the slow pace of reform and appointed Marouf al-Bakhit, a former army general and ambassador to Israel. A new 26-member cabinet was sworn in on Feb. 10., 2012.

The demise of King Hussein, a ruler for 46 years, left Jordan struggling for economic and social survival, as well as regional peace. His son, Abdullah, the new king faced the task of maintaining stability while accommodating calls for reform. A blueprint for sustainable political, economic and social change – has yet to be implemented.

Tunisia

Protests continued in Tunisia – despite President Zine al-Abidine Ben Ali's decision to step down. The trigger was pulled by a young unemployed man on December 17. Mohamed Bouazizi imolated himself when officials prevented him from selling vegetables on the streets of Sidi Bouzid without permission. The violent response of the police ignited further protests which ultimately led to the president's downfall. Parliamentary Speaker Foued Mebazaa took oath as interim president and asked Prime Minister Mohammed Ghannouchi, head of the government since 1999, to form a national unity government. The prime minister pledged to step down after elections in about six months' time.

Morroco

Morocco's main opposition warned the "autocracy" to sweep away unless there are big economic reforms. It has announced an increase in state subsidies to counter commodity price rises. Morocco's reputation was diminished after Wikileaks leaked out allegations of corruption involving the royal family and the people close to King Mohammed VI. The king, the fight against poverty was a priority, earning him the name "guardian of the poor." Economic liberalisation has attracted foreign investment and officials felt better basic services in shanty towns and rural areas. But poverty still widespread and unemployment remained high. Morocco, like Egypt and Algeria, allowed limited freedom of expression and contained protests. Like Jordan, monarchy with strong support among sections of the public remains non-vulnerable

Bahrain

Protesters gathered at capital Manama after two days of clashes with police in which two people died. The unrest emerged because of discontent among its majority Shia population against the ruling Sunni dynasty.The Al-Khalifas have ruled the country since the 18th century. Protesters grived of economic hardship, lack of political freedom and discrimination in jobs in favour of Sunnis.

Since ascending to power in 1999, King Hamad bin Issa Al- Khalifa introduced economic and political reforms to enhance relations with the

Shia community. The country, is a regional banking, trading and Islamic finance hub, became a constitutional monarchy in 2002.

Iran

The government in Tehran called for a rally to express hatred for the opposition movement. It was assembled demonstrations organised by the regime's two main opposition leaders earlier in support of the unrest in neighbouring countries. The protest immediately turned into anti-government unrest which left two people dead and others injured. Iran's complex and unusual political system had elements of a modern Islamic theocracy with democracy.

A network of unelected institutions, controlled by the highly powerful conservative Supreme Leader, is countered by a president and parliament elected by the people. President Mahmoud Ahmadinejad, elected in 2005, a hard-liner vowed to supress any protests against the regime, and accused demonstrators of wanting to "tarnish the Iranian nation's brilliance."

6. Principles of Social Media in Building Public Perception

Ten core principles underlie the value of social-media solutions, and, in combination, serve as the defining characteristics that set social media apart from other forms of communication and collaboration.

6.1. Participation

Successful social-media solutions tap into the power of mass collaboration through user participation. The only way to attain substantial benefits from social media is by motivatingthe community to contribute. To obtain the "wisdom of the crowds", participation is mondatory.

6.2. Collective

Varied definitions and applications of the term "collective" abound and attains a wide spectrum of meanings. Here, as a core principle of social media, the use of the term "collective" is tightly aligned with its root origins "to collect." With social media, participants "collect" around a unifying entity.

People gather around the Facebook social graph to contribute their profile information. People collect on Wikipedia to add encyclopaedic articles. People gather on YouTube to share videos. In social media, people collect around the content to contribute rather than individually create the content and distribute it.

6.3. Transparency

A social-media solution provides transparency, participants are privy to each other's participation. They get to see, use, reuse, augment, validate, critique and rate each other's contributions. In absence of transparency, there is no participant collaboration on content. Due to transparency, the community improves content, unifies information, self-governs, self-corrects, evolves, creates emergence and otherwise propels its own advancement.

6.4. Independence

The principle of independence counotes that any participant can assist completely independent of any other participant. This is also called anytime–anyplace collaboration. Generally, there is no workflow or document check-in/check-out that can check collaboration and effect the scalability needed for mass collaboration. No coordination between collaborators is needed.

6.5. Persistence

It differentiates social media from synchronous conversational interactions, where much of the information exchanged is either lost or captured, most often only in part, as an extra scribing activity.

6.6. Emergence

It is the recognition that one benefit of social media is as an environment for social structures to emerge. These symmetyries may be hidden organisational structures, expertise, work processes, content organisation, information taxonomies, etc..

Social media are best understood as a group of new kinds of online media, which share most or all of the following characteristics:

6.7. Openness

Most social media services are exposed to feedback and participation. They assist voting, comments and the sharing of information. There are rarely any barriers to accessing and making use of content – password-protected content is frowned on.

6.8. Conversation

Whereas traditional media are about "broadcast" (content transmitted or distributed to an audience) social media is better seen as a two-way conversation.

6.9. Community

Social media allow communities to form quickly and communicate effectively. Communities share common interests, such as a love of photography, a political issue or a favourite TV show.

6.10. Connectedness

Most kinds of social media thrive on their connectedness, making use of links to other sites, resources and people.

7. Findings and Conclusion

There are various statistical findings that account for social media usage and effectiveness for individuals worldwide. Some of the most recent statistics are as follows:

Social networking now accounts for 22% of all time spent online in the US. A total of 234 million people aged 13 and older in the U.S. used mobile devices in December 2009. Twitter processed more than one billion tweets in December 2009 and averages almost 40 million tweets per day. Over 25% of U.S. internet page views occurred at one of the top social networking sites in December 2009, up from 13.8% a year before. Australia has some of the highest social media usage statistics in the world. In terms of Facebook use Australia ranks highest with almost 9 hours per month from over 9 million users. The number of social media users age 65 and older grew 100 percent throughout 2010, so that one in four people in that age group are now part of a social networking site.

The statistics itself suggests the penetration of Social Media among public. The numbers signifies the role of social media in building the public perception and its effect in good governance in a politically active society. In this new world, peoples' sins can be broadcast from the rooftops quickly, and political leaders can be compelled to follow higher standards in their personal and career actions or be forced to resign by the people.

References

1. Framework: The Social Media ROI Pyramid.
2. European Journal of Social Psychology.
3. Research Survey.
4. Inc. Technology Brent Leary Article.
5. Edelman 2010 Trust Barometer Study.
6. Benkler, Yochai (2006), The Wealth of Networks, New Haven: Yale University Press.

7. Gentle, Anne (2009), Conversation and Community: The Social Web for Documentation, Fort Collins, Colo: XML Press.
8. http://www.tednguyenusa.com
9. www.reuters.com
10. www.suite101.com
11. english.aljazeera.net
12. www.usip.org
13. www.quora.com
14. www.eurasiareview.com
15. Johnson, Steven Berlin (2005), Everything Bad Is Good for You, New York: Riverhead Books.
16. Li, Charlene; Bernoff, Josh (2008), Groundswell: Winning in a World Transformed by Social Technologies, Boston: Harvard Business Press.
17. Scoble, Robert; Israel, Shel (2006), Naked Conversations: How Blogs are Changing the Way Businesses Talk with Customers, Hoboken, N.J: John Wiley.
18. Shirky, Clay (2008), Here Comes Everybody, New York: Penguin Press.
19. Surowiecki, James (2004), The Wisdom of Crowds, New York: Anchor Books.

8

Challenges before Traditional Media in the Age of Digital Media–How to Integrate it with the Digital Media–The Way Ahead

1. Introduction–The definition and Periphery of Digital Media

Basically digital media refer to any type of electronic media be accessed in many ways, including devices like mobile phones, laptops, desktops, mp3 players, and more. Digital media must be stored in an electronic way. The digital content on the internet today, includes text content, pictures, audio content, as well as video content. Emerging with the history of internet, digital media have been improving in various stet ways. (A) Type of digital media is text; which in fact represented the very first explosion of this type on the Internet. When the Internet first got big, an explosion of content on the web existed especially with all the text editors and word processing options. The internet definitely permitted a great manner to share, transfer, and store content as well. As the Internet grew, images started to appear. In shape of text e-mails, photos, and soon photo sites for sharing photos began to crop up. In the middle 1990s, audio began to become an important part of digital media with the mp3 fileseasy in use. Soon music and more was shared online. Last in the digital media development was video. YouTube definitely made video sharing a much popular form of modern media distribution, with further rapid growth in perspective. Now with new technology like the iPhone, this new form of virtual media is available in handheld devices as well, with much scope to grow in the future.

1.2. How they Help

Businesses are harmezzing digital media for marketing more realisation that there is a huge marketing field available and that they can help to draw in more visitors and with provisions of better search engine visibility. Text content can be kept well updated on site and helpful content is a great part of good marketing.

Expertise in particular field can really help one's business and get traffic flowing into the business website. Photos, charts, diagrams' and models are ever with repute online and helps to get more visibility as well. Audio permits to use music on pages or to do podcasts for business.

The creation of videos is a popular method of digital media marketing today, do very well in search engines. With the popularity of digital media, it is definitely important to create and use it for good marketing and business results.

2. Facts about Traditional Media in Indian Context

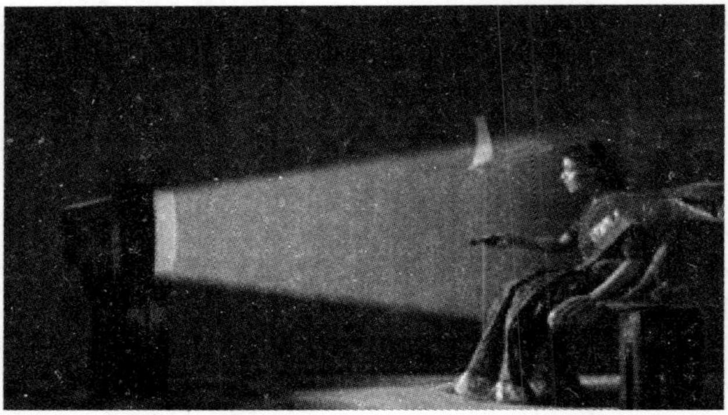

2.1. Television

Television first came to India in the form of Doordarshan (DD) on Sept 15, 1959, the National Television Network of India, the largest broadcasting houses in the world. With the emergence of several Indian private broadcasters and the introduction of international satellite services. In fact, over the last 10 years, the industry has witnessed a massive networking where there are currently 300 channels available – with 30 news channels in almost all of the 22 official languages in India.

Presently around 50% of Indian households own a television, an increase from less than a third in 2001. India's television business has an estimated $3.4 billion in revenue in 2005, according to PricewaterhouseCoopers. The major players in the television industry are:

- Doordarshan
- STAR TV
- Zee Television
- United Television
- CNN
- Sony Television
- ATN (Asia Television Network)
- BBC World
- SUN TV
- Discovery Channel

Satellite services are slowly being embraced by Indian households. The number satellite households in India grew by 9% in 2008. The Direct-to-Home (DTH) digital market is expanding on fat pace and is calculated to be accessed by 10 million households.

The average time given by viewers in India is calculated to be about 145 minutes/day, while more time is given watching channels in digital homes. Once the DTH market achieves important mass, niche broadcasters will be in an empowered position to capitalise on the upmarket viewers through advertising and marketing channels. Television is the favourite medium of advertising by businesses, according to a report done by WebChutney.

In 2008-2009, television took for 51.4% of the total advertising expenditure in India. Though estimates suggest a slight fall in 2009-2010 due to increased adoption of online advertising, television remains an important medium that businesses utilise however.

2.2. Print

The printed press industry a declining in in Europe and the United States, in India, is booming due to rising literacy rates and increasing advertising expenditure. India has emerged as the largest newspaper market in the world, according to World Association of Newspapers (WAN) released on 1 October, 2009.

India has taken primacy over China as a leader in 2008 and the country is home to 20 of the 100 largest newspapers in the world. Currently 62,000 newspapers circulated in India, with further oztimated growth.

The increazing growth of non-English press casts the broadening appeal of newspapers in India. The readership of Hindi newspapers available has risen from less than 8 million in the 1990s, to more than 25 million today with 3,200 newspapers published in Hindi, more than 3 times that of English papers available.

The newspaper's importance in India remains static or growing free from competition of the Internet. Newspapers are the more accessible alternative, even for rural areas; being dependent on other factors such as infrastructure or availability of electricity.

After television, print is the second most favoured medium by businesses for advertising. 27.4% of the total advertising expense is taken by the print industry in 2008-2009. This is estimated to decline in 2009-2010, to 25.7% due to increased competition from the online medium.

2.3. Radio

According to the latest Indian Readership Survey all India radio reaches 24%, of the urban population. There are 238 FM radio stations owned by 40 broadcasters. In 2008s the radio industry had growth at a fazt speed which cThe same year, new markets emerged for private Frequency Modulation making this sector grow by 62%. The radio is restricted by the government giving the audience not a big variety in programmes.

The popularity of radio is also assisted by the fact that local advertisers can reach a large audience in rural areas. Telecom Regulatory Authority of India is expected to introduce many reforms to further stimulate revenue growth.

The following players have the most operational stations:

Broadcaster	# of Stations
Big FM	44
Radio Mirchi	32
Radio City	21
South Asia FM	21
My FM	17

Some play in joint ventures because the government limit the amount of stations per broadcaster, making the actual amount of stations bigger than those stated in the table.

2.4. Advertising in Traditional Media

The Indian advertising and marketing market is estimated worth a total of $4 billion with most of the expenditures in the traditional media. 82% of the top 500 marketers pay only 5.4% of their budget online. Businesses keep advertising through traditional mediums due to the Internet-penetration in India is low compared to the other media. Another remarkable point is that the sectors accounting for a total of 70% of advertising expenditure are accountable for only 30% of online-advertising expenditure.

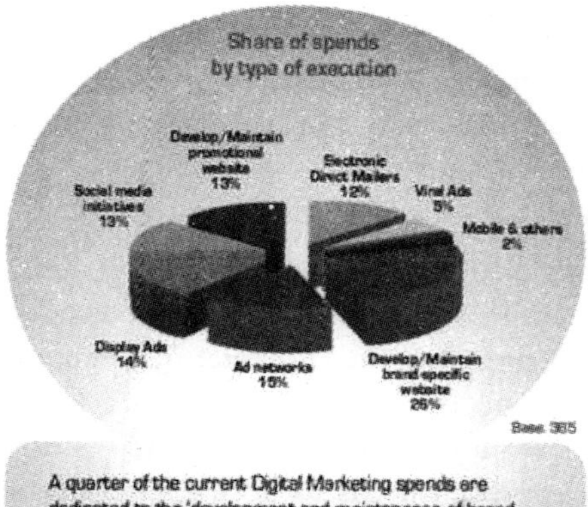

A quarter of the current Digital Marketing spends are dedicated to the 'development and maintenance of brand specific and promotional websites'. About 34% is spent on 'advertising' through pure display ads, viral ads and ad networks. It is a welcoming change to see that almost 13% of spends go into social media initiatives and 2% towards mobile and other initiatives.

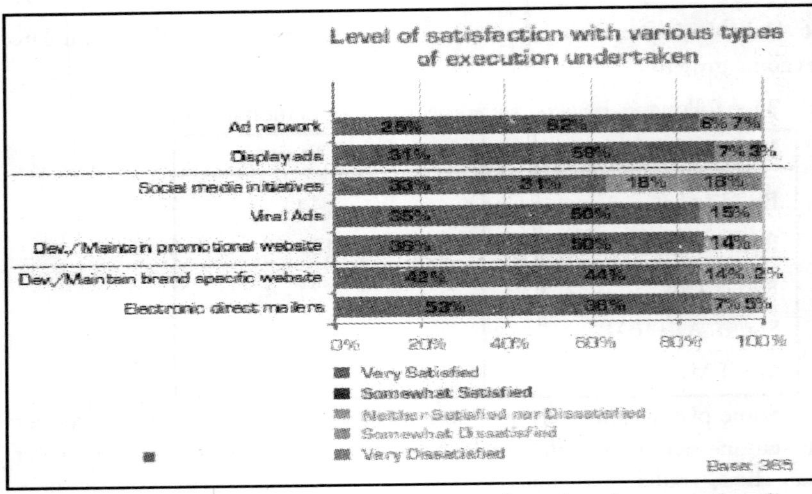

This is so because the bigger companies view Internet for direct marketing rather than a platform for creating conversations. Moreover, research said about another important aspect of Internet advertising is to generate leads and the satisfaction of using social media as an advertising medium is very low. However, as it is likely the advertisement spending will fall by 10% while an increase of 44% is expected to be seen in digital media advertising.

3. Problems in Traditional Media

There is a transition to digital, but still have to pay the bills and maintain margins. To make the transition new skills are needed to be learned. More importantly, they need to unlearn some things they knew about how to make money in media. The problem with most traditional media companies that they're old, but that they're too balkanised. Business and creative sides have been historically adversarial that puts it hard to build the collaboration needed for digital media.

The problem is that very few media people are generalists, they immediately try to address new media problems using the few tools they know. However, digital media require greater integration. To be successful, traditional media need to learn about new media, and old media as well. Print is needed to learn broadcast, creative people understand more about business, etc. This approach needs to be absorbed into every facet of the business: strategy, hiring, training, organisational structure, etc.

4. Examples of Digital Media

The following list of digital media is based on a rather technical view of the term media. Other views might lead to different lists.

- Cellular phones
- Compact discs
- Digital video
- Televisions
- e-books
- Internet
- Video games
- e-Commerce
- Game consoles
- Computers
- Interactive media

5. How Traditional Forms are Digitised

In digital art computers played a role in production or display of the artwork, which can be an image, sound, animation, video, CD-ROM, DVD-ROM, videogame, web site, algorithm, performance or gallery installation. Many traditional disciplines are now associating with digital technologies and, consequently the lines between traditional works of art and new media works created by computers has been blurred. Often, the medium itself is considered the artwork. As a result, defining computer art by its end product can thus be significantly tough Comic book artists in the past generally sketched a drawing in pencil before drawing again with India ink, using pens and brushes. Magazine illustrators often worked with India ink, acrylics or oils. Currently, an increasing number of artists are now creating digital artwork. As our culture becomes increasingly digitised, digital artists are leading the way in exploring and defining this new culture.

Digital Artists use a medium nearly immaterial, that being binary information. Taken as a whole an image consisting of pure light is the feedback device to tell an artist what is being made and simultaneously stored on the computer's hard drive. Digital Artists apply many types of user interfaces corresponding to the wide variety of brushes, lenses, or other tools that traditional artist use. These electronic brushes and tools allow an artist to translate hand motions, cutting and pasting, the chemical darkroom techniques to effect the arrangement of screen pixels and create a picture.

In addition, digital art may be appreciated directly on a computer screen in gallery situations, or simultaneously in every place on the globe with access to the web.

6. Digital Media–Danger for Traditional Media

Putting the spotlight on digital media, exchange4media convened the first ever Digital Media Conference in Mumbai on March 11, 2010, the theme being 'Insights into the digital business'.

Mahendra Swarup, Chief Mentor, Smile Interactive, and President, Indian Venture Capital Association on Emerging Digital Trends, predicted the print medium would wane out even as the electronic arena was growing at an extremely fast pace, and along with were growing the content owners, advertisers and distributors. "With the advent of digital, the paradigm of advertising will change. While traditional media currently are a one to million medium, digital facilitates a one to one interaction. Thus, more and more advertising will be done on a one to one basis. The launch of 3G in India, which is expected in April, will further grow the digital medium."

Swarup cited the example of Coke and Pepsi and said, "Brand is the creation of advertisers. For example, Coke and Pepsi have some adverse effects on health, but the advertisers will never disclose those. Thus, brands have to be present in the digital world to build greater connect. Consumers can take more informed decisions.Thanks to digital media. For instance, one can simply do a Google search and do a comparison of all the toothpaste brands and decide on which one is the best."

Digital media are powerful in the West. Currently, digital media are worth Rs. 120-150 million in India. Today, there are 50-plus million Internet subscribers in India, with a scope for this medium to grow in future.

Mobile is a P2P device, however, mobile advertising is catching on in a big way here, as well as to play a key role in decimating information. The brands making disappropriate advertising on television will make less in digital.

India is going to adapt digital at a faster rate in times to come, however, the challenge is that digital advertising is not growing at the required pace. Use of landline phones is declining lower while mobile usage is increasing on rapid pace. Today there are 100 million TV households in India, but the distribution cost of DTH is met condusive. Print is surviving, On the other face of coing, of digital is increasing. Internet will become cheaper in coming days. As for Internet speed, laser broadband facilitates download in less than 3 minutes, and India goes to be an early adapter of laser broadband.

7. How Digital and Traditional Media Functions?

7.1. Print Companies Make Money by Selling Space

In print, advertisers want top titles. High demand culminates into more space sold at higher rates. A good print salesperson is one who sells a lot of pages, but a great print salesperson creates pages by working closely with advertisers on non-standard advertising targeting small consumers.

7.2. Managing Inventory is the Core Competency of Broadcasters

While print businesses can increase page counts to suit demand, broadcast companies fix inventory. There are so many ad spots in an hour with average ratings unchanged very much in a year.

A good broadcast salesperson sells a very high percentage of inventory at good rates. They are cautions about their limited prime time and package in as much fringe time as they can. By selling the weakest time slots they win big profit margins. In fact, selling broadcast is like selling a mortgage bond. What's significant is packaging a portfolio that imparts the advertiser maximum coverage at minimum cost. There is very little migration between print and broadcast sales. The two activities demand very different sets and volumes of skill.

7.3. Successful Digital Media Businesses Create and Manage Inventory

Digital media has limited premium inventory but unlimited fringe inventory. Moreover, more fragmented than print itpackages even better than broadcast.

Digital strategy is, to a large extent, a trial and error process. You have to fail often and fail cheaply.

Nevertheless, these three strategies the help increase margins:

7.4. Integrate Social Functionality

Much like broadcast, it's not so easy to make money in digital premium space alone. Adding social components to branded content is a great way to increase loyalty and engagement, and to create lots of new, albeit cheaper, inventory.

7.5. Satellite and Aggregated Sites

Users want to find relevant information in as few clicks as possible. For that, they choose a portfolio of sites, that suit their interests. A great way to take advantage of that is by strcturing new sites with existing content. This can be done by either creating satellite sites for a general product or by aggregating related niche sites together into a more general portal. There are several benefits in doing this.

It dovetails very well with integration of social functionality as different content brands initiate different discussions. Moreover, by linking to the source of the original article, you enjoy SEO benefits on the original site. Finally, you introduce more inventory to sell.

Unlike in print or broadcast, this is comparatively cheaper and easier to do as long as one was CMS and related templates established. The point is to build fast and simple, the users will show you where to develop further.

7.6. Package Aggressively

Packaging effectively is important for making money online. It is needed to protect the prime and sell as much fringe as possible. There's no point in selling out the home page while everything else is filled with self promotion. Moreover, packaging opportunities are more extensive online. It can be created run-on-site and run-on-network packages, thematic channels, performance and CPA pricing, e-commerce partnerships, etc.

With virtually unlimited inventory, the options are nearly unlimited as well. Many companies want to farm out their fringe inventory to a banner network and keep higher margin space and sponsorships in house.

8. Conclusion: Towards Integrative Solutions-The Way Ahead

Many old media skills are still relevant in the digital world. In fact, many best practices off-line will lead to failure online. The problem with most traditional media companies is that they're Business and creative sides have been historically adversarial which makes to build the collaboration needed for digital media-hard.

Very few media people are generalists, which is why they immediately try to solve new media problems using the few tools they know. Digital media know no bounds and therefore require greater integration.

To be successful, traditional media need to learn about new media, and old media as well. Print needs to learn broadcast, creative people need to comprehand more about business, etc. This approach needs to be taken into every facet of the business: strategy, hiring, training, organisational structure, etc.

If media incumbents are to be successful in the digital realm, they need to integrate skills and develop new principles, instead of depuding on old ones. New Media certainly need new thinking process to make a way for integration of traditional media with the digital one.Only then we can project an adoptable theory for digital and traditional both the media.

References

Leah A. Lievrouw, Sonia Livingstone (ed.), The Handbook of New Media, SAGE, 2002.

Logan, Robert K. (2010), Understanding New Media: Extending Marshall McLuhan, New York: Peter Lang Publishing.

Reed, TV, "Will the Revolution be Cybercast?"

Thompson, John B. (1995), The Media and Modernity, Cambridge: Polity Press

Long, Paul and Wall, Tim : Media Studies: Text, Production and Context, Pearson Education, 2009, http://www.doingmediastudies.com

How Old Media Can Survive In a New World, Wall Street Journal.

http://comm215.wetpaint.com

9

Changing Mutual Perception of TV News Viewers and Programme Makers in India–A Case Study of CNN-IBN and Its Unique Initiative of Citizen Journalism

1. Introduction

The Indian television system is one of the systems in the world. Terrestrial broadcasting, broadest the sole preserve of the government, provides wide television coverage to over 90% of India's 900 million people. By the end of 1996 nearly 50 million households had television sets. International satellite broadcasting, introduced in 1991, had swept across the country because of the rapid proliferation of small scale cable systems. By the end of 1996, Indians had dozens of foreign and local channels and the competition for audiences and advertising revenues was one of the hottest in the world.

In 1995, the Indian Supreme Court held the government's monopoly over broadcasting was unconstitutional, setting the stage for India to grow into one of the world's largest and most competitive television environments.

2. The Satelite Television in India

The journey of satellite broadcasting was started in the form of the famous Satellite Instructional Television Experiment (SITE) in 1975-76. It was arrested the American satellite ATS-6 and transmitted development programmes via direct transmission to 2400 remote villages located in six different states of the country. SITE proved India's capability of using improved technology and learn to the socio-economic necessities of the country. The success was technological, managerial, programme production and research. INSAT facilitates satellite based national transmission in the form of direct reception from the satellite or through a hybrisystem of receiving it from the satellite and re-transmit it terrestrially through low or high power transmitters, which provided communication umbrella to the whole country. The Gulf war of 1991 was another very major landmark effecting television scene in the country, CNN was first to beam transnational signals on the war, opening up enormous possibilities.

A large number of small enterprising youngsters started distributing satellite signals through a cable network to individual households. The cable operator received the satellite channels and distributed them through a cable network to the household subscribers for a small fee. Along with CNN many other foreign private satellite channels found the huge market with India. Amongst the earliest initiatives came from Rupert Murdoch's Star TV. 1992 was the beginning of Star TV network through the Asiasat-1.

3. Growth of Television in India

Indian Television idiot box has thousands of programmes in all the states of India. The has produced numerous celebrities of their own kind attaining national fame. TV soaps are extremely popular with housewives as well as working women. Approximately half of all Indian households own a television. The Ramayana and Later on Mahabharat was the first major television serial produced. This serial notched up the world record in viewership numbers for a single program.

By the late 1980s people started to own television sets. With single channel, television programming had reached saturation. Hence the government opened up another channel known as DD 2 later DD Metro. Both channels were broadcast terrestrially.

3.1. Post-Liberalisation Television

Under the new policies, the government allowed private and foreign broadcasters to engage in limited operations in India. Foreign channels like CNN, Star TV and domestic channels such as Zee TV and Sun TV began satellite broadcasts. Starting with 41 sets in 1965 and one channel, by 1991 TV covered more than 70 million homes giving a viewing population of more than 400 million individuals through more than 100 channels.

3.2 Cable television

India had over 130 million homes with television sets, of which nearly 71 million had access to cable TV. The overall Cable TV market grew at a robust 8-10%. The cable TV industry exploded in the early 1990s when the broadcast industry was liberalised, and saw the entry of many foreign players like Rupert Murdoch's Star TV Network in 1991, MTV, and others. The emergence and notification of the HDVSL standard as a home grown Indian digital cable standard can bring an era of interactivity on cable networks.

Sun TV (India) was founded in 1992 as the first private channel in South India. Today it has 20 television channels in the four South Indian languages – Kannada, Malayalam, Tamil and Telugu. Channels of the Sun TV network are also available outside of India. Five new channels belonging to the Hong Kong-based STAR TV gave Indians a fresh outpage in communication. MTV, STAR Plus, Star Movies, BBC, Prime Sports and STAR Chinese Channel were the 5 channels.

Zee TV was the first private owned Indian channel to broadcast over cable. Later CNN, Discovery Channel, National Geographic Channel made a foray into India.

Star expanded its bouquet introducing STAR World, STAR Sports, ESPN, Channel Vandalso thrived, STAR Gold. Regional channels flourished along with a multitude of Hindi channels and a few English channels.

By 2001 HBO and History Channel were the other international channels to enter India. By 1999-2003, other international channels such as Nickelodeon, Cartoon Network, VH1, Disney and Toon Disney came into foray. In 2003 news channels started introducing their boom.

3.3. Audience Metrics

Television Metrics in India have gone through several phases in which it fragmented, consolidated and then fragmented again.

3.3.1. DART

During the days of Doordarshan monopoly, DART (Doordarshan Audience Research Team) was the sole metric available. This used the notebook method of recordkeeping across 33 cities across India . DART continues to provide this information independent of the Private agencies. DART till this date is the sole rating system that still measures audience metrics in Rural India .

3.3.2. TAM and INTAM

In 1994, claiming a heterogeneous and fragmenting television market ORG-MARG introduced INTAM (Indian National Television Audience Measurement). Ex-officials of DD (Doordarshan) opined that INTAM was inducted by vested commercial interests to break the monopoly of DD. Moreover, INTAM was significantly non-competent in sample size, rigour and the range of cities and regions assessed. In 1997, a joint industry body appointed TAM with AC Nielsen) as the official recordkeeper of audience metrics.

Due to the differences in methodology and samples of TAM and INTAM, both provided different results for the same programs. In 2001, the two measurement systems merged into TAM . For several years after this, in spite of misgivings about the process, sample and other parameters, TAM was the de facto standard and monopoly in the audience metrics game.

3.3.3. Conditional Access System

CAS pay (conditional access system) is a digital mode of transmitting TV pay channels through a set-top box (STB). The transmission signals are encrypted and viewers need to buy a set-top box to receive and decrypt the signal. The idea of CAS was mooted in 2001, due to a furore over charge hikes by channels and subsequently by cable operators. Poor reception of certain channels; arbitrary pricing and increase in prices; bundling of channels; poor service delivery by Cable Television Operators (CTOs); monopolies in each area; lack of regulatory framework and redress avenues were some of the core issues remained to be addressed by implementation of CAS.

It was decided by the government to introduce CAS first in the four metros. It in Chennai since September 2003. It has been introduced out recently in the other three metros of Delhi, Mumbai and Kolkata.

3.4. Satellite television

Over 300 TV Satellite television channels broadcast in India. Include Doordarshan, STAR TV, Sony Entertainment Television, Sun Network and Zee TV. Direct To Home service is provided by Airtel Digital TV, BIG TV, DD Direct Plus, DishTV, Sun Direct DTH and Tata Sky.

These services are facilitated by locally built satellites from ISRO such as INSAT 4CR, INSAT 4A, INSAT-2E, INSAT-3C and INSAT-3E as well as private satellites such as the Dutch-based SES, Global-owned NSS 6, Thaicom-2 and Telstar-10.

3.5. Direct to Home

DTH is defined as the reception of satellite programmes with a personal dish in an individual home. DTH does not compete with CAS. Cable TV and DTH are two methods of delivery of television content.

CAS is integral to both the systems in delivering pay channels. Cable TV is through cable networks and DTH is wireless, reaching direct to the consumer through a small dish and a set-top box. India currently has 6 major DTH service providers and a total of over 5 million subscriber households. Dish TV(a ZEE TV subsidiary), Tata Sky, South India Media Giant Sun Network owned 'Sundirect DTH', Reliance owned BIG TV, Videocon D2H, Bharti Airtel's DTH Service 'Airtel Digital TV' and the public sector DD Direct Plus.

3.6. Internet Protocol Television (IPTV)

IPTV launched only in some cities around 2006-2007 by MTNL/ BSNL later expands to many urban areas and still expanding. Private Broadband provider Bharti Airtel also starts its IPTV service in Delhi, NCR region. 2009-2010 IPTV in India was scarcely making any impact in the market. But IPTV and Online Video Services in India have incrative markets. Screen Digest estimates broadband penetration of TV households to increase from 4.2 percent in 2009 to 13.4 percent in 2013 .

4. The Citizen Journalism–History, Growth and Expansion of Citizen Journalism Worldwide

4.1. Definition of Citizen Journalism

Citizen journalism (also known as "public", "participatory", "democratic" or street journalism)is the concept of members of the public "playing an active role in the process of collecting, reporting, analysing and disseminating news and information," according to the seminal 2003 report We Media: How Audiences are Shaping the Future of News and Information.

Bowman and Willis say: "The intent of this participation is to provide independent, reliable, accurate, wide-ranging and relevant information that a democracy requires."

Citizen journalism ought not to be immdled out with community journalism or civic journalism, which are practised by professional journalists, or collaborative journalism, which is practised by professional and non-professional journalists working together.

Mark Glaser, a freelance journalist who frequently writes on new media issues, said in 2006:

The idea behind citizen journalism is that people without professional journalism training can use the tools of modern technology and the global distribution of the Internet to create, augment or fact-check media on their own or in collaboration with others. For example, you might write about a city council meeting on your blog or in an online forum.

Or you could fact-check a newspaper article from the mainstream media and point out factual errors or bias on your blog.

Or you might snap a digital photo of a newsworthy event happening in your town and post it online. Or you might videotape a similar event and post it on a site such as YouTube.

4.2. Background

The roots of citizen journalism lie in the self-printed pamphlets distributed on the street-side. However, byfacilitating everyone to report news without the permission like news organisations or editors, social media has democratised journalism and mad it enriched by bringing in a diversity of views and voices to told.

There are four aspects of citizen journalism.

a. News blogging: Re-blogging, commenting on, giving context on, or curating news often reported in traditional media. WATBlog and Pluggd.in, for instance, curate news on the IT/ Telecom/ Media industry in India.

b. Local blogging: Blogging about local news not usually reported in traditional media. For instance, the Metroblogging network, which has chapters in Mumbai, Chennai, Bangalore and Hyderabad, is focused on covering local city news.

c. Change blogging: Blogging about a cause or an issue. The Blank Noise Project, which communicates against street sexual harassment. The Indian Water Portal Blog is another, especially Sharda Prasad's K2K project.

d. Crisis reporting, which involves live blogging about a crisis. Often, these are game-changing events that bring citizen journalism into the mainstream, for citizen journalism is often the fastest and the most inclusive/ interactive source of news on these events.

Examples include the Tsunami in 2004 and the Mumbai terror attack in 2008. While blogs like T sunamiHelp and MumbaiHelp have played an important role in coordinating such efforts, they are essentially distributed efforts.

Of times media, corporates have done experiments with their own citizen journalism initiatives, like MTV India's My India Report and IBN Live's Citizen Journalist. Similarly, there are citizen journalism websites like NowPublic, GroundReport, Merinews and Instablogs. Still, citizen journalism remains a non-consolidated phenomenon.

4.3. The story of CNN-IBN–The First Channel to start Citizen Journalism in India

CNN-IBN is a partnership between Global Broadcast News (GBN), a Network18 Company, and Turner International (Turner) in India.

The 24-hour, English-language news channel is spearheaded by famous television journalist Rajdeep Sardesai, the Editor-in-Chief. He is supported in the initiative by the Network18's experience and infrastructure in India and by CNN's global news network.

IBNLive.com is the online version of GBN with stern news as its core contribution and interactivity as its main component. Along with a plethora of mobile- and multimedia-enabled content, IBNLive is a multi-platform offering that, for the first time, assists viewers/users chance to bestow to the news process and respond with editors and reporters.

Manned 24x7, IBNLive.com is empowered not just by CNN-IBN journalists but also by Network18's team of over 1,000 news professionals. CNN-IBN will offer recebt high quality news from every corner of India and relevant global news from CNN, the world's news leader, on the same platform with a target to provide the comprehending viewers with a complete dedication to the needs and ambitious of the Indian viewer, while CNN International will to deliver global news to Indian viewers.

Mr. Sardesai, the Editor-in-Chief, eloberates "The news channel is built on the age-old ethic that editorial sovereignty is inviolable – and this shall be a cornerstone of GBN's partnership with CNN. It will be a journalist-driven channel rooted in the realities of modern India. With nationwide news gathering capabilities, superior journalistic talent, and a passion for news, the new service will endeavour to get the news first and direct from the ground. In a fast-globalising India, access to CNN's global news network will add immense value for our audiences."

"This service will complement CNN International's global news offering and marks another milestone in CNN's efforts to move closer to its audience though local partnerships. The coupling of CNN's global resources and GBN'S local expertise will take news broadcasting in India to a whole new level," told Chris Cramer, Managing Director, CNN International.

"The alliance is the first of its kind for CNN and Turner in the Asia Pacific. The service will leverage the combined international and local journalistic expertise of each partner to provide Indian news viewers unparalleled coverage of global and local events as they unfold, from an Indian perspective," told Anshuman Misra, Managing Director, Turner International India Pvt. Ltd.

Headquartered at a world-class facility in New Delhi, the channel is supported by over 20 bureaus nationwide, along with a team of well-versed newspersons and production staff, backed by Network18's state-of-the-art broadcast infrastructure and newsgathering technology. GBN, a Network18 Company, is a 74:26 joint venture between the Network18 and professionals - Rajdeep Sardesai, Sameer Manchanda and Haresh Chawla.

GBN's charter is to launch channels in the general news space under the editorial leadership of Sardesai, one of India's most renowned TV journalists. The Network18 Group is India's leading and most successful business news broadcaster in both English and Hindi. CNN is the world's leading global 24-hour news network and one of the world most wondered and trusted sources for news and information. The CNN brand responds to two billion people through 18 CNN branded TV, internet and mobile services produced by CNN Worldwide, a division of Turner Broadcasting System Inc. and a Time Warner company. CNN International is the international directorate of CNN Worldwide and distributes news via 14 services in seven different languages. CNN International can be seen in more than 257 million households and hotel rooms in over 200 countries and territories worldwide, including more than 37 million across the Asia Pacific region and online at www.cnn.com/international.

7. Popular Shows of CNN-IBN

7.1. Face The Nation

The idea behind this show is to obtain the top newsmakers or those associated with the big story of the debate. Jointly hosted by Sagarika Ghosh and Bhupendra Chaubey, it a show based on British Parliamentary debating style, the host first sets up the topic for debate with his own comments and asksed the three guests to respond in half hour duration show. The uniqueness is that it's also a debate being taken place at an interactive level as well. While the guests on the channel are commenting on the question, viewers are offered to take part in this debate through online voting or sms. The way it works is :

QOTD: Should Pakistani terrorists targetting India be hanged? Type QOTD Y for yes, QOTD N for no. Sms your responses at xxxxx or log on to IBNLIVE.COM to send in your responses.

Now this subject is debated extensively and looked at from all angles.At the end of the day, the viewers are going to vote on this subject and assest the final verdict on the channel.

7.2. Citizen Journalism Show

So far the basic tenet of journalism was always to give some kind of a route to people. But now at CNN-IBN, this show attempted to change this basic principle. It makes the viewer the central character of this show. It asks viewers to get in touch on any basic issue. Something as basic as lack of water, electiricty, bad road, health care, schools anything with an impact on the daily life of the viewer. A team visits the concerned person. He explains on camera abentitute issue. The process is sent to the old school of journalism to seek anwers from the supposed. The viewer with the team visits to the relevant authority and seeks answers from them. This show has revolutionised Indian TV. We call it the CJ awards, which is now an annual affair, for those who made some difference in society with the help of this show.

7.3. Late Night Edition

It's a crisp wrap up of the days top news stories packaged in half an hour. The idea is to just present the facts. This is a show which is a daily news bulletin and is put on air at 11 pm. People like to the news stories before they go to sleep.

7.4. India@9

Now the 9 pm show is also a bit about views. The fundamental challenge in Indian news television at present is how to balance the nuance of reporting on a story and at the same time, in the span of a 24 hour wheel take it forward as well. India@9 is the show where we deal with this challenge practically on a daily basis. Viewers are interested in news and wants WHY behind WHAT has happened! Marketing agencies divide viewership patterns as 4+, 15+ and 25+ in terms of age groups. Data is also available in terms of male viewing habbits and female viewing habbits. The top headline is essentially what you can expect to read in the newspapers the next day on the front page. The format would be first giving the story and then maybe have a couple of people who are associated with that story giving their inputs on it. The show is hosted by the editor in chief of the network. An hour long show would have the top news story, voices associated with that story for the first half anhour. The next ten minutes would be dedicated to giving the other day developing stories leading upto sports. The last 10 minutes of the show are always reserved for entertainment.

At 4 pm everyday, the editorial staff of the channel meets to figure out what are the kind of stories we would be showcasing in our 9 pm show. At 7.30 the editor-in-chief himself sits with the editorial staff to make a few last minute changes if required.

8. Conclusion–Impact of Citizen Journalism on Society-

Citizens need information about the political, economic, and cultural systems that structure their lives in a democratic order to act on them effectively. The pamphleteers of the American Revolution were, in their way, citizen journalists. Many of the newspapers in the 19th Century were started by non-professionals, who understood a need in local communities and began publishing a mix of news, advertising, and gossip. Newspapers were professionalised in the 19th Century, but professionalisation discounted the underlying truth claims on one side or another and led to a decline of independent judgment and, sometimes, support for the status quo.

In terms of content they alternate fact-oriented reporting of locally based participants in the context of a global network, to self-expression of opinion. What defines citizen journalism, is a networked structure of storytelling based on the following premises: a) openness of information; b) horizontal linkage structures rather than vertical flows of information; c) blurring lines between content production and consumption; d) diffused accountability based on reputation and meaning, rather than on structural system hierarchies.

In Korea it has served to open the political spectrum and in the United States to redefine the news agenda. At least in theory it could represent an important pathway in the development of a networked civil society that brings about democratisation change.

References

1. In India, the Golden Age of Television Is Now, New York Times.

2. Scatindia.
3. Identity and Consumerism on Television in India, AEJMC Archives.
4. DART report shows DD scoring high among rural audiences
5. Why is TRP a contentious issue? Screen India.
6. Company Profile tamindia.com
7. How real is Tam/Intam rating? The Times of India.
8. TRP rating: The slip is showing Business Standard via Rediff.com
9. Security Check: TAM, INTAM Try To Ensure Data Sanctity Express cricket.
10. Quibbles apart, TAM is only currency industry can use, indiantelevision.com
11. New TV rating system to challenge TAM monopoly, The Times of India.
12. Map brings TV ratings online, Hindu Business Line.
13. Ratings COS fight for market share, Business Standard.
14. Rival to stare TAM in eyeball, Financial Express.
15. "Indiantelevision dot com's Satellites over India", Indiantelevision.com.
16. Map secures Tata Sky DTH audience measurement biz Indiantelevision.com
17. TV and Video Portals in India, International Television Expert Group.
18. Broadband Penetration Forecast for Indian TV Households (2000-2013), International Television Expert Group.
19. Chatterji, P.C. Broadcasting in India, New Delhi: Sage, 1991.
20. Desai, M.V. Communication Policies in India, Paris: UNESCO, 1977.
21. Mehra, M. Broadcasting and the People, New Delhi: National Book Trust, 1976.
22. Mehta, D. S. Mass Communication and Journalism in India, New Delhi: Allied Publishers, 1992.
23. Rajagopal, A. "The Rise of National Programming: the Case of Indian Television," Media Culture and Society (London), 1993.
24 Sinha N. "India: Television and National Politics", In, Raboy, Marc, editor. Public Broadcasting for the Twenty-First Century, Montreal: World Radio and Television Council, 1996.

10

Community Radio–Evolution, Growth, Challenges and Status of it with Special Reference to India

Introduction

In the UK, the idea of community-based services can be traced back at least as far as the original concept for BBC local radio in the early 1960s. Since, various land-based unlicensed pirate radio stations (East London Radio, and Radio AMY (Alternative Media for You)) during the proliferated during the late 1970s and early 1980s were joined by they these by to minority immigrant communities (Afro-Caribbean and Asian etc.), broadcasters in cities such as London, Birmingham, Bristol' and Manchester.

Although, "community radio" remains synonymous with "pirate radio" for some people in the UK. Most minority immigrant stations attended purely on specific musical genres and were operated on a profit basis. Community radio services in the UK are operated on a not-for-profit basis with community ownership and control built into their structures.

Following an experiment started in 2001 by the former UK broadcast regulator The *Radio Authority*, since 2005 some 200 such stations were licensed by the UK broadcasting regulator (Ofcom). The stations broadcast on FM and on AM (medium wave), particularly in more rural areas. In the U.S., community radio stations are non-profit, community-based operations licensed by the Federal Communications Commission for broadcasting in the non-commercial, public portion of the FM band.

These stations are distinct from other public radio houses in the U.S. by allowing community volunteers to actively participate as broadcasters.

Pirate radio is virtually unknown in Australia due to the strictly limited allocation of broadcasting frequencies, and the likely application of severe, legislated penalties, including jail, for offenders.

Vision and philosophy behind CRS

Community radio means to cover the news and information programming geared toward the local area, particularly immigrant or minority groups, poorly served by other major media outlets. More specialised musical shows are also often a feature of many community radio stations. Such stations typically avoid content soared on commercial outlets.

Models of community radio

Philosophically two distinct approaches to community radio can be attended to, though the models are not necessarily mutually exclusive. While one emphasies over service or community-mindedness the other does on involvement and participation by the listener. Within the service model localism is often prized, focused on a more local or particular community than larger operations. Within the United States, many stations syndicate content from groups such as *Pacifica Radio*, Democracy Now, on the basis that it provides a form of content not otherwise available, because of such a program's lack of appeal to advertisers or politically controversial nature. Within the access or participatory model, the participation of community members in producing content has been seen as a good in itself. While this model does not necessarily despatch from a service approach, there remains a tense environ between the two, as outlined, for example, in Jon Bekken's *Community Radio at the Crossroads.*

Growth and Development of Community Radio

(References with major countries operating CRS)

Australia

Community Broadcasting, Australia's third media sector, at June 2005 with 442 fully-licensed community radio stations, fulfills a broad, but largely unacknowledged role as a source of local content. According to a 2002 report, 20,000 (or 0.1% of all Australians) volunteers are on a regular basis, and volunteers equate for more than $145 million in unpaid work each year. Nationally more than 7 million Australians (or 45% of people over 15) listen to community radio in each month (source: McNair Ingenuity).

The role of community broadcasting in Australia, the *Community Broadcasting Association of Australia* states, is to supply a diverse range of services meeting community needs in ways that are not met by other sectors. Community broadcasting is assisted by the principles of access and participation, volunteerism, diversity, independence and localism. Community radio stations sometimes represwent themselves as specialist music stations. Others might broadcast talks and current affairs programs filling perceived gaps in commercial or government radio content. Although community radio has developed immensely over the years, both in terms of the number of listeners and the number of stations, the sector is largely under-funded which results in spending much of their time financing their community service activities.

53% of community radio stations assist to build an array of different communities of interest including: Indigenous and Ethnic, people with a print disability, young people, older people, arts/fine music, religious, gay and lesbian. The remaining stations provide generalist services which address the interests of communities in particular geographic locations.

Canada

Community radio stations (volunteer-run by cooperatives) in Canada most commonly target commercially underserved minority language communities such as Franco-Ontarians, Acadians or First Nations, although some communities also have English language community stations. In larger cities, community-oriented programming more commonly airs on campus radio stations.

Most community stations in Canada are members of the *National Campus* and *Community Radio Association*, or *NCRA*. Most of Canada's French language community radio stations are members of either *l'Association des Radiodiffuseurs Communitaire du Quebec* (ARCQ) or *l'Alliance des radios communautaires du Canada inc (l'ARC).*[3] The province with the largest number of community radio stations in Canada is Saskatchewan. The majority of those stations are affiliated with Missinipi Broadcasting Corporation, an aboriginal public radio network.

Community stations are controlled and regulated by the Canadian Radio-television and Telecommunications Commission's (CRTC) community radio policy.[4]

In this policy, the CRTC needs community stations to facilitate community access to programming; promote the availability of training throughout the community; and provide for the ongoing training and supervision of those within the community wishing to participate in programming. It also needs stations to broadcast diverse programming that represents the requirements and interests of the community including: music by new and local talent; music not generally broadcast by commercial stations; spoken word programming; and local information.

The CRTC maintains a list of community stations. In Canada, call letters and frequencies are regulated by Industry Canada's Spectrum Management.[6]

India

In India, the campaign community radio started in the mid 1990s, after the Supreme Court of India ruled in February 1995 that "airwaves are public property". This came as an inspiration but only educational (campus) radio stations were permitted under non-condusive conditions. Anna FM is India's first campus 'community' radio, launched on 1 February, 2004, run by *Education and Multimedia Research Centre* (EM^2RC), and programmes are produced by the students of Media Sciences at Anna University. On 16 November, 2006, the government of India notified new Community Radio Guidelines which allowed NGOs and civil society organisations to own community radio stations.

By 30 November, 2008, the ministry of Information and broadcasting, government of India, had received 297 applications for community radio licences, including 141 from NGOs and other civil society organisations, 105 from educational institutions and 51 for 'farm radio' stations to be run by agricultural universities and agricultural extension centers ('Krishi Vigyan Kendras'). By 30 November 2008, there were 38 operational community radio stations in the country.

The first community-based radio station, licenced to an NGO (as distinct from campus-based radio) was launched on 15 October, 2008, when '*Sangham Radio*' in Pastapur village, Medak district, Andhra Pradesh state, was switched on at 11.00 am. Sangham Radio, which broadcasts on 90.4 MHz, is licensed to Deccan Development Society (DDS). The second NGO-led community radio station in India was launched on 23 October, 2008 at Taragram in Orchha, Madhya Pradesh state. Named '*Radio Bundelkhand*'; the radio station is licensed to the Society for Development Alternatives (DA), a Delhi-based NGO.

According to the Ministry of Information and Broadcasting said, 47 community radio stations were operational in India by 1 November, 2009, including 45 campus-based stations and two CRS run by NGOs. By December 2009, the number of CR stations run by civil society groups had seven, including *Sangham Radio* (Pastapur, Medak District,

Andhra Pradesh), *Radio Bundelkhand* (Orchha, Madhya Pradesh), *Mann Deshi Tarang* (Satara, Maharashtra), *Namma Dhwani* (Budikote, Karnataka), *Radio Mattoli* (Wayanad, Kerala), Kalanjiam Samuga Vanoli (Nagapattinam, Tamil Nadu) and *Barefoot* (Tilonia, Rajasthan).

By 4 December, 2009, the Ministry of Information and Broadcasting had issued '*Grant of Permission Agreements*' (GOPA) for 62 community radio stations, mostly to educational institutions.

Amongst the campus-based community radio stations started in 2009, SARANG 107.8 is the only one in Karnataka, though few more have received SACFA (Standing Committee Clearance for Frequency Allocation). Two other campus-based stations are already operational in Bangalore, Karnataka.

SARANG 107.8 is run by St. Aloysius College (Autonomous), Mangalore, Karnataka. SARANG 107.8 FM means 'all colours' of Mangalore signifying various social, religious, linguistic communities and their harmonious existence. The local communities of farmers, fisher folk, medical/legal experts, students, workers assist regularly to this radio. Health and hygiene, agricultural messages, fisher folk issues, road safety, water conservation, rain water harvesting, folk culture and life, original entertainment by locals and students are the major activities of this radio. Currently by the end of July 2009. *SARANG* 107.8 broadcasts in Konkani, Kannada, Tulu, and English languages regularly, in addition to occasionally broadcasting in Malayalam and Beary languages.

United Kingdom

Community radio stations operated on cable systems from 1978 onwards and mostly situated in new town areas and staffed and operated by volunteers.

In the late 80s and early 90s the newly formed Radio Authority licensed "Incremental" to a number of new, ex-pirate and cable based community ventures.

Notable stations included *Radio Thamesmead* (later *RTM Radio*), on the rediffusion cable system in South-East London area in 1978. The old breed of community radio stations managed their financers by selling air space and by receiving donations or grants.

United States

U.S. community radio stations have usually volunteers and air a wide variety of programming. They have smaller budgets than *National Public*

Radio (NPR) network houses, because of the small listener group of potential contributors and/or business donors. Community radio stations are different from NPR stations in that most community radio programming is locally incorporated by non-professional disc jockeys and producers, where NPR tends to rely more on syndicated programming, both from its own sources and other houses such as PRI; NPR stations almost pay staffs to handle most duties.

Community stations often try, as a matter of principle, to belittle their dependence on financial contributions from corporations (and even governments) in comparison with other public broadcasters. Many community stations are licensed as full-power FM stations, while others under low-power broadcasting rules.

Many were founded in the 1960s and 1970s, when cultural experimentation (e.g., the New Left) in the U.S. had a significant following, especially among the young. The *National Federation of Community Broadcasters* was formed in 1975 as an umbrella organisation for community-oriented, non-commercial radio stations.

The NFCB produces handbooks for stations and lobbies on behalf of community radio at the federal level. It is criticised for encouraging the homogenisation of community stations through its *Healthy Station Project*. The project motivated stations to scale back volunteers' power over management and the content of their programs, as well as embrace more predictable "strip" programming.[9]

The Grassroots Radio Coalition was formed as a reaction against increasing commercialisation of public radio and lack of support for volunteer-based stations. Some stations have membership of both groups.

The Social Impact of Community Radio

Population Media Center President William Ryerson demonstrated, an empirically proven fact based on quantifiable and statistically analysed results. Focusing on women's rights promotion, HIV rates reduction, family planning, reproductive health issues, and prevention of child trafficking, the Center uses community radio to produce behavioural change among large audiences in 15 countries in Africa, Asia, and Latin America, educating through entertainment, including with soap opera characters.

The highly important results of pre and post-broadcast random-sample surveys, *Ryerson* saw, pointed to positive changes in the behaviour of the listeners. In Ethiopia, listeners to special programming on HIV were more likely to be tested for the virus than non-listeners. According to the estimates of a project in Tanzania, the cost of getting people to take steps to avoid HIV infection was eight cents per listener.

William Siemering, president of *Developing Radio Partners* and founding member of N*ational Public Radio's Board of Directors,* defined the work of community radio developers as "scattering seeds"–alluding to the original meaning of "broadcast"–the results of which take time to ripen. He said, community radio is "a simple, effective solution" to achieve development goals, to check "fragile states from becoming failed states," and further to help people celebrate their own culture.

Community Radio is most particular in areas having practically no other access to information, and donors should, therefore, realise the significance of investing in it as a means of making information available. Donors need avoid imposing models for individual stations to adopt, but let it be develop naturally and out of necessity.

Community Radio is generally the best tool for getting information to illiterate and poor communities, as needn't reading skills or money to buy newspapers. Since in many countries most media are centred in capital cities and most populated areas, and even national media was limitations to reach remote areas, community radio brings the chances of "reaching powerless communities and giving them a voice."

The participants also considered contexts where community radio development is infeasible. One implementer suggested engaging appointed and elected officials as part of community radio projects to build a strong linkage between governments and local media. The guidelines outlined for donors can prove irrelevant in regions where governments and the legal and regulatory environment limit community radio development.

In the Middle East and North Africa region, discussions on the effect of community radio matter but after there is legal reform for the licensing and establishment of independent community radio stations. In terms of inadequacy of community radio development, an implementer strongly warned against supporting initiatives, in case of evidence that the majority does not protect the rights of the minority within the community radio and will take advantage of community radio to further reinforce the disparity, be it on ethnic, political, or social basis.

Sustainability is the biggest challenge for community radio; they manage to generate revenue through paid announcements, through funding from side businesses : or through a barter system, allotting priority air time to an advertisement. Active participation by volunteers, however, is the key to success for many community radio stations.

As a representative that provided initial operational funding to a community radio station in northeastern Congo put it. If people donate their time and resources in something without any pay, it is an indication of commitment and sustainability. With community radio development, ensuring the financial sustainability of stations should not be the primary objective.

"When I start worrying about sustainability and stop worrying about my listeners, that's when my stations get into trouble," an implementer with vast experience in community radio development commented. However, all aspects of sustainability social, institutional and financial– must be incorporated into the overall strategy of community.

Challenges to Sustainability and Funding Perspectives of Community Radio

The issue of sustainability is not only limited to the financial standing of a station. In northern Uganda they sold airtime to humanitarian organisations, but only one of those stations managed to keep editorial control and reproduce the information as opposed to the other stations, which simply aired the material as provided to them. Donor funding can often have an adverse impact on the sustainability of community radio stations, as many focus on areas which attract donations at the expense of local community needs.

Out of five Serbian-language stations in eastern Croatia, the only station that maintained its community nature and survived and resisted donor funding. It maintained its sustainability through a number of auxiliary activities, including airing concerts sponsored by a local bar.

In some countries, to establish a station is a challenge because of the lack of supportive legislation permitting it to operate freely, or the existing laws are not properly implemented. Daoud Kuttab, a Ferris professor of journalism at Princeton University, shared his experiences in founding community radio in an non-conduzive legal and political environment.

Identifying the need for local and interactive news in the Middle East and North Africa (MENA) region, Kuttab in 2002 introduced the creative approach of launching *AmmanNet*–an Internet-based radio channel, thus avoiding a prohibition that was available at the time against founding an independent radio station in Jordan. Four years later, the Jordanian government began granting licences to private FM stations for $40,000 for entertainment-oriented stations and $60,000 for those seeking to broadcast news and cover politics.

AmmanNet went on air to carry out a community radio mission with a commercial model. The station's programming had a significant impact both on policy-makers and traditional media practices. The station a pioneered in providing live broadcast of Jordan's parliamentary sessions. Airing live voices and news content focused on local developments, the station launched a new practice of radio reporting that was adopted by other media. "In a country such as Egypt with almost 100 percent radio and television penetration, why aren't media used for development purposes?" a radio activist rhetorically inquired.

Community Radio–The Indian Perspective

Community radio movement in India

Until late 2006, only educational institutions were supported with authority to set up campus radio stations having a transmission range of 10-15 km. The scope was only recently spread to include non-profit agencies, agricultural research institutes, and schools, to set up community radio stations.

Today there are four stations that are broadcasting, and around six stations that are in advanced stages of their application approvals. The importance of community media for community empowerment and democratisation is well known. However, despite radio being an efficient channel for voice-based community media, communities and independent organisations were forbidden to set up their own radio stations. Pioneering organisations such as *Voices* and *Drishti Media* therefore opted for a concept called *narrow casting* to circumvent the policy restrictions. They worked with NGOs *Myrada* in Bangalore and *Kutch Mahila Vikas Sangathan* in Gujarat to train rural community reporters to compose audio programs. But the programs were played out over loud-speakers in common community meeting points or within "listener groups" of women working together in self-help groups. The audio production was itself done in a small studio .

Namma Dhwani (meaning, our voices), the setup at the village of Buddikote near Bangalore, even pioneered a new concept called *cable casting* where they used the cable TV network in the village for broadcast. *Namma Dhwani* could purchase air time cheaply for their own programs. The channel did not have any video but given the high penetration of television in the community, it was a fantastic outreach channel. Both the experimental setups near Bangalore and in Gujarat were extremely fruitful in empowering communities, helping them realise their rights, and assemble for their demands from local authorities.

Given ready evidence, enterprising activists from organisations such as *Drishti, Voices, Ideosync, Maraa, One World South Asia*, and many independent individuals continuously assembled for a policy reform to get permission for radio broadcast. Their efforts were rewarded in late 2006, but the policy still remains mired with many complications.

Community Radio Policy in India

Points of dissatisfaction amongst the CR community:

Only non-profit communityu radio stations more than 3 years old can apply for a CR licence. Although this clause is present to help ensure accountability, it is restrictive for new organisations. The older non-profits that are submitrting for licences have been experiencing in varied streams such as micro-finance, low-cost housing, health, etc., and tend to look upon CR as an outreach channel for their existing programs.

The licence process can take well over a year. It needs the approvals of almost five different ministries, and if the application stops at any point, it is hard to find out. Updates are hardly available on the government websites.

The complete process is also very inconvenient for the applicant organisations because they are often asked to supply more details within sudden deadlines, or needed to appear in person in New Delhi without any warning.

One of the most important formalities to maintain during the application process is a community survey supposed to be filled out by over 1000 respondents. The specific survey needed by the government is available only in English, with amusing questions that are completely irrelevant to community radio. Many people feel that a *one-fits-all* survey is not suitable in the diverse Indian context, and applicants should be permitted to design their own surveys structured upon certain specific directives laid down by the government.

Prior to *Nomad*, the transmitter equipment was made available at a prohibitively enormous cost from the other vendors. At *Gram Vaani*, even lower cost alternatives exist, but given the approval difficulties development efforts on the transmitter front differ and now it is decided to focus on other components of the CR technology in priority.

The policy mandates that the CR station should be owned by a non-profit organisation. The non-profit organisation in India may or may not opt to listen to feedback from the local community, and there have been reports where feedback from certain community individuals was undermined because these people did not take part in the other development programs assisted by the non-profit organisation. In the same manner, as the community also may not incur any clearly-observable liability from a failure of the CR station, it would impact on their levels of engagement with the radio station.

Role of Community Radio in Education and Entertainment in rural India–A Report

(Here is a report about role of community radio in India to educate and inform the society) (By Hartfried SCHMID, APEID/ ICT)

Ramvati Adivasi didn't let the fact that she can't read or write stand in the way of her burgeoning radio career. Today she's conducting interviews, editing programmes on the computer and performing scripts as a member of a newly inaugurated local radio station, Dharkan 107.8 FM.

"My name is known in the community as a radio person," said Ms. Adivasi, who wore a beautiful blue sari and sparkling red bangles. Traditional tattoos decorated her arms. Her work at the station has brought her new respect, she added.

Residents of Shivpuri, located in India's Madhya Pradesh State, turned out in force for the recent launch of the station, which will broadcast to scores of villages in a 15-km radius of the city. Traditional musicians beat drums, while girls with bells tied around their ankles danced in celebration.

The crowd burst into peals of laughter when a programme was played, featuring Ms. Adivasi as a difficult mother-in-law arguing against exclusive breastfeeding.

Rather than preaching educational messages, the station uses humour and local entertainers to inform its audiences.

Dharkan 107.8 FM is collaboration between the community near Shivpuri, the district administration, two non-governmental organisations – Ideosync Media Combine and Sambhav – and UNICEF. Besides education, the station's goals include improving community participation and giving villagers a voice in media.

A large proportion of the Shivpuri community is made up of traditionally disadvantaged groups. Nineteen per cent are so-called "scheduled tribe" members, like Ms. Adivasi, and 11 per cent are "scheduled caste" members.

A recent survey found that radio was the medium most readily accessible to the community; more than half of respondents said they tuned in several times a day. The survey also found that the audience wanted to participate in programming.

Radio technology has advanced so far that it doesn't take much more than mobile phones and laptop computers to get a radio station off the ground. The project in Shivpuri costs only a few hundred US dollars per month to maintain.

"Electronic media was once accessed only by the elite in cities," said N. Ramakrishnan of Ideosync. "Now mobiles, the Internet and globalisation have changed that entire process. It's a liberating communication that gives people a platform."

Community members, who may have little or no formal education, can use icons to perform basic editing, said Mr. Ramakrishnan. "It's quite easy to do, because they all know how to listen. You are only limited by your imagination," he said.

Vandana Dube, the station's first manager, helps to produce programmes on hygiene, health and the importance of education. She said that listening groups, which have formed throughout the district, are having a major impact.

In particular, more women are now contributing to important debates on caste discrimination, female foeticide and female empowerment – issues that concern them directly.

"People listen to the radio very seriously," said Ms. Dube. The medium, she believes, "will have a real impact and help them to speak out."

Ms. Dube works long hours, often arriving home at 10 pm or even later. But her family is so committed to her blossoming career that they have relocated to be near the station. "My daughter says, 'I will be an NGO worker like you,'" she said proudly. "She wants to be like her mother."

In 2005, Shivpuri was selected as a UNICEF-supported integrated district. As part of this project, representatives of the panchayat, or councils, at the village level were elected to identify community needs.

Today, more than 1,500 village volunteers are working to advocate for the rights of children by connecting families with available services.

"This huge mobilisation of community leadership has dramatically improved the use of government services," said UNICEF's Chief of

Field Office in Madhya Pradesh, Hamid El Bashir. "Many didn't even know services were available," he said.

Ms. Adivasi herself serves as a bridge between the community and health services, referring expectant parents to ambulances so that their babies can be delivered at a hospital. Between 2000 and 2005, maternal deaths in India declined from to 540 to 300 deaths per 100,000 live births. The number is continuing to fall.

Organizers of the radio project hope that such information, when provided by Dharkan 107.8 FM, will move the community to adopt improved sanitation and health practices. The station also hopes to improve low literacy rates through continuous dialogue and education awareness.

Story by Angela Walker, UNICEF

Future of Community Radio in India (Reference of a seminar)

Here is a reference of a seminar held at India's top communication institute IIMC, New Delhi in March 2007 which put light on future of community radio in India.

India to establish 4000 community radio stations under new community radio policy

15-03-2007 (New Delhi), In the next few years 4000 community radio stations will have sprung up in India under the new enabling community radio policy announced by the Government, says Shri S.K. Arora, Secretary, Ministry of Information and Broadcasting of India.

This was announced during the 'National Consultation on Community Radio for practising and potential Community Radio Operators in India', at the Indian Institute of Mass Communication (IIMC), New Delhi, 6-7 March, 2007.

The Ministry of Information and Broadcasting, Government of India in collaboration with the United Nations, led by UNESCO, organised the consultation meeting attended by over 150 representatives from Government of India, bilateral agencies, umbrella NGOs, grass roots community workers, both mainstream media and community radio enthusiasts., The Consultation achieved its aims of raising awareness about the processes involved in community radio (CR) licensing in India, and taking the dialogue forward.

Based on presentations from Community radio operators in South Africa, Philippines, Nepal, Sri Lanka and India relating to crucial aspects ranging from policy to operation, organisation and management, programming and technical aspects and sustainability, it showcased different models/experiences in South Asia and other regions and focussed on contextualising them to meet the Indian situation.

The National Consultation, envisaged as a precursor to a series of regional workshops to spread awareness of community radio and encourage community groups to set up community radio stations, was further encouraged by the Government's proposal to follow up with a "touring technical exhibit" of technology options for this purpose.

Other proposals emerging from this meeting related to the establishment of a pro-active national community radio association to build peer pressure for trustworthiness; voluntary mechanisms for dispute resolution that may also form a link to a national broadcast complaints commission; development of mechanism for on-going dialogue on policy; professionalisation of community radio; lowering of entry barriers in an effort to reach the Government target of establishment of 4000 community radio stations by 2008; maintenance of community radio networks for information sharing and capacity building; continued targeted advocacy to involve communities in taking the lead to spread the community radio movement in India; and publication of a source book on technical facilities available in the country.

In his inaugural address, Shri S. K. Arora, Secretary, Ministry of Information and Broadcasting anticipated that in the next few years 4000-5000 community radio stations will have sprung up in India and that it was indeed helpful for community radio operators (practising and potential) in India to understand different aspects from others' experience. According to him, "The Indian Government has been extremely supportive of NGOs functionning. The mass media factor had been missing in this support. This gap will be filled up by community ratio operations." He further added, "Community radio focuses on low cost and low return pattern of operations, which are aimed at educating and entertaining the community using their own idioms and language in contrast to the private FM radio which is primarily driven by entertainment and business considerations".

W. Jayaweera, UNESCO Director, Division for communication development, Paris, in his keynote address reminded one and all that community radio was all about community engagement by harmonising local potential. "CRS can prove to be an excellent tool for managing plurality in a society and fostering the democracy."

In the welcome remarks delivered by Jocelyne Josiah, Adviser in communication and information, the meeting was reminded of the added power of community radio when combined with multimedia devices as practised in the four experimental Community MultiMedia Centres (CMCs) in India promoted by UNESCO.

UN Resident Coordinator and UNDP Resident Representative Maxine Olson said that UNESCO is training 150 personnels for Radio Banasthali in Rajasthan. She also referred to the support being lent by United Nations in Andhra Pradesh and Karnataka in the setting up of Community radio stations.

This National Consultation comes in the wake of the November 16, 2006 the Union Cabinet clearance of the community radio policy allowing non-profit organisations with a three-year track record to set up and run stations. A modification of an earlier policy that let 'reputed educational institutions' have radio stations, this one permits civil society organisations to have their own transmission. Ownership over transmission was one major point of contention by NGOs; they could use campus radios and buy time on All India Radio (AIR) earlier, but didn't own the transmitters.

Radio is the main source of news and entertainment for most of India. AIR is the top tier in radio coverage, as the public service broadcaster. Private FM has now become the second tier. Community radio promises to be the third tier, closest to the people.

Community radio in India has many advantages over AIR and private FM. Programmes, nearly always in the local languages deal with local issues involving ordinary people so that villagers and townspeople understand what they are about. The government's broadcasting code notwithstanding, audio programmes have exposed corruption. Just hearing themselves on radio is an empowering experience for people, who realise that this, truly, can be their voice and help them get a better deal from the government and other castes. It is the first time Dalits, tribals and women have found an opportunity to speak out.

Conclusion: Input about challenges before Community Radio in India

There are still a lot of problems which CR stations face, the foremost ones being financial sustainability and technology.

CR stations are allowed only 5 minutes of advertising per hour, practically infeasible for resource-crunched CR station operators to obtain business skills and see for advertisers while they also creatye good quality radio content. *Gram Vaani* look for advertising on their behalf will be very helpful. But it is also important to create other revenue sources for community radio.

Although simplicity is good, the want of interactive systems such as telephones, field reporting tools, and content sharing, leaves it harder to persist engagement from the community. Software used in the radio station can have an important impact on its success. Most CR stations currently use *Winamp* to broadcast radio programs, and resort to hacks to do live broadcast, or interleave advertisements between programs.

A professional radio automation system is very essential to scale activities, but presently there is no free and open-source system to provide a one-stop solution to playout, broadcast, telephony, SMS, and Internet content sharing.

The current push behind the CR movement

Gram Vaani is among the early players in the area of improving technology for community radio, and structuring a business model shaping making CR stations financially sustainable. The *Gram Vaani* team and other CR activists form part of the Community Radio Forum, a pan-India collective mandated is to assemble for legislative changes on the CR policy front. The third annual meeting of the CR Forum was held at Orchha, in the Bundelkhand region of India, chosen because the very first community radio station licensed under the new policy was established there by *Development Alternatives.* Anita Iyer from *Radio* and *Music* detailed the meeting.

The enthusiasm and commitment of the CR community in India is undying, and will prolong purposefully.

References

1. Dunaway, Ph.D., David (2002), Jankowski, Nicholas W.; Prehn, Ole, eds. "Community Radio at the Beginning of the 21st Century: Commercialism vs. Community Power", Community Media in the Information Age: Perspectives and Prospects (Cresskill, NJ: Hampton Press).
2. http://www.javnost-thepublic.org
3. CBONLINE Culture, Commitment, Community: the Australian Community Radio Sector: Susan Forde, Micahel Meadows and Kerrie Foxwell [1].
4. Jesse Walker, Rebels on the Air: An Alternative History of Radio in America (New York University Press, 2001), pp. 147-149.

   Bekken, Jon, "Community Radio at the Crossroads: Federal Policy and The Professionalisation of a Grassroots Medium" in Sakolsky, Ron and S. Dunifer (eds.) Seizing the Airwaves: A Free Radio Handbooks.

5. Girard, Bruce (ed.), "A Passion for Radio: Radio waves and community".
6. UNESCO, "How to Do Community Radio: A Primer".
7. TQM Communications – AM/FM newsletter number one – Spring 1990.
8. Smith, Mike "UK Radio, A Brief History – Other Media Developments".
9. Working Group Report, Oct. 2007, Centre for International Media Assistance, Washington–Its Impact and Challenges to Its Development.

11

Media and Disaster Management : Early Warning

1. Introduction – What is a disaster?

Disaster can be defined as a sudden, calamitous event causing great damage, loss destruction and devastation to life and property. It causes immeasurable damage and differs with the geographical location, climate and the type of the earth surface. This exerts influences on the mental, socio-economic, political and cultural state of the affected area.

Generally, disaster has the following effects, namely, it completely disrupts the normal day to day life; It negatively influences the emergency systems; and Normal needs and processes like food, shelter, health, etc. are affected and deteriorate depending on the intensity and severity of the disaster.

A disaster can be termed as "a serious disruption of the functioning of society, causing widespread human, material or environmental losses which exceed the ability of the affected society to cope using its own resources."

It can also be termed as, "situations characterised by surprise, high threats to important values, and a short decision time", or "A disruption that physically affects a system as a whole and threatens its basic assumptions, its subjective sense of self, and its existence core".

The dictionary defines *disaster* as: An occurrence causing widespread destruction and distress. A grave misfortune; a total failure; an evil influence of a celestial body; a calamity of great destruction; Hardships and loss of life; Grief; and tragic outcome with irreparable loss.

In production units, it defines disaster as: "An extraordinary event or series of events that adversely affect the integrity of the product the reputation or financial stability of the organisation or health of the well-being of employees, community, or the public at large."

2. What Is Disaster Management?

Emergency management or disaster management is the discipline that involves preparing for disaster before it occurs, disaster response (e.g., emergency evacuation, quarantine, mass decontamination, etc.), and supporting, and rebuilding society after natural or human-made occurence of disasters is a continuous process to manage hazards in an effort to avoid or ameliorate the impact of disasters resulting from the hazards.

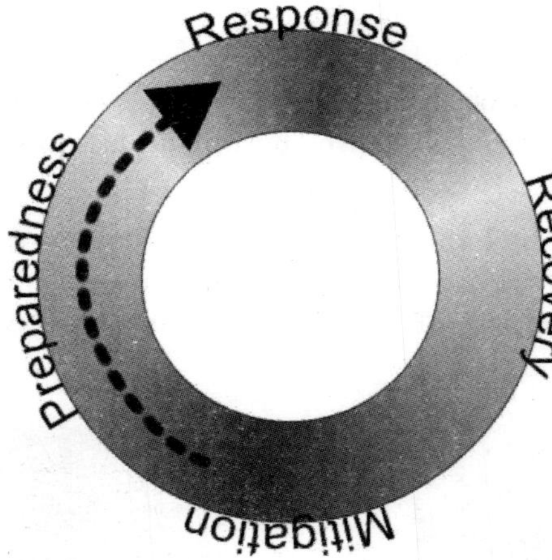

Effective emergency management depends on thorough integration of emergency plans at all levels of government and non-government involvement, the other levels. Emergency management is sometimes referred to as business continuity planning, in the private sectors. Emergency Management a terms coined coined since the end of the Cold War, have largely replaced Civil defence, originally focussed to was protect civilians from military attack. Modern thinking replicates as to protect the civilian population in times of peace as well as war. An academic trend is towards using the term disaster risk reduction, particularly in a development management context, which focuses on the mitigation and preparedness aspects of the emergency cycle.

What is Early Warning System

A warning system is any system of biological or technical nature employed by an individual or group to inform of a future danger, to enable the deployer of the warning system to prepare for the danger and act accordingly to mitigate against it.

The Indian Ocean Tsunami Warning System is set up to provide warning to inhabitants bordering the Indian Ocean. It was agreed to in a United Nations conference convened in January 2005 in Kobe, Japan as an initial step towards an International Early Warning Programme.

Nanometrics (Ottawa, Canada) and RESULTS Marine Division (Chennai, India) successfully installed 17 Seismic VSAT stations with 2 Central Recording Station to help the seismic event alert to the scientists through SMS and E-mail automatically within 2 minutes. It was cereated by the 2004 Indian Ocean earthquake and resulting tsunami, which tolled some 230,000 people. Many analysts claimed mitigated if there had been an effective warning system in place, citing the well-established Hawaii-based Pacific Tsunami Warning Center.

After July 2006 Java earthquake, the Indonesian government received tsunami warnings from the Hawaii center and the Japan Meteorological Agency but failed to relay the alert to its citizens. At least 23,000 people made the coast vacant after the quake, fearing a tsunami or the destruction of their homes.

It is suggested in Muslim-dominated coastal areas, the loudspeakers of the mosques could be used to flash warnings.

PM applauds media role in tsunami disaster

PTI, Jan 11, 2005, 09.18pm IST`

KOLKATA: Complimenting the media for playing the role of an "early warning system" during the tsunami disaster, Prime Minister Manmohan Singh on Tuesday said that it was the press which had first brought the world's attention to the disaster. "Media arethe best early warning system which help in acute crisis," Prime Minister said, inaugurating the diamond jubilee celebrations of Kolkata Press Club, here. "Although I have appealed to the scientists to address the problem, there is no substitute for the learned and energetic media," Singh said.

Applauding the media's role in the tsunami tragedy, Singh said that it was the press which had first captured the world attention to the disaster and that prompted the local administration and the government to act quickly."I greatly value and salute the media in this situation," the Prime Minister said. "I pay special tribute to you (mediapersons)," Singh said. The Prime Minister said the government was able to collect more money in the initial periods of tsunami disaster than during the Gujarat earthquake just because the media had motivated the people.

Singh repeated that he was thankful to the media for sensitising the administration on the magnitude of the disaster that tsunami had caused to the nation.

Commenting on the importance of free press, the Prime Minister said that it was a continuous reality check on the authorities despite increasing pressures of commercialisation.

"I am for a free Press as free Press is the ultimate check on tyranny by authorities," he said. Referring to Nobel laureate Amartya Sen, he said that the noted economist had also acknowledged the role of the media during the Bengal famine which was depicted in glowing terms in the press.

3. Phases and Efforts During Disaster

Mitigation

Mitigation refers to knowing and avoiding unnecessary risks. This includes an assessment of possible risks to personal/family health and to personal property.

For example, mitigation avoids buying property that is exposed to hazards, e.g., in a flood plain, in areas of subsidence, or landslides. However, specialists conduct risk identification and assessment surveys. As such purchase of insurance covering the identified risks is a common measure. Personal structural mitigation in earthquake prone areas incorporates installation of an Earthquake Valve to immediately shut off the natural gas supply to a property, seismic retrofits of property and the securing of items inside a building to enhance household seismic safety.

In flood prone areas, houses can be built on poles, as in southern Asia. In areas prone to prolonged electricity black-outs, installation of a generator is an example of an optimal structural mitigation measure. The istallation of storm cellars and fallout shelters are further examples of personal mitigative actions. Mitigation involves Structural and Non-structural measures taken to check the interest of disasters.

Structural Mitigation

This involves proper layout of building, particularly to make it resistant to disasters. This also involves measures taken other than enhancing the structure of building.

Personal preparedness grips on preparing equipment and procedures for use when a disaster occurs, i.e., planning. These measures can take many forms such as the construction of shelters, installation of warning devices, creation of back-up life-line services (e.g., power, water, sewage), and rehearsing evacuation plans. Two simple measures can assist prepare the individual: for evacuation, a disaster supplies kit may be prepared and for sheltering purposes a stockpile of supplies may be created. The preparation of a survival kit such as a "72-hour kit", is often advocated by authorities, which includes food, medicine, flashlights, matches candles and money.

The *response* phase begins with search and rescue but in all cases the focus quickly turns to fulfilling the basic human needs of the disaster in flicted population, provided by national or international agencies and organisations.

Effective coordination of disaster assistance remains crucial, especially when organisations respond and local emergency management agency (LEMA) capacity exceed on the demand, or diminish by the disaster itself. On a personal level the *response* can take the shape either of a shelter in place or an evacuation.

In a shelter-in-place scenario, a family prepares to fend for themselves in their home for many days without any outside support. In evacuation, by mechanical transpsortation or on foot, a family transports to other places taking with them the maximum amount of supplies sufficient to protect human life. On foot transpportation includes carrying at least three days of supplies and rain-proof bedding, a tarpaulin and a bedroll of blankets.

The *recovery* starts after the immediate threat to human life has been prevented, or naturally calmed down. During reconstruction it is said to consider the location or construction material of the property. The most extreme home confinement scenarios include long time war, famine and severe epidemics. Planners for these events usually arrange much foods and appropriate storage and preparation equipment, and eat the food as part of normal life.

A simple balanced diet can be prepared from vitamin pills, whole-meal wheat, beans, dried milk, corn, and cooking oil, added by vegetables, fruits, spices and meats.

4. The Media in Disaster Management and Early Warning

The media, by the informing to the people and the concerned authorities sufficiently in advance, enables them to take the necessary steps to prevent and minimise the loss of life and property. While the disaster is prolonging the media plays the role of communicating the measures being taken and monitoring them, warming the affected or to be affected people about the Dos and Don'ts, of scotching rumours and checking panic and confusion of identifying the grey spots and targeting attention on them, and generally by helping the authorities, voluntary organisations and volunteers in reaching, informing and assuring the affected people of the help and the measures taken, for their relief.

During disaster, the utmost importance is to keep the morale of the people high, to build self-confidence in them, to check panic and to maintain order by making available the necessary help readily. The rescue, relief and rehabilitation measures are assisted by integrated and co-coordinated approach and for that purpose all agencies, have to collect their resources together for efficient, expedient and effective work on all fronts.

The policy of material resources and the enlisting of man-power are as much crucial as their effective utilisation. The mention of devastation and human misery through the media many times by itself acts as an appeal to the people to come forward to offer help in various ways. In addition, the particular appeal made for relief by the media, brings in sizeable aid in the requisite form. Meanwhile it becomes necessary to keep a watch and report on some anti-social elements who try to take advantage in the like situations. Disasters like floods, cyclones and droughts have been a periodic feature of Indian national life.

The worst sufferers are ever the weaker sections of the society. They are not able to shift from their places, due to their sources of livelihood and other essentials. They are rarely remembered and the measures for the permanent solution of their circumstance are hardly ever discussed in the media. The media can also focus its attention on this problem.

A prompt presentation of the real state of affairs by our media or the news-agencies, and the correction of the misrepresentations by them will go a long way in dispelling the wrong impressions framed abroad which may otherwise have adverse effect on the administration, the economy and the polity of the country. In the past the media fulfilled its responsibilities in full measure while on other occasions it was found wanting.

However, if the media have to day their role on such occasions, it needs to have a complete cooperation between it and all governmental and non-governmental agencies.

Media reportage of Disasters: Interview with Mark Tully

Excerpts from an interview on media and disasters

"How can the media change the perception about disaster-affected people from "helpless victims" to "partners in change"?

My own feeling is that, in the media, we fall into the difficulty of portraying victims really in a way as victims rather than as individuals. A lot of journalists try to get around this problem by telling individual stories of people. Even then I feel that what we have to do more is to make sure to emphasise that it is people who suffer and somehow try to tell the reader what their suffering is like.

I will give you an example of a human-made disaster. I was to make a film 10 years after the Bhopal gas tragedy. I saw some of the other documentaries. What struck me in these documentaries was that the victims were somehow presented as examples rather than as human beings. It was like showing examples in a museum. When we went to shoot, we went out of our way to humanise the characters. We tried to bring out the subtleties of each individual's story.

I think it is very important that we should make it clear that the victims of disasters are the people who also have the courage to survive that disaster. Far too often the stress is on aid... a fact, which is important in itself.

"Suffering makes a good story". Reportage is dominated by stories of "starving children" in drought-hit areas or the homeless in cyclone situations. Reports of atrocities dominate the reportage on riots, but reportage on the possibilities to minimise the impact of disasters is virtually non-existent. What role could the media play to prepare and help people survive a disaster?

There is a role that the media can play, and to some extent have played, in preparing people for disasters. I think, for instance, in the situation of Bangladesh, the widespread reporting of cyclones there has been a major factor that led to a much more effective relief system than there was before.

I think a more careful analysis of the causes of communal riots sometimes could help. If it is made absolutely clear as to what the reasons behind the riots were and who has created them, and why, then the public outrage may be awakened. The local people might become more aware of what is happening when badmash and goondas come into their area instigating trouble. Then they may be on their guard against rumours. I think that is quite important.

The Indian media are trying to fudge everything by saying there is a riot between two communities without mentioning their names, I think they are not helping anyone by doing that at all. I think such issues should rather be faced by being absolutely fair and square, as to what has happened. Make people understand how it has happened, and also present the story in a manner that may arouse public awareness against it.

"The media have been known to be choosy about which disasters to cover, depending on sensational value and, sometimes offensively, their own circulation and advertising exigencies. How do you view this?

I have no direct evidence to support that view. All I would say is that it is true, in general, that media organisations are being more and more dominated by commercial considerations rather than by old-fashioned editorial values. That, in my view, is one of the crucially important factors in favour of public service broadcasting. Public service broadcasting need not be dictated by commercial considerations. But even the commercially motivated media organisations have to cover the main news agenda, otherwise people won't watch their news. There are pressures on them. Equally, I wouldn't deny that there is a tendency to cut down on news and dub it down because of increasing commercial pressure.

The media are metro-centric. If there is a fire in Delhi, in an office building, it will get national coverage. A worse fire in the Orissa will probably be reported only in Orissa papers. In some ways you can't help this just as you can't avoid celebrity news.

In India there is a real problem. Certain disasters, which recur frequently, like bus accidents and people getting killed at railway level crossing do not get covered. The numbers involved are very large. The media can think of a campaign on such issues. Level crossings are often unmanned; the approaches are too narrow and badly designed. The Railways should be taken to task for ignoring this safety aspect.

5. Media Role in Disaster Risk Management

The media can enhance lobbying for political commitment to make the leaders be more responding to the vulnerable communities' needs and demands through consistent reporting. They can also influence the government to give4 priority to disaster risk issues into a development component through expanded research and regular reports on natural perils. The media can create early caution systems by providing to policy makers adequate information on risks integrated into a development or management concept.

They can arrange donations from the international community as well as court governments to enhance budgetary allocations for disaster response programmes. The media can improve integration and coordination of risk assessment by the policy makers and donor communities to save lives of the affected population or vulnerable communities.

How to achieve?

There is need for media to be more proactive in reporting on drought or disaster risk related issues. Media people need to be trained regularly on disaster management to increase their understanding of the key disaster terms and scope of the perils. The policy makers should work hand in gloves with the press to publish positive stories that can offer solutions in the disaster prone areas. Capacity building for journalists with close monitoring of their progress should be improved.

There is need to develop a journalist disaster risks guide book besides holding workshops for them to shape them more pro-active in reporting disaster issues. It helps to establish an online magazine for disaster stories and to appoint a team of online editors and sub-editors to receive the stories from field and post them on Web magazine. The journalists must help coordinate the process with commitment in managing disaster. It can be formed a forum of competition and give annual awards for best researched stories on disaster by journalists as a mark of appreciation to help combat disasters. Exchange programmes can be organised where journalists can the experience of the effects of disasters affecting their countries. The central function of the media should influence the policy makers them to act by exposing the high dangers or risks facing the people and the doings of the governments towards readers.

6. Media Use in Early Warning and Preparedness

Nyondo, 1988 looked. at the ancient narratives from different African countries. In these narratives, myth, folklore and stories, there are several related to warning about disasters; The Beautiful Giraffe; The Ancient and Wise Python; The Millipede. These ancient narratives make one know the disasters not to be a modern phenomena. Based on these narratives, the question one should be asked is; How come we have not learned on how to cope with them?

The media that can be used in early warning and preparedness instead of storytelling take modern technology that can reach beyond the fireside of a village hut; Technical Communications systems; Disaster sites of communications; Organisational Communications; Communication for scientific development, which always misses in developing countries; and Providing Analytical Information:

As a means of preparedness, the media are good at reporting events and functions.

Fred H. Cate, 1990, says, humankind possesses the means to minimise the impact of disasters to save lives and reduce damage to property. If we do not accurately document and analyse our present disasters, we will never learn to cope up with them. When we die we will take all our experience and knowledge with us to the grave.

Medium to be Used for specific Disaster

Research shows that during earthquakes, volcano ruptures and other related disasters the one item that people picked from their homes to escape with is a radio. A similar research done in El Salvador shows even dead bodies were found with a radio in their hands or in the vicinity. Radio is a very important medium in disasters. However, the most recent research preferred to have was found to be the internet. In Africa less than 2% of the population have reach to a computer, Internet, or Websites. However, more than 99% of media houses both electronic and print, do have access to some computer, internet, or websites. The so-called medium if properly utilised can reach the grassroots in a matter of hours or minutes. It is, therefore, time for experts on each disaster to: create websites for each disaster they foresee in the region; give correct information before the disaster occurs; give responsible and accurate information after and during disaster period; provide accurate analysis of the future ramifications and prevention of repetition of the disaster;and provide address and contacts of relief services. Moreover, the public need regular education on all possible disasters, which include early warning, planning, prevention and mitigation.

Traditional

Face-to-Face communication will never be surpassed by any modern medium. Education and training done by extension workers can be more productive. Story telling warns people about possible disaster. The story of The Millipede; The story of the beautiful giraffe; The python that are found in every African language do reveal that disasters of drought, floods etc. have remained a common phenomena in history ever.

Village meetings, debates, discussions, and deliberations took place at Indaba. Every village had these forums where issues were put openly and deliberations taken. They were effective because everybody took part in decision-making. When we scrutinise communication models we view that development in Africa has delayed because we jumped the ancient village forum to the modern communication where information descends from above to the grass roots, undermining the participatory aspect.

One very effective mode of communication is drama or Theatre for Development (TFD) in urban areas as well as rural areas. These are very optimistic particularly if followed by a group discussion facilitated by some experienced personnel.

Electronic

The most common of them all in terms of MASS COMMUNICATION is radio. In Zambia and in most parts of Africa every citizen has access to a radio and that more than 95% of the households have a radio–*Kasoma 2001*. The creation of a winding radio that need not batteries is a great improvement for Africa where power is limited and during disasters one need not look for batteries or power. The creation of community radio stations in Africa will bring great improvement in development if properly utilised. According to *Kasoma 2001*, the moment Community radio will assume the property status of the community and operated by the community without interference, development in Africa will make a difference.

Media such as TV, slides, videotapes etc. can be very effective in the education of the public. This media can be quite expensive both in production and circulation of the product. When deciding on what medium to use for 'In-House Training' to prevent factory disasters or mine disasters, television, videotapes, or a slide montage would be the best. This way, one receives inter-personal communication and a professional presentation.

Film and network video are very different from the "in-house" production. Though educational they are the element of entertainment surpasses that of educational tool. We can recollect the many films or TV programmes we relished as well as learned a lot from them. The element that made us enjoy the production and persevere in watching it was the entertainment value. Because of the aesthetic elements in these productions we attach the word fiction to them.

The satellite communication has shaped the world into a global village. We get news from all over the world within a few hours or minutes of occurrence. We watch the events as they occur – LIVE. We access information, research from various universities and other Academic and research institutions.

The new technology of cell phones has brought another element in the highlightingof disasters. The first pictures of tsunami disaster on *CNN* and *BBC* were taken by tourists on the spot.

The practicality of print materials gives one cosy set-up to go back to it, refer to it and study the material at own convenience time. However, during disaster it is difficult to concentrate and comprehend sophisticated information. The best print media able to disaster information are pamphlets, brochure and small leaflets. and made of such materialspoertable in nature.

Finally, modern telecommunications like Internet, W@P, SMS should also be taken into account. There might be a problem that users should be "active" and open "specific pages" first themselves to receive warning or other needed information. These modern means can be utilised for graphical presentation of warnings and other essential news not only for public but also for professionals involved in EW system. In some cases also Teletext should be used for warning communication. Newspapers and other printed readings can be used for additional information, but they are slow media for direct warning in urgent and quick events.

7. Radio in Disaster Management, Reduction and Early Warning

During disasters, amateur radio is most frequently taken to use as a means of emergency communication when other means of the wireline, cell phones and other conventional means of communications fail. It is dispersed throughout a community without "choke points" such as cellular telephone sites that can be overloaded. Amateur radio operators are acquinted with improvising antennas and power sources and most equipment today can be powered by an automobile battery. Yearly "Field Days" are organised in many countries to revise these emergency improvisational skills.

Amateur radio operators can use hundreds of frequencies to establish networks tying disparate agencies together to enhance inter-operability. In the 2001 attacks on the World Trade Center, the 2003 North America blackout and Hurricane Katrina in September 2005, amateur radio coordinated disaster relief activities when other systems failed. On September 2, 2004, ham radio to informed weather forecasters on Hurricane Frances live from the Bahamas. December 26, 2004, an earthquake and destroyed tsunami across the Indian Ocean destroyed all communications with the Andaman Islands, except for a DX-pedition that provided a means to coordinate relief efforts.

Recently, Amateur Radio operators in China provided emergency communications after the 2008 Sichuan earthquake and US hams during Hurricane Ike.

How it worked in Haiti?

From the CQ / World Radio Online Newsroom:

All radio amateurs are requested to keep 7045 kHz and 3720 kHz clear for possible emergency traffic related to today's major earthquake in Haiti. International Amateur Radio Union (IARU) Region II Area C Emergency Coordinator Arnie Coro, CO2KK, reports that as of 0245 UTC on January 13, nothing had been heard from radio amateurs in Haiti, but that the above frequencies were being kept active in case any Haitian hams manage to get on the air, and in case of other related events in surrounding areas, including after shocks and a possible tsunami.

Orissa : How radio worked?

Bhubaneswar

While people of all hues paid tributes to the victims of the devastating super cyclone on Thursday, the state government was busy putting in place hi-fi mechanisms to combat the recurrence of such high-voltage natural disasters in future.

On the occasion of 10th anniversary of the 1999 super cyclone, Chief Minister Naveen Patnaik inaugurated community radio station and stressed on the use of technology to help reduce damages caused by natural calamities.

"We have taken steps for preparedness so that during the time of calamities, we remain prepared as best as possible to look after the people of our state and minimise the loss of human lives," Naveen said. The community radio is connected with 21 radio stations in calamity-prone areas in the state which can play a crucial role in establishing communication at a time when all the other modes of communication fail during natural calamities, like flood and cyclone.

The super cyclone of 1999 was certainly one of the worst disasters in recent history, Naveen said and claimed that better communication infrastructure was now in place.

While there was only one satellite phone with the state government during the 1999 super cyclone that killed at least 9885 people, now all district headquarters are equipped with it.

"Apart from police VHF network, we have a dedicated civil wireless network system connecting 414 locations, including district headquarters with blocks and disaster-prone gram panchayats," he said adding 21 community radio stations have been set up in vulnerable areas.

Apart from this, facility for timely weather forecast and obtaining data about impending calamities through upgraded satellites was also inaugurated. The government informed that 203 multi-cyclone rehabilitation centers have been established and additional 22 cyclone and 50 flood rehabilitation centers would be set up soon.

While five Orissa Disaster Rapid Action Force (ODRAF) units exist at present, additional five units would soon be constituted and 220 automated weather stations and four Doppler radars will be established in the state.

"At present both ODRAF and fire units have been equipped with modernised instruments and gadgets to carry out relief and rescue operations during any kind of disasters," Nikunja Kishore Sundaray, the special relief commissioner informed. A disaster risk reduction programme with the help of UNDP is on in the state. Under the UNDP-assisted Disaster Risk Management (DRM) programme, Village Disaster Management Plans have been prepared in more than 23,000 villages in 16 districts.

Emergencies Involving Amateur Radio

Natural or man-made disasters have occurred at various parts of the world inflicting heavy loss of human life and damage to property.

The list shows some of the disasters where Amateur Radio operators worked as volunteers in emergency communication after the failure of infrastructure dependent communication modes such as mobiles and land lines:

United States

- tornado outbreak – February 2008
- Oregon Storms – 2007
- Hurricanes Katrina and Rita – 2005
- Hurricanes Charlie, Frances, Ivan, and Jeanne in Florida –2004
- Severe weather in Virginia – May 2004
- Tornadoes in Illinois – April 2004
- Earthquake in Central California – December 2003
- Hurricane Isabel – September 2003
- Northeast blackout – August 2003
- Midwest tornadoes – May 2003
- Shuttle Columbia recovery effort – February 2003
- World Trade Center and Pentagon terrorist attacks – September 2001
- Flooding in Texas and Louisiana (Storm Allison) – June 2001
- Fires in Los Alamos, New Mexico – May 2000
- Hurricane Floyd – September 1999
- Hurricane Mitch in Central America – November 1998
- "500-Year Flood," Grand Forks, N.D., and East Grand Forks, Minn.– April 1997
- Western U.S. floods – January 1997
- Hurricane Fran – September 1996
- TWA plane crash – July 1996
- Oklahoma City Bombing – April 1995

India

- Latur Earthquake, 1993
- Orissa Super Cyclone, 1999

- Gujarat Earthquake, 2001
- Indian Ocean Tsunami, 2004
- Aila Cyclone, 2009

8. Types of Disaster we face in general

1. Air Crashes
2. Avalanches
3. Drought
4. Earthquakes
5. Extreme Weather

6. Fire Emergencies
7. Floods
8. Hazardous Materials
9. Hurricanes and Tropical Storms
10. Landslides
11. Mass Trauma
12. Natural Disasters and Hazards
13. Nuclear Accidents and Radiation
14. Pollution
15. Severe Storms
16. Terrorism
17. Tornadoes

18. Tropical Storms
19. Tsunami
20. Volcanoes

9. Role of Media in the Aftermath of Disaster

Disasters happen though monitored, yet beyond predictions of exact timing, the devastation and destruction. Perhaps there is no escape. This background paper brings information on the role of media as a conduit with the rest of the world at the time the grieving try to start their lives afresh on the rubble.

Media programmes should care for a balance between unwarranted intrusion and reporting; neither grief and suffering should be exploited, nor sanitised the news, keeping the viewer away from the complete the information of the disaster.

Covering of disasters or tragedy can never be a detached business. Yet some form of detachment is important to escape the repart overburdened with the emotion of the moment, stripped of context and meaning.

Media officers are news managers; the investigative journalism, then, is pushed inevitably into the heart of the story, searching out people's truths, on apparent dichotomy – public interest demanding personal intrusion.

Imperatives

During crisis situations there is a role for mass media to play; to use the right to safeguard citizens' lives and to inform the living regarding disasters and on safeguard measures. Media have to inform the citizens regarding the danger of furutre and present and the specific solution programmes.

Moreover, the media is given an imperative to inform the citizens about the relief supplies available and the place of availability so that the victims can have direct access. They remain perpatual remembering to assist the government and the non-governmental organisations providing relief supplies to the people.

Reporting genuine facts with constructive criticism by media would greatly help in restoring the order. Building the morale of the afflicted and those engaged in relief operations begs unavailable importance. Media has to guard itself against vested interests and should not create chaos and discord among the different sections of society on limited grounds.

The communication revolution, has reduced the possibility of excuses and increased accountability. Through the media, the public has acquired a new face and a voice of assertiveness. People spoke up identified the problems, the need they wanted redress.

The constant stream of information and two-way communications has always helped react with a greater sense of urgency. The informed magnitude of suffering goods and urgency into doing something about it.

Sebastian D'Souza / AFP

Case study Analysis

Union Carbide Bhopal Pesticide Plant

Pre-crisis situation

Jackson B. Browning (1993), a former executive in charge of safety for the Union Carbide Corporation, informed that in the early hours of December 3, 1984, a toxic cloud of methyl isocyanate (MIC) gas spread through the hundreds of shanties and huts surrounding a pesticide plant in Bhopal, conducted by Union Carbide India Limited (UCIL). The deadly cloud slowly drifted through the streets. By the time the gas cleared at daybreak, 1,430 people were left dead and thousands injured.

The first report of the disaster did not reach Union Carbide executives in U.S.A until 12 hours after the incident. By 6 am in the morning Union Carbide executives started gathering with technical, legal, and communications staff at the company's headquarters.

Post-crisis situation

The first press inquiry had come at 4:30 am, which roses 500 calls a day for several weeks. This front page disaster story appeared later for months. As was discovered two years later, the accident was caused by a disgruntled employee who wanted to ruin a batch of MIC by adding water to a storage tank.

The water brought a reaction to turn the chemical compound into a lethal gas. The first contact from plant officials to Browning revealeed that an accident had occurred, no employees had been injured, but 8 to 12 civilians had been killed. In his 1993 article, *Union Carbide: Disaster at Bhopal*, Browning informed as he was listening to the radio on his way to the 6 am meeting he heard the death toll rose to 50. Because the Union Carbide headquarters was serving as a crisis response center, the first press conference was held at a nearby hotel at 1 pm that day in the USA.

Union Carbide sent medical and technical experts to aid the people of Bhopal, to help dispose of the remaining MIC, and to investigate the cause of the tragedy. The press conferences served as a more efficient made to answer the hundreds of questions and phone calls from all over the world.

10. How NASA Operates

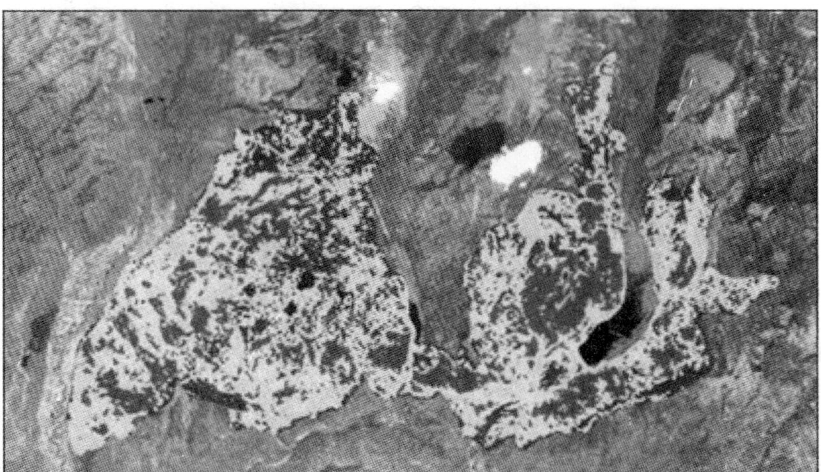

Preliminary Burn Severity
unburned low moderate severe

The U.S. government allocates yearly billions of dollars in aid to regions impacted by disasters. Community planners need access to the most accurate and timely environmental information to respond to these extreme events, along with to know how vulnerable their approaches are to any of these phenomena in order to plan for proper redress. They also need advanced warning to know about the extreme weather events to occur, to minimise their impact. Objective forecasts of natural phenomena prove to be vitally important to allow for proper evacuation and damage mitigation strategies.

NASA works with the Federal Emergency Management Agency (FEMA), the National Oceanic and Atmospheric Administration (NOAA), the U.S. Department of Agriculture (USDA), and the U.S. Geological Survey (USGS) on this effort. *NASA Earth* science data are being incorporated into an advanced decision support system (DSS) created by FEMA to meet the requirements of planners, early warning systems and first responders, and to assist the impact assessments, risk communication, mitigation, and implementation of relief works.

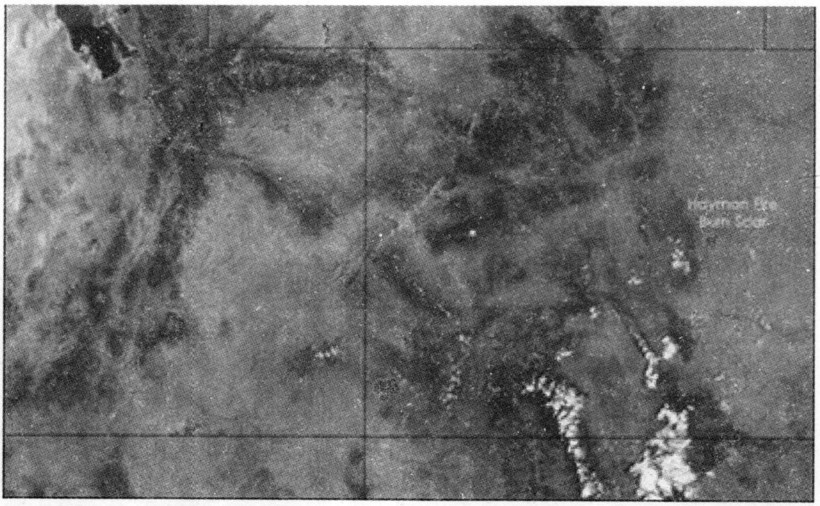

Photo: June 30, 2002 the Hayman Fire, the largest wildfire on record, was still not fully contained, Colorado (right) continued to be plagued with other forest fires throughout the state, including the Missionary Ridge Fire north of Durango in the southwest, and the Spring Creek Fire several hundred miles to its north. In Utah (left), the Rattle Complex burned more than 40,000 acres and a new fire sprung up due west of the larger one. The Hayman Fire was about 90 percent contained, and dropped below MODIS' fire detection threshold, but the large dark burn scar is quite apparent.

The Moderate Resolution Imaging Spectroradiometer (MODIS) Land Rapid Response System exemplifies the NASA data making a difference in responding to disasters. This system serves the need for quick access to products from the MODIS instrument–onboard NASA's Terra and Aqua satellites–when disaster occurs. NASA with the University of Maryland, the USDA's Forest Service (USFS), and NOAA provides firefighters with the most up-to-date maps and satellite images from Terra and Aqua, which assist their strategic response. Afterwards land managers can use the information for rehabilitating the burned area and protecting water quality in the affected area.

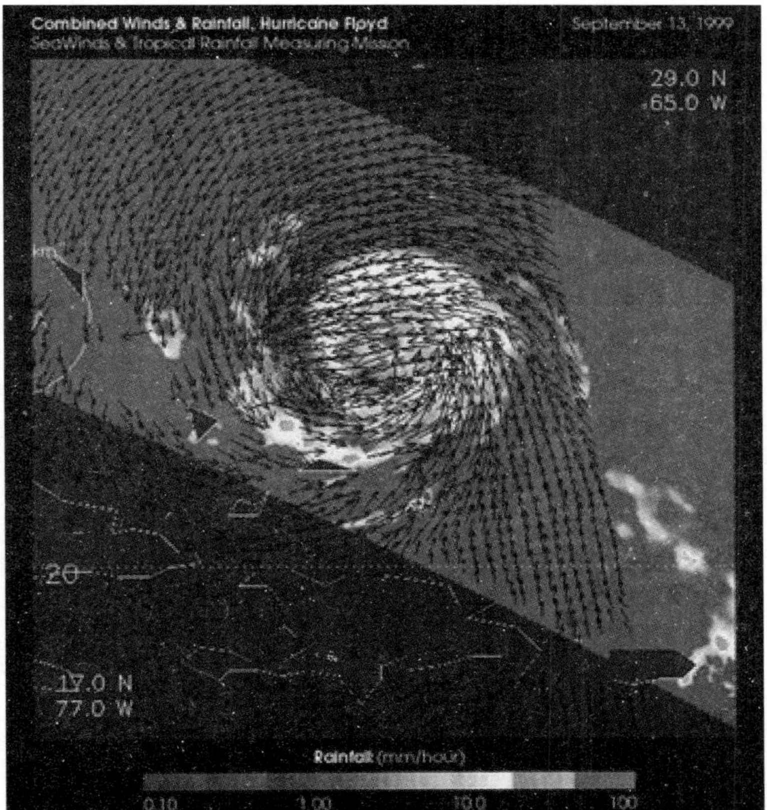

Image: This image of Hurricane Floyd combines rainfall data from the Tropical Rainfall Measuring Mission (TRMM) with wind data from QuikSCAT on SeaWinds. This combined data allows scientists to study the interplay between precipitation air currents.

NASA satellite missions data also contribute significantly contributions in the area of hurricane and flood prediction. NOAA combines satellite-derived estimates of precipitation from the Special Sensor Microwave Imager (SSM/I) and from the Tropical Rainfall Measuring Mission

(TRMM), with winds from QuikSCAT. This substantially inhances the accuracy of forecasts for landfall, track and intensity of hurricanes, and increases the lead-time for warnings for both hurricanes and floods. Moreover, accurate forecasts, enable improved decision-making assisting in more enhanced community preparedness for these disasters.

11. What Government of India is Doing?

The National Disaster Management Authority of India, a government agency to the Ministry of Home Affairs manages emeregencies. Now the shift from response and recovery to strategic risk management and reduction, and from a government-centred approach to decentralised community participation hsas been introduced. Survey of India, Ministry of Science and Technology, works in this field, brings the academic knowledge and research expertise of earth scientists to the emergency management. Government has in recent times formed the Emergency Management and Research Institute (EMRI). Which represents a public/ private partnership, funded primarily by Satyam Computer Services to improve the general response of communities to emergencies. This effort lays as layout for emulation by all of India, as well as, it operates in the Indian states of Andhra Pradesh, Uttarakhand, Goa, Tamil Nadu, Rajasthan, Karnataka, Assam, Meghalaya and Madhya Pradesh using a single 3-digit toll-free number 1-0-8. such practical devices protect from many of the disasters.

India is prove to natural disasters on account of its unique geo-climatic conditions. Floods, droughts, cyclones, earthquakes and landslides have remained a recurrent phenomena. About 60% of the landmass is vulnerable to earthquakes of various intensities; over 40 million hectares to floods; about 8% of the total area to cyclones and 68% of the area is prove to drought.

In the decade 1990-2000, an average of about 4344 people were left dead and about 30 million people got affected by disasters every year. The loss in terms of private, community and public assets has been phenomenal.

Globally there has become risen concern over natural disasters. DEsp;ite tremendous scientific and material progress, the loss in terms of lives and property due to disasters has not benumbed. The United Nations General Assembly, in 1989, declared the decade 1990-2000 as the International Decade for Natural Disaster Reduction with the objective to lesson the loss of lives and property and prevent socio-economic damage through integrated international action, particularly in developing countries.

Earthquake in Gujrat

The super cyclone in Orissa in October, 1999 and the Bhuj earthquake in Gujarat in January, 2001 underscored the need to opt for a multi-dimensional effort involving diverse scientific, engineering, financial and social processes; multi-disciplinary and multi-sectoral approaches and incorporation of risk reduction in the developmental strategies.

The Government of India over the past years have have been exposed to a paradigm shift in the approach to disaster management. The new approach proceeds from the conviction that development cannot be sustainable unless and until disaster mitigation is structured into the development process.

Another cornerstone of the approach is that mitigation has to be multi-disciplinary across all sectors of development. The new policy also rises from the belief that investments in mitigation are much more cost effective than expenditure on relief and rehabilitation.

Disaster management covers an important space in this country's policy framework as the under-privileged are worst affected on account of calamities/disasters.

The steps adopted by the Government are taken from the approach outlined above; translated into a National Disaster Framework [a roadmap] covering institutional mechanisms, disaster prevention strategy, early warning system, disaster mitigation, preparedness and response and human resource development.

The roadmap comprises of the expected inputs, areas of intervention and agencies to be involved at the National, State and district levels. Ministries and Departments of Government of India, and the State Governments/UT Administrations have beenoffered advise to develop their respective roadmaps taking the national roadmap as a broad guideline. There is as a result now a common strategy underpinning the action being taken by all the participating.

Early Warning System

Cyclone Forecasting

Tropical Cyclones (TC) are intense low pressure systems which are formed over warm sea. Such cyclones are capable of affecting immense damage due to wild winds, rains and storm. The frequency of the TC in the Bay of Bengal is 4 to 5 times more than in the Arabian Sea. About 35% of initial disturbances in the north Indian ocean access TC stage of which 45% become severe.

Indian Meteorological Department (IMD) monitors and gives warnings regarding Tropical Cyclone (TC). Monitoring process has been transformed with the arrival of remote sensing techniques. A TC intensity analysis and forecast scheme has been taken into work using satellite image interpretation techniques which facilitate forecasting of storm surges.

Data resources are said to be crucial to early forecasting of cyclones. Satellite based observations are being extensively work out . Satellite integrated automated weather stations are established on islands, oilrigs and prove coastal sites. Buoys for supplementing the surface data network in the tropical ocean have been deployed.

The Government have also began a National Data Buoy Programme. A set of 12 moored buoys have been deployed in the northern Indian Ocean to provide meteorological and oceanographic data.

Flood Forecasting

Floods ravage due to is caused by the inadequate capacity between the banks of the rivers to contain the high flow brought down from the upper catchments due to heavy rainfall. It is caused further by accumulation of water resulting from heavy spells of rainfall over areas, which have got poor drainage.

Flood made more grave by erosion and silting leads to meandering in plains and reduction in carrying capacity of the rivers. Floods are aggravated by earthquakes and landslides, leading to changes in the course of river and obstructions to flow.

Synchronisation of floods in the main rivers and tributaries and retardation of flow due to tidal effects lead to major floods.

Scientific flood forecasting was started in November, 1958 by Central Water Commission when a Flood Forecasting Centre was set up at its Headquarters, at Delhi, for timely forecasts and warnings of the incoming floods in the river areas around Delhi. The network has spread out and the Central Water Commission (CWC) assesses all the major flood prone inter-state river basins in the country.

Pictures of some natural disasters occurred in India in recent past.

Courtesy: thetelegraphindia.com, asianmedia.com, terradaily.com, agricorp.com, tribuneindia.com

The Flood Forecasting involves the following four main activities:

(a) Observation and collection of hydrological and hydro-meteorological data;

(b) Transmission of Data to Forecasting Centres;

(c) Analysis of data and formulation of forecast; and

(d) Dissemination of forecast.

On an average, 6000 forecasts at various places in the country are issued during the monsoon season every year. The analysis of the forecasts indicates about the accuracy of forecasts consistently increased from around 81% to 98%. Forecast is considered accurate if forecast water level is within ± 15 cm. of actual water level of the inflow forecast (i.e. discharge) is within ± 20% of actual discharge. The economic future of the state of Gujarat is threatened by an ever-growing water shortage. The semi-arid districts of north Gujarat such as Mehsana, Patan, Banaskantha, Surendranagar, and Kutch, receive scanty rainfall, on average 400 mm of rainfall.

Drought is a recurring phenomenon in these regions, with a normal drought occurring once in 3 to 7 years, a severe drought once in 7 to 10 years, and a very severe drought, once in 14 to 20 years. Since 1960 four repeat droughts in Gujarat have occurred, the most recent one in 1999, 2000-2001.

The short length of the rivers and the steep slope to the sea causes high run-off and floods during monsoons.

By the similar vain every third year there is a flood in Gujarat's rivers and every tenth year almost half of the state suffers from flash floods. Falling ground water tables and salinity further exacerbate the water situation in Gujarat (Source: Barot, 1996).

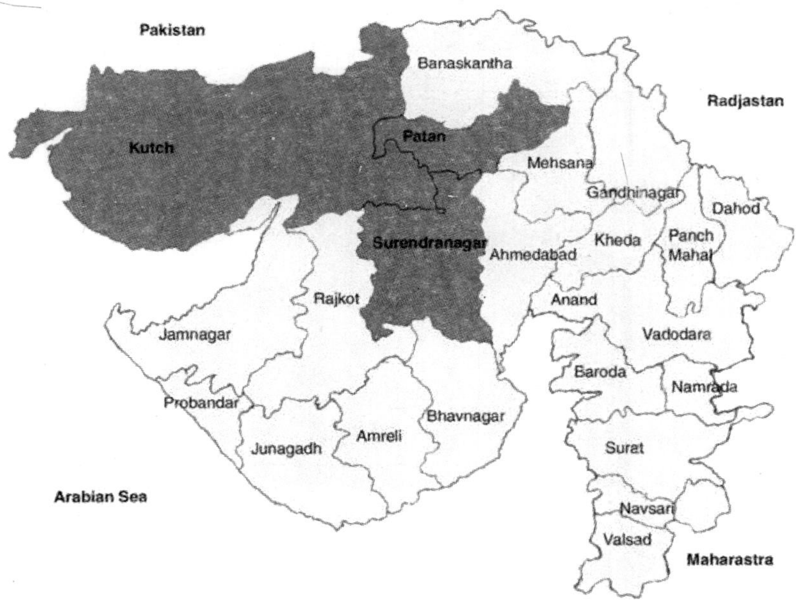

Fig. 1 : Patan, Kutch, and Surendranagar district

Due to the dependency on rain-fed agriculture, the frequent droughts that erode any livelihood gains and keep them in the poverty trap. Women are especially hard hit by the crisis. IRC International Water and Sanitation Centre (IRC), Self Employed Women's Association (SEWA), and the Foundation for Public Interest (FPI) found women spending an average of three hours a day on arrangement of water that can be spent on income generating activities. In addition, health problems caused by carrying heavy loads of water over long distancesare not rare in such women folk.

Pictures of Flood in Mumbai, 2005

Tsunami of 2004

12. Conclusion: The Way Ahead

Media play a vital role in educating the public about disasters; warning of hazards; collecting and promulgating information about affected areas; cautioning government officials, organisations and the public to specific needs; and facilitating discussions about disaster preparedness and response. For the media to work effectively, the scientific and disaster mitigation organisations need to strengthen working rapport with the media. Peter Hansen, United Nations Under-Secretary General for Humanitarian Affairs, challenged disaster mitigation organisations to "act to sensitise the media" and to "make ourselves a reliable source of usable information for journalists." Roundtable stressed the importance of providing dependable information to the media, earlier in a concise and comprehensive form, and linked to newsworthy events.

Asian Disaster Preparedness Center in Bangkok, stressed the need of creating and taking advantage of mechanisms for journalists and disaster mitigation officials to spend more time together and learn about each other's work. Moreover, the experience, sensitivity, and trust that such programmes facilitates allocate to the quality and focus of media coverage of to disasters. Effective working relationships require the media, NGOs (non-governmental relief or development organisations), scientists, government agencies and international organisations to understand their distinct objectives and needs. Many participants noted the importance of recognising those differences and of working together for a comprehensive outcome. It is also important to recognise differences among media and practice their distinct characteristics, potential, and needs. Moreover, the media and relief organisations, challenge each other and ask difficult, penetrating questions. It is through the media that the agencies are accountable to the public.

D.R. Sikka makes some observations and suggestions regarding mutual co-operation between the weather and climate experts and media. The regional and national newspapers could solicit special articles before the advent of the adverse weather season with advice on steps needed to minimise the impact. In the hours and days before a big storm is expected to hit an area, the weather report can become a front-page story for the newspapers....

Met office is suggested to "make increasing efforts do develop good media relations", placing immediate responses and authentic information to media inquiries on weather, preparing special information kits for the media before the beginning of each season, etc.

These steps are necessary, and a change in attitude of the media towards natural disasters. The issue includes the human beings who suffer – women, men and children. Their voices are to be transmitted by the media to their fellow beings the readers, as well as the powers to prevent or at least mitigate such sufferings. Moreover, it is the regular news items which most of the readers notice and draw their conclusions from, special articles are less read, less understood and less relied upon. The sub-editors need to be sensitised much more on the gender and human rights aspects of the disaster reports.

References

1. http://www.vu2.in
2. http://www.vu2.in
3. http://www.arrl.org
4. http://www.vu2.in
5. http://www.vu2.in
6. http://www.keele.ac.uk
7. http://www.unisdr.org
8. http://nasascience.nasa.gov
9. Photographs of some disasters happened worldwide. Courtesy – noblis.org, shemford.com, rgc.salford.ac.uk, geoscientific.net, bu.bournemouth.ac.uk, nema.gov.ng
10. http://www.annenberg.northwestern.edu
11. http://www.helpageindiaprogramme.org
12. www.undp.org
13. www.dimarsi.org

12

History of Communication and its Application in Multicultural, Multilingual Social System in India Across Ages

1. Introduction–History of Communicaton

The history of communication dates back to the earliest signs of cavemen. Communication ranges from very subtle processes of exchange, to full conversations and mass communication. Human communication got revolutionised with speech perhaps 200,000 years ago, symbols came in vogue about 30,000 years ago and writing about 7,000. On a much shorter scale, there have been major developments in the field of telecommunication in the past few centuries.

Speech

Evolution of the brain differently put humans from animals, as among other things it permitted humans to master a very efficient form of communication – speech. A mutation of the FOXP2 gene, in *homo sapiens* about 200,000 years ago, was likely responsible for much of this change. Speech greatly helped the transmission of information and knowledge to further generations. Experiences passed on through speech became increasingly rich, and allowed humans to adapt themselves to new environments much more quickly than was possible before; in effect, biological human evolution was overtaken by technological progress and socio-cultural evolution.

Speech meant easier coordination and cooperation, technological upliftment and development of complex, subtle concepts such as religion or science. Speech gave humans at the top of the food chain, and assisted human colonisation of the entire planet.

Symbols

The imperfection of speech eventually resulted in the creation of new forms of communications, improving both the range at which people could communicate and the longevity of the information. All of those inventions were based on the key concept of the symbol: a conventional representation of a concept.

Cave paintings

Just as the small child first learns to draw before it masters more difficult forms of communication, so Upper Paleolithic *homo sapiens*' first attempts at passing information through time took the form of paintings. The *oldest* known cave painting is that of the Chauvet Cave, around 30,000 BC.

Though not well shaped, those paintings contained increasing amounts of information: Cro-Magnon people may have developed the first calendar as far back as 15,000 years ago. The connection between drawing and writing is further shown by linguistics: in the Ancient Egypt and Ancient Greece the concepts and words of drawing and writing were one and the same.

Pictograms

A pictogram (pictograph) is a symbol representing a concept, object, activity, place or event by illustrious. Pictography is a form of proto-writing whereby ideas are promulgated through drawing. Pictographs were the steps further in the evolution of communication: the most important difference between petroglyphs and pictograms is that petroglyphs are simply showing an event, but pictograms are telling a story about the event, ordered in chronological order. Pictograms were used by ancient societies all over the world since around 9000 BC, when tokens marked with simple pictures began to be used to label basic farm produce, and got increasingly popular around 6000-5000 BC. They were the basis of cuneiform and hieroglyphs, and developed into logographic writing systems around 5000 BC.

Ideograms

Pictograms, in turn, evolved into ideograms, graphical symbols that represent an idea. Pictograms could represent only something similar to their form: therefore a pictogram of a circle could represent a sun, but not concepts like 'heat', 'light', 'day' or 'Great God of the Sun'.

Ideograms, on the other hand, could convey more abstract concepts, so that for example an ideogram of two sticks can counete not only 'legs' but also a verb 'to walk'. Because some ideas are universal, various dissimilar cultures created similar ideograms. For example an eye with a tear means '*sadness*' in Native American ideograms in California, as it does for Aztecs, Chinese and Egyptians. Ideograms were *precursors* of logographic writing systems such as Egyptian hieroglyphs and Chinese characters.

Writing

The writing began primarily logographic, based on pictographic and ideographic elements. Most writing systems can be broadly clasasified into three categories: logographic, syllabic and alphabetic (or segmental); however, all three may be found in any given writing system in varying proportions, often making it difficult to categorise a system particularly.

The development of the first writing systems coincide contemporary with the beginning of the Bronze Age in the late Neolithic of the late 4th millennium BC.

The first writing system is generally attributed to have been developed in pre-historic Sumer and improved by the late 3rd millennium into cuneiform. Egyptian hieroglyphs, and the undeciphered Proto-Elamite and Indus Valley scripts also date to this era, though a few scholars have questioned the Indus Valley script's status as a writing system. The original Sumerian writing system was adjusted to clay tokens used to represent commodities.

By the end of the 4th millennium BC, this (Summerian) had evolved into a method of keeping accounts, using a round-shaped stylus impressed into soft clay at different angles for recording numbers. This was by degrees taken with pictographic writing using a sharp stylus to indicate the commodities to be counted. Round-stylus and sharp-stylus writing was by degrees overtaken about 2700-2000 BC by writing using a wedge-shaped stylus (hence the term cuneiform), at first only for logograms, but include started phonetic elements by the 2800 BC.

About 2600 BC cuneiform storted to m ean syllables of spoken Sumerian language. Finally, cuneiform writing was taken to a general purpose writing system for logograms, syllables, and numbers. By the 26th century BC, this writing system had been adapted to another Mesopotamian language, Akkadian, and onwards to others such as Hurrian, and Hittite.

Scripts similar in appearance to this writing system are Ugaritic and Old Persian.

Alphabet

The first pure alphabets 'abjads', evolved around 2000 BC in Ancient Egypt, but by then alphabetic principles had already been included into Egyptian hieroglyphs for a millennium. By 2700 BC Egyptian writing had a set of some 22 hieroglyphs to represent syllables starting with a single consonant of their language, plus a vowel (or no vowel) to be arranged by the indigenous speaker. These glyphs were used as pronunciation guides for logograms, to write grammatical inflections, and, later, to transcribe loan words and foreign names.

2. DEFINITION OF COMMUNICATION

Communication is the particular acumen to share information. Based on necessitated reasons by its evolution communication is well needed for human existance. It assists people in trouble to contact police, fire departments, ambulances and doctors. Transportation and food supplies would not meet the needs of the people without it. We can lose contact with our families and friends that live far away. Society would surely not be the same as it is now.

Someday, we will have wrist telephones, televisions with only interactive 3D programming. Computers will be able to visually connect with anyone in the world, without cameras... Only the future will tell... after all, 100's of years ago no one would have dreamed of all the things we have today.

3. TIME LINE

3000 B.C. - The Egyptians created a picture language called hieroglyphics.

105 A.D. - Chinese began using paper and ink.

450 A.D. - Asia used Block Printing.

1539 A.D. - Mexico began using the first printing press in the Western Hemisphere.

1639 A.D. - The first press in the American Colonies was established in Cambridge, Mass.

1665 A.D. - The "London Gazette" was the first English newspaper.

1738 A.D. - The first daily newspaper was the "Pennsylvania Evening Post and Daily Advertiser".

1828 A.D.	-	The first comprehensive dictionary was published by Noah Webster.
1844 A.D.	-	Samuel Morse transmitted the first public telegraph message.
1858 A.D.	-	The first Transatlantic cable was laid.
1876 A.D.	-	Alexander Graham Bell invented the telephone.
1878 A.D.	-	Thomas Edison invents and patents the recording of sound onto cylinders and discs.
1906 A.D.	-	First wireless communication of human speech.
1919 A.D.	-	First broadcast radio station KDKA licensed in Pittsburgh, Pennsylvania.
1936 A.D.	-	First television broadcast made in London, England.
1941 A.D.	-	First commercial television began in the United States.
1941 A.D.	-	Z3 computer developed by German engineer Konrad Zuse.
1954 A.D.	-	Color television broadcast standards are set in the U.S..
1957 A.D.	-	Satellite first sent information back to earth.
1959 A.D.	-	U.S. and Russian rockets sent information back to earth from distances beyond the moon.
1962 A.D.	-	"Telestar I", a satellite, first beamed television programs between the U.S. and Europe.
1971 A.D.	-	Intel 4004 chip developed an integrated microprocessor chip, for the computer, that could be programmed for different needs.
1976 A.D.	-	JVC markets the first VCR with the VHS (instead of Beta) format.
1985 A.D.	-	Television began to be broadcast in Stereo.
1994 A.D.	-	High Definition TV standards agreed on in the U.S..
1999 A.D.	-	Intel introduces the Pentium III processor, taking personal computing to new highs.
2050 A.D.	-	......???......Give us your input. Tell us where you think we will be in the year 2050, on our questionnaire.

4. PICTORIAL PRESENTATION

Cave drawings were murals painted onto the walls of caves and canyons to tell stories of battles, hunts and culture.

Storytelling both fiction and nonfiction was a way for families and communities to pass on information onward to the careing one.

Drums sent signals to neighboring tribes and groups. The sound of the drumming patterns communicated them of the concerns and events.

Smoke signals sent messages to people who were not close enough to use words with.

5. PRINTING PRESS

The oldest printed book is a Chinese religious book, The *Diamond Sutra.* Other books like this were printed with wood blocks, usually made from Mulberry wood. Johann Gutenburg invented an actual printing press in 1450, it was a screw press He discovered a good ink print with metal type. Gutenburg was the first to use a press to print the Bible, it is the oldest full length volume printed. From Mainz in Germany, printing spread all over Europe.

Rome developed a printing press in 1465, but, the rulers of countries realising the power of the printed word strictly controlled the amount of material that printers were allowed to produce. Printing did not really grow again until the 18th century. Between 1450 and the 1800s, power press was introduced. By the 1600's the art of printing was started in business. Printed news sheets, called corantos, were somewhat like present day newspapers.

In 1728, Ben Franklin opened his own printing office in Philadelphia. He printer by the age of 17. Ben Franklin printed newspaper *The Pennsylvania Gazette* and the *Poor Richard's Almanac.*

He began printing cartoons and illustrated news stories. Which he became famous for. He believed in the power of the press and brought the news to the people. He was an ardent reader and founded the first Public Library in 1731. He wanted to use the printing press to help all people to understand the world around them.

Today we use modern versions of these printing presses to print books, magazines, and newspapers.

6. TELEGRAPH

The idea for the electric telegraph was thought up on the deck of a sailing ship Scully, in the middle of the Atlantic Ocean. The inventor was Samuel Finley Breese Morse in 1832, the most famous artists in the United States. Morse thought in a discussion on electromagnet if electricity travelled a short distance through wire, long distances through wire can be traveled, too.

On May 24, 1844, Morse from Washington D.C. to Baltimore, New York sent the message, "What hath God wrought!" through the telegraph machine. The telegraph was a success,

In 1874, Thomas Edison invented quadruplex telegraphy, where two messages could be sent in each direction at one time.

In 1915, the multiplex telegraphy allowed eight or more messages be sent at one time. In additions the invention of the teleprinting machines during the mid-1920s made the things most possible.

7. TELEPHONE

A telephone is an electronic device that makes speech travel by means of electricity. The word telephone comes from Greek meaing far and sound. The telephone is one of our best ways to communicate. It saves time. With a telephone one can call almost anywhere in the world.

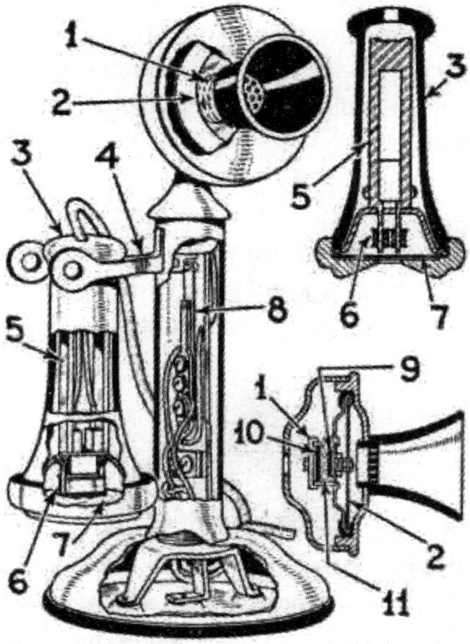

View, partly sectional, of a typical modern Telephone, with cross-sectional views of Transmitter and Receiver. 1, 1 Transmitter Button (containing 9, 10, and 11); 2, 2 Transmitter Diaphragm; 3, 3 Receiver; 4 Receiver Hook; 5, 5 Permanent Magnet; 6, 6 Receiver Coil; 7, 7 Receiver Diaphragm; 8 Contact Springs which close the circuit when the receiver is lifted from the hook; 9 Front Carbon Electrode; 10 Rear Carbon Electrode; 11 Carbon Granules.

Alexander Graham Bell invented the telephone in Boston in 1876, 120 years later there are over 360 million telephone numbers, and that figure grows each year.

Some phones have option like holding multiple calls or transferring calls to other phones. An intercom allows you to talk to other people in other rooms. Speaker phones have a microphone and a loud speaker. Cordless phones do not have wires connected to them; Cellular phones are true wireless phones.

8. RADIO

Radios are used for many purposes; as navigation and television broadcasting. Radios affect everyone's life in many ways; to get the weather reports, tyo help NASA speak to astronauts, etc.

Radios send messages through a process called electromagnetic waves; measured by a metric measurement called a hertz, one kilohertz is equal to 1,000 hertz and a megahertz is 1,000,000 hertz.

The term hertz is baptised after the early radio pioneer Heinrich Hertz. Because electromagnetic waves run in a straight line and earth is round, long distance travel for radio waves are made in the ionosphere, known as short wave signals or low frequency. Wave length in short distance communication is called high frequency does not use the ionosphere to reflect signals. Radios are made up of two main components; a transmitter and a receiver that send signals back and forth.

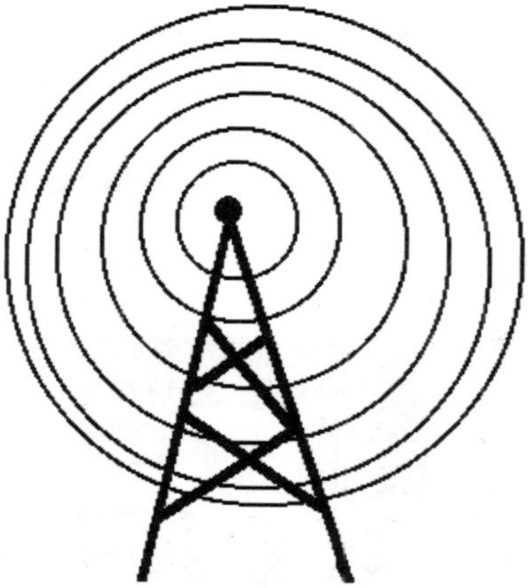

9. TELEVISION

Television is not just about entertainment, it is about news and lots of information. Television makes it possible to teach lessons for kids and also allows workers to watch over radioactive materials.

Light forms scenes you see on the television screen. In television, images and sounds travel by means of electrical energy.

A television camera changes the light reflected from a scene into electronic signals. Transmitter sends out the signals; finally, a television receives the signals and changes them back into sound and picture images. Television camera has lenses to concentrate light to form images of objects.

10. COMPUTER

Konrad Zuse is popularly recognised in Germany as the "father of computer" and his ZI, a programmable automation system built between 1936 and 1938, as the first computer in the world. Konrad Zuse constructed a system capable of doing sequences of mathematic operations. He had no formal training in electronics and basic technological ideas, which allowed him solve problems with original solutions.

Herman Hollerith was the first American to promote invention of the computer in 1890. He invented the Tabulating Machine used by the U.S. Government. His company Computing-Tabulating-Recording Company changed its name to International Business Machines, as IBM, the world largest computer company.

The ENIAC (the Electronic Numerical Integrator and Computer), built at the Moore School of Electrical Engineering of the University of Pennsylvania in 1943-1945, is said to be the world first large scale general purpose electronic computer.

In the 1940-1950's, one single computer filled an entire room and weighed about 30 tons. In the 50's and 60's the computers, smaller and faster, were still too big and expensive for home use.

In the 1970's, smaller computers designed for smaller businesses and the microprocessors were now small enough for use in homes and schools. We still use computers with microprocessors and they keep getting smaller and smaller in size and price.

The computers in the future will be smaller, faster, more affordable and able to process and store even more information.

11. COMMUNICATION IN ANCIENT INDIA

India is the land with the highest number of post offices and the most eclectic, yet effectual modes of mail conveyance ever used. The evolution and systemic growth of postal communications in India can be traced over a span of centuries.

An pertinent aspect of the development of communication system, has been its adaptability to the geographical environs of the country. So the routes and modes that have evolved over the centuries, befit the different topography and compelling historical developments of this region.

Communications in India have ever remained typically endemic to the Indian sub-continent.

Beginning with the early era, one comes across these visually enduring practices of that period. The primitive drawings and heliographic characters found in caves, the carvings of ancient temples and pillars, or the stone tablets that have been of great help to archaeological discoveries. In fact, the visual modes maybe interpreted as symbolic of the ethos traversed across a timeline of centuries. Most unique to this country is her wealth of oral communication, weaved within narratives and carried down generations as part of oral histories. Genealogical studies and postal histories of Indian Princely States are incomplete without these oral time-honoured communications. As the needs of men became more demanding, the methods used to communicate were manifested in various ways designed to meet the challenge of the times. Many of the old Hindu scriptures carry references to such remarkable 'carriers' of message. The 'RigVeda' cites the use of a dog called 'Sarama' to carry message, even as the 'Atharvaveda' records the use of couriers going by the term 'Palagala'.

The 'Ramayan' cites instances of Hanuman being sent by Ram to covey messages. In 'Mahabharata', King Drupad dispatched the message to King Dhritirashtra to give away half the kingdom. through the Royal Priest. Chanakya's 'Arthashaastra' also calls attention to the efficient manner of collecting information and revenue data using doots, who doubled up as spies for the King. The practice of using pigeons as courier also prevailed from the earliest times in India. The 'pigeon carriers' are still officially in use by government departments in remote areas, in the State of Orissa.

Camels were in rampant use in the desert areas of present Rajasthan and arid zones of Orissa. The use of horses for carrying mail was chiefly for military purpose. Then, there is the legendary Harkara, the relentless dak or mail runner, through rain and storm, deliver his epistle contained within a bundle on his stick.

The exchange of communication obviously was a part of ancient maritime activity, though records are mostly unavailable except for the random reference as Greek and Deccan Indi records.

The earliest evidence of a systematic postal service with foot messengers has been traced back during the reign of Chandragupta Maurya (322-298 B.C.). A courier service between the capital and the outlying provinces of the vast kingdom served the needs of intelligence gathering and collection of revenue data, whence regular messengers, *doots* (emissaries) and pigeons were used for conveying the royal communiqué.

Emperor Ashoka however devised a very efficient means of communication that proved to be successful in building a vast empire, using a combination of mail runners, horse couriers, pigeon carriers and camels for official communication. This was efficiently operated communication system gave essential fillip to effective governance and the extra edge to an aggressive ruler.

12. A HISTORICAL PERSPECTIVE OF COMMUNICATION IN INDIA

(with emphasis on Overland Routes)

In India, overland routes and merchant links were established at very early stages, much before the Portuguese demarked sea routes in the 15th-16th centuries. These overland routes took a general South-Easterly sweep from Turkey through Middle-East.

The early postal systems in India with well-laid out routes and messenger systems emerged from the trade movements and the dissemination of Buddhism, in the Northern and North-Western frontiers. We find the early and subsequent development of mail systems in India were contributed by the Persians, Greeks, Arabs and Mongols. The movement of nomadic tribes, explorers and invaders established the principal routes with Central Asia and the Far East. The centre of silk trade activity in 4th century A.D. was Asia, chiefly controlled by the silk traffic. The important land routes connecting the Silk Route necessarily linked India. A royal highway connected Taxila with Pataliputra and terminated at Tamralipti, the main port in the Ganges delta.

On the western coast the major port of Bhrgukaccha (modern Bharuch) was connected with the Ganges Valley via Ujjain. From the Narmada valley, the routes went into northwestern Deccan and continued along rivers flowing eastward to various parts of the peninsula.

Persian influence

The ancient overland routes stretching from Persia to India were primarily nature-made paths and ruts created by hoofs of animals, and most likely centuries of human traverse. For safety and practical purposes, they travelled in caravans of oxen and carried letters and messages for fellow tradesmen and private individuals. The military envoys and Generals conveyed important letters and *firmans*. The imperial system was more organised and speedy.

The swiftness of the horse messengers played a key role in communications, and shaped the subsequent historical events in India.

13. CONCLUSION

LANGUAGES AND "UNITY IN DIVERSITY"

Sanskrit has a profound impact on the languages and literature of India. Hindi, India's most spoken language, is a "Sanskritised register" of the *Khariboli* dialect. In addition, all modern Indo-Aryan, Munda and Dravidian languages have borrowed many words from Sanskrit, or indirectly via middle Indo-Aryan, languages. Words evolving in Sanskrit constitute roughly fifty percent of the vocabulary of modern Indo-Aryan languages, and the literary forms of (Dravidian) Telugu, Malayalam and Kannada.

2001 India census suggests Hindi to be the most spoken language in India, followed by Bengali, Telugu, Marathi and Tamil. In contemporary Indian literature, there are two major literary awards; these are the Sahitya Akademi Fellowship and the Jnanpith Award. Seven Jnanpith awards each have been awarded in Kannada, six in Hindi, five in Bengali, four in Malayalam, three each in Marathi, Gujarati, Urdu and Oriya.

Since the late 16th century India was under the influence of the British Empire until 15th August, 1947. But though we speak different languages yet we are all Indians. 'Unity in Diversity' has been the distinctive feature of our culture.

In our struggle for freedom people from different communities participated keeping one thing in mind that they all are Indians first. this peace and understanding among different communities has been SET ON PERIL lately. India at present is facing many problems, the biggest is the problem of communalism. In fact, it is the biggest threat to humanity and to the unity and integrity.

None can claim single identity. Modern India presents a picture of unity of different faiths and beliefs, together in peace and harmony.

References

1. Tarikh-i-Sher-Shahi by Abbas Khan Sherwani,translated in vol. 4 of Elliot and Dawson's History of India as told by its own Historians
2. Mughal Administration by JaduNath Sarkar
3. http://www.columbia.edu
4. http://stampsofindia.com/
5. http://library.thinkquest.org/
6. http://www.festivalsinindia.net

13

International Terrorism–Role, Responsibility and Operation of Media Channels During Terror Acts

1. Introduction

"Terrorism" was used extensively to characterise enemies of the United States and its allies.President Reagan's asserted in 1985, that Libya, Cuba, Nicaragua and North Korea constituted a "confederation of terrorist states" intent on undermining American attempts "to bring stable and democratic government" to the developing world. Conversely, Argentina waged a full scale internal war against "terrorism", loosely implying a definition to embrace almost every criticiser the regime. Television journalism in Britain has faced a particular problem in reporting "the Irish Question" as the Republican movement has adopted a dual strategy the ballot box and the bullet, for the ultimate reunification of Ireland electorally, through the legal political party, Sinn Fein, and militarily, through the campaign waged by the illegal Irish Republican Army.

The Prime Minister Thatcher argued in 1990, although "they are at war with us.... we can only fight them with the civil law." Then Home Secretary, Douglas Hurd, admitted in 1989 that, in his view "with the Provisional IRA...it is nothing to do with a political cause any more. They are professional killers... No political solution will cope with that. They just have to be extirpated".

Television journalists' tries to discover these contradictions produced two of the bitterest peacetime confrontations between British broadcasters and the British state. Television's acumen to strike this balance is not just a question for news, current affairs and documentary production however.

The images and accounts of terrorism offered by television fiction and entertainment are also important in orchestrating the continual contest between the discourse of government and the state, the discourses of legitimated opposition groups, and the discourses of insurgent movements. This struggle is not simply for visibility – but also for credibility – to have one's views discussed sincerely and one's case examined with care. The communicative weapons in this battle are unevenly distributed.

New, a relatively closed form of television programming, it privileges the views of spokes people for governments and state agencies which generally organise stories to stand around officially sanctioned resolutions. Other programmes like documentaries, are potentially, more open, allowing a broader spectrum of perspectives into play, including those that voice alternative or oppositional viewpoints, they may offer debates and pose awkward questions rather than offering familiar answers. Television in a democratic society requires the greatest possible diversity of open programme forms to address the issues raised by terrorism in the complexity they merit. Whether the emerging forces of technological change, in production and reception, channel proliferation, increased competition for audiences and transnational distribution, will advance or block this ideal is a question well worth examining.

2. OBJECTIVE OF RESEARCH PAPER

The objective studies the responses of media channels after 9/11 across the terror hit countries to put a case study of two most watched western media channels (*BBC* and *CNN*) and one arabic channel *Al-Jazeera.* The objective is to understand the response of these channels while covering 9/11 and its consequences.

3. THE WAR ON TERRORISM ACROSS THE WORLD AFTER 9/11, AND ROLE OF MEDIA CHANELLS

Introduction

Since September 11 attacks on the United States, the world has suddenly grown a more uncertain and fearful place. Almost a year on, these fears have been confirmed. The declaration of a "war on terrorism" by the United States and its international coalition has created a dangerous situation in which journalists have become victims as well as key actors in reporting events. Inevitably, it has created a pervasive atmosphere of paranoia in which press freedom and pluralism have suffered. Moreover, it has also led to casualties among media staff. The brutal killing of Daniel Pearl in Pakistan at the start of 2002 – chillingly filmed by his media savy murderers – symbolised the appalling consequences of September 11 for journalism and for freedom of expression.

Pearl's murder, together with the deaths of Marc Brunereau, Johanne Sutton, Pierre Billaud, Volker Handloik, Azizullah Haidari, Harry Burton, Julio Fuentes, Maria Grazia Cutuli and Ulf Strömberg in Afghanistan, is a grim indicator of the dangers facing journalists. Today people essentially comprehend the context and complexities of this new confrontation. They largely dep;end on journalists for reliable and timely information. It was recorded, during the American terriorism war against in Afghanistan about 3,500 correspondents were covering the war story. But war was rarely been considered good news for journalism. While media covers aghost, risks governments influences media and coverage their conveniet to their own political and strategic interests.

The post-September 11 media crisis is all pervasive. From countries like Australia, Zimbabwe, Colombia, Russia, UK, India, Afghanistan United States and Uganda, politicians have raised the banner of "anti-terrorism" against their political opponents, and have tried to strengulate free journalism along the way.

Today, media must lodge a resistance against the pressure politicians have superimposed who will to sacrifice civil liberties and press freedom to win their propaganda battles. The priority must always be p0laced to the right to publish these words and images – however unpalatable – which help the people understand the roots of conflict better.

Australia

September 11 media coverage was comprehensive, all-pervading and, professional. Journalists at both the tabloid and broadsheet ends in the mainstream media were responsible in handling issues of tolerance. However, among radio commentators, there has been a serious increase in, at best, lack of care in handling issues of race and, at worst, open racism against people from Muslim backgrounds, partly due to the attacks traggered against a pre-existing background of racial tension within Australia garnered by the debate over asylum seekers, particularly asylum seekers from Afghanistan and Iraq.

By records only a small number of asylum try attempt to enter Australia, arriving by boat through Indonesia. The number of such refugees mark nmopt more than 5,000 a year, at the most.

Colombia

Human rights' groups puts; Colombia's worsening internal armed conflict affects virtually every part of the country and has tolled more than 60,000 people since 1985 – around 20 people every day. Journalists with more than 80 killed in the past ten years are among the victims. Thousands of civilians fear of being kidnapped, killed or "disappeared"; again thousands have fled from their respective homes, lands, livelihood, for warring factions don't guarantee their safety respect their right not to be drawn into the conflict.

Around 80% of victims are civilians, killed outside combat.

Cyprus

Media coverage has been generally extensive and well informed, with no problem of intolerance in reporting. The Attorney General announced the drafting of a new anti-terrorism bill which may create perils for free speech and civil liberties and the only relevant law introduced was one ratifying the International Convention of the United Nations on the Suppression of Financing of Terrorism. The authorities say not to impose anything putting a peril overhead the press freedom, and the Union of Cyprus Journalists opened to follow the situation closely.

European Union

After September 11 states of European Union promptly formed a joint approach on counter-terrorism actions with the United States. Cooperation was demonstrated most dramatically one day after the attacks on the World Trade Center when NATO first time invoked its Article 5, which declares an attack on one to be an attack on all. European combat forces, aircraft and ships at once came committed to support the U.S. strike on Afghanistan.

Within few months, the European Union had a common legal definition of terrorism, a list of suspects closely in line with that of America and more than 100 million dollars in assets frozen. EU adopted a common arrest warrant to prevent suspected terrorists from evading arrest by crossing the EU's largely unchecked internal borders.

France

French media coverage says the SNJ-CGT can be summed up by the September 12 editorial of Le Monde: We are all Americans Now. While one cannot talk of intolerance, much of the coverage was in want of analysis of American policy. Unfortunately, many journalists errored of ignorance by confusing Arab, Muslim and Islamic and they strengthened the view of many in France that "Muslim" is "terrorist".

The SNJ-CGT a press release criticised this approach, not reported. The union reports a number of media organisations took advantage of the uncertain times to announce cutbacks (job losses, salary cuts) in the days immediately after the terror attacks.

The government legislated new anti-terrorist legislation, including surveillance and tracking of Internet messages. Many journalists fear under the pretext of the urgency of the situation and the tracking of terrorist networks, the government is preparing to adopt, in haste yardsticks to have serious implications for press freedom and civil liberties.

Germany

The coverage of September 11 was uniform and provided continual repetition of the incidents with vivid portrayals from *CNN* used by German private channels. The incidents brought journalism and public closer and they together did not require additional "sensational" reporting.

Pictures and information about the attacks were distributed and exchanged between media without competition. The public service broadcaster ARD had the largest audience followed by private RTL network and then ZDF. As in many other countries, advertisements were avoided in the first hours.

Great Britain

In terms of covering ethnic/religious differences, the UK press has performed smortly. The ethnic riots in some British cities between white racist youth and Asian Muslim youth had forced government and press to pull back from racist coverage. UK media follow the government in such times. "The *BBC* goes straight into "Ministry of Information" mode", says the NUJ, "imagining at some level of its collective consciousness that it is holding the nation together in the face of a Nazi invasion."

India

Despite a general climate of understanding over the need for counter-terrorism in the nation, journalists have protested strongly over recent changes to law curbing on civil liberties. The National Union of Journalists (India) and the Indian Journalists Union report that the media coverage of attacks on New York and Washington was unbiased and a section of the media attended on Islamic fundamentalism presumably to equate the terrorist attacks on the US with terrorism in India. However, the "global campaign" appears as a selective and brutal military campaign to protect the global strategic interests of the West. Media can ensure the focus of the campaign remains on terrorism and diplomatic ways to redress the problems.

Ireland

The national mood reflected the strong ties between the United State and the Republic of Ireland. But a media controversy was due to the decision of the Irish Government to declare a National Day of Mourning. *The Irish Times*, observed on the National Day of Mourning. This caused outrage within the paper's Editorial committee, National Union of Journalists office branch, who complained the decision to be taken only for commercial and operational reasons, and felt to give the paper out free better.

Israel

Israel responded *the attacks* by declaring its full support to the "War. On Terror" and linked it to the conflict in Palestine. Prime Minister Benjamin Netanyahu in the very September expressed before the Congress of the United States the international terrorist network to be based in Iraq, Iran, Syria, Taliban Afghanistan, Palestinian authority, Sudan and other Arab regimes. The Israeli response to Palestinian attacks during 2002 has been read as the "war on terror" with its actions against the Palestinian *Intifada.* That the Palestinians have been harboring terrorist groups such as Osama bin Laden in Afghanistan, Hizbullah in Syrian Lebanon, and other terror organisations based in such capitals as Damascus, Baghdad, and Khartoum. That these states and terror organisations. network among for operations as well as political ends.

Jordan

Recently Jordan is considered to be with the most press freedom among the Arab countries, however, the representative government has started taking advantage of the instability and anti-terrorism campaign through repressive measures against the press. In October 2001 Prime Minister Ali Abul Ragheb, said about the amendments to penal code and press law in order "to cover all the needs that we are confronting now." The government now can close down any publications publishing "false or libelous information that can undermine national unity or the country's reputation," and prescribed prison terms "that undermine the king's dignity", or information against the reputation of the royal family. The events on-going tensions between Muslim and Christian communities precipitate an urgent response on the part of journalists and media people.

Pakistan

Pakistan became a crucial ally of the United States in its war on the Taliban in Afghanistan meanwhile in a form of military rule that challenged its commitment to democracy. However, the United States autocratic regime as a close player because the regime aligned proved against Taliban and al-Qaeda fighters coming to Pakistan from Afghanistan.

The country's media largely engaged in the fierce rivalry with India over the disputed Kashmir region remains being accused of providing propaganda to suit their own political claims. Journalists did not access to high profile court hearings, such as Wall Street journalist Daniel Pearl. After 26/11 U.S.A. exerted a tremendous pressure over the leadership to act against the terrorism.

Palestine

The bottlenecks which the journalism faced grew more difficult in the period aftere September 11. On October 8, in Gaza, journalists from covering an anti-American demonstration were prevented by the police. This latest press freedom violations since the international crisis caused by the terrorist attacks on the United States intensified. The latest strike by Israeli forces in Gaza (Dec. 27, 2008) was covered by media channels satisfactorily.

Russia

The Russian media covered objectively the events in New York and Washington, reported the Russian Union of Journalists. The basic theme taken attended to the hostile methods of terrorism and the need of an international response. Since September 11, international concern for human rights abuses in Chechnya waned. However, since the attacks at least one person per week has "disappeared" from custody of the Russian forces.

Uganda

President Yoweri Museveni highlighted the differences between fighting for freedom and terrorism and gave words to "firmly deal with those elements that plan to destabilise Uganda." *The Suppression of Terrorism Bill*, 2001, which incorperates a mandatory death sentence for terrorists and any person who aids, abets, finances or supports terrorism was tabled before Parliament the same time. It gives the High Court "extra-territorial jurisdiction" to try any offence relating to terrorism committed within or outside Uganda and gives extra-ordinary powers to officers engaged in anti-terrorism investigations to carry out surveillance against suspects including accessing suspects' bank accounts and intercepting their phone calls, faxes, e-mail and other communicative devices.

U.S.A.

The US news media, changed buddenly its credibility face face after the September 11 attacks. The Newspaper Guild-CWA, the IFJ found journalists expected to become "patriots first, and journalists second". The Congress moved rapidly to adopt repressive new immigration and wiretapping laws and other anti-terrorist measures raising serious concerns about civil liberties.

According to Linda Foley, President of The Newspaper Guild-CWA, journalists and media staff acted responsibly. The unprecedented atrocities of September 11 and other such events where journalists themselves were the targeted victims, has seen the professionalism of media to the full.

The media supported for the tough measures enacted by the government, though the civil liberty implications of changes in law raise some understandable questions.

Linda Foley, "Despite some early backlash against Arab-Americans and Islam, much of it an emotional and fearful reflection of anxiety in the wake of September 11, there has been a high level of professionalism and racist attitudes have been largely sidelined".

In the first week after the attacks, "an unprecedented 89%" of the public gave the media a positive rating, the *Pew Research Center for the People and the Press.*

However, when media sought more access and information than the Pentagon and the White House on the military actions, the problems began. The Bush administration called on all news networks to "exercise judgement" in broadcasting statements by Bin Laden and his associates, and warned against coded incitements to violence. The Newspaper Guild-CWA established a website to publicise attacks.

4. WESTERN MEDIA CHANELLS AND INTERNATIONAL TERRORISM—IS OBJECTIVE JOURNALISM POSSIBLE (THE CASES OF BBC AND CNN)

This study seeks an analysis of the concept of "objectivity" applied to the role played by *CNN* and the *BBC* in covering major news events within and outside the West World. It intende to show how CNN and BBC are changing with their roles. With a brief description and comparison of thestructure, history, ownership and finances of the two networks, and with the description of political and professional environments, it highlights the political culture and the media of the USA and of the UK, and makes an analysis of the role, image and impact of CNN and the BBC on the public sphere and political mobilisation.

It further refers to everyday practice and the theories of objectivity as a concept and as a journalistic value, the question of absolute or contextual objectivity. Investigating coverage of war and terrorism, the author analyzes whether indications are there of Samuel Huntington's "Clash of civilisations" theory. The debate on his ideas is important for the media as it might help shape their approach to covering the world and their reflections on the possibility of objective journalism that shows respect for both sides of a conflict. The concept of globalisation or internationalisation of certain wars and international conflicts, might open up better opportunities to journalists in democratic countries to improve their coverage. The context stands that of the corporate structure, of the nation state, of the journalistic culture and of the global environment.

The context of the corporate structure

The *BBC* is publicly financed UK's most visible medium in the world. The BBC's journalistic and ethical standards and the level of independence from government and political parties make this media organisation unique. The late 1990s brought a moderate deregulation and the duopoly of the BBC and ITV / Channel 4.

CNN, once owned privately by Ted Turner and now part of Time Warner, is now only one of several leading news channels in the US, but was the first of its kind.

Due to different structure they differ in self-perceptions, transportation. The commercial broadcaster CNN was economically successful until Gulf War II for its journalists' co-operation. When *Fox News* challenged CNN economically with patriotism, CNN's reinforced its reputation with a more pro-American, less global attitude. Meanwhile, BBC, consequently due to a discussion on its financing status tended more towards commercialisation, e.g. via *BBC World.* The BBC is still protect, its "public values", as the discussions following the crossfire of the Hutton Inquiry in the wake of the Kelly Scandal 2003/04 show, seem to be a strong backbone, requiring journalistic impartiability.

The political power of CNN and the BBC is a myth. The CNN, through any acting broadcaster cannot drive policy, nor does the BBC have the power sometimes attributed to it. The Kelly-Scandal indicates the BBC, the emblem of impartiality is driven by the government; it does no longer drive the government.

5. INTERNATIONAL TERRORISM AND ARAB MEDIA CHANNELS (THE CASE OF AL-JAZEERA)

Its daring and engaging journalistic style has formed za rapport with more than 40 million Arab viewers worldwide. Its uninhibited critique of authoritarian governments, exclusive broadcast of tapes by Osama Bin Laden and his lieutenants, and its reporting on the wars in Afghanistan, Iraq and Lebanon have placed it into the international media spotlight.

This Qatar-based *Al-Jazeera* satellite channel, the first 24-hour all-news network in the Arab world has fared much controversy since its inception. Deflying all odds it came out in a region established unknown for a GOOD media environment; it was launched by a small peninsular country in the Persian Gulf which courted hardly any impact on the Arab media scene this; challenged the Western news networks' monopoly over the global news flow; and gave the Arab people a platform through which they expressed their opinions without red lines. It covers different points of view and bold political debates which ever remained under the carpet of government censorship before the advent of Al-Jazeera.

The channel with motto "the opinion, and the other opinion," has generated its admirers who towards it as a beacon for freedom of expression. Its critics have accused this channel of sensationalism and biased reporting. Viewing gaccusations this study looks into the "objectivity" as an idealistic, abstract notion, as it incorporates in the role played by *Al-Jazeera* in covering American responses and other major news events and conflicts inside and outside the Arab world. However, it is felt to be futile to expect *Al-Jazeera*, or other network, to be absolutely objective, because broadcasting networks are products of the cultures from which they originated.

"...journalistic methods and ideals are no guarantee of 'truth,' but vary according to the environment and media landscape. Journalists, decision-makers and audiences are confronted with a fundamental contradiction in journalism between impartiality and loyalty to audiences in this new culturally relativistic broadcasting landscape..." (Riegert, 2005).

Al-Jazeera: Brief History, Ownership, and Financing

Al-Jazeera, "the island" in Arabic, was establishedby Qatar's progressive emir Sheikh Hamad bin Khalifa Al-Thani, in November 1996, as part of his democratisation process moved in his tiny state in the Persian Gulf.

"The British-educated emir, who overthrew his father after a non-violent coup in 1995, planned for Al-Jazeera to be an independent and nonpartisan satellite TV network free from government scrutiny and manipulation" (el-Nawawy and Iskandar, 2003, p. 33).

The establishment of *Al-Jazeera* terminated contract April 1996 between the Rome-based Saudi-owned *Orbit Radio and Television Service* and the *Arabic TV* division of the BBC News Service. It was reported, the Saudi investors limited their financial support of the project following an argument over the broadcast of a documentary about executions in Saudi Arabia. The venture having failed, the majority of the *BBC's Arabic TV* service editorial staff members were recruited by *Al-Jazeera*, which also inherited the *BBC* network's editorial spirit, freedom, and style (el-Nawawy, 2003).

6. How 9/11 Changed the Evening News

The attacks of September 11 and the resulted wars increased the coverage of foreign policy and global conflict on the network evening news, *Tyndall Report* made by ADP research. The traditional hard news and feature of lifestyle coverage, meanwhile, has remained virtually the same on the evening newscasts. The number of minutes devoted to coverage of foreign policy was up 102%, armed conflict 69%, of terrorism 135%. There has been a serious decline in reporting about domestic issues. Coverage of crime and law enforcement dropped to 47%, science and technology coverage to 50% and coverage involving alcohol, tobacco and drugs by 66%.

The effect of the shift in coverage on the overall tone of the newscast is less obvious. The balance between "hard news" and softer features, interviews, and commentaries remained unchanged after 9/11. Moreover, the minutes devoted to hard news courted a growth of 2% after the attacks while the airtime given to softer coverage decreased by only 5%.

The jump in minutes devoted to coverage of foreign policy, armed conflicts, and terrorism seems to be in sync with the concerns of citizens as measured in a Sept. 6 *Pew Research Center for the People* and the Press poll.

In that survey, 51% of the respondents said the 9/11 attacks changed life in America drastically and 82% compared the assault to the seriousness of the Dec. 7, 1941 attack on Pearl Harbor that brought the US into World War II.

7. THE RECENT TERRORIST ATTACKS IN INDIA AND COVERAGE BY MEDIA CHANNELS

While international felt restraints covering the terror attacks in Mumbai, Indian media placed the details about the strength and location of NSG commandos, and marcos involved in operation *black Tornado.*

Ten terrorists came by sea route and seiged the Taj Hotel, Oberai Trident hotel, CST Terminal, Nariman House and few other places, Nov. 26th and ended up on Nov. 29th. The forces guned down all the 9 terrorists capturing the lost.

The broadcasters association in India resolved the Television channelsto should observe for self-regulation while covering such events. It was studied that certain media channels while broadcasting live footage of NSG commandoes involved in operation wanted their reporters cover each of the details of operation and activities of forces,likely to have resulted in a leak of crucial informations to terrorists linked with their commanders at other locations. Broadcasters association demanded the visuals of the tragedy and information about closed ones of victims be prevented from relaying.

8. CONCLUSION

The war on terrorism can be won, not with the help of the strategies of fear, ignorance and intolerance. Since September 11, 2001, the democracies of Europe and North America tre4mendously ambivalent about their commitment to citizens' rights and press freedom. This shows cynicism in autocratic regimes about Western commitment to fundamental rights and, media oppression.

After 26/11 in India, a debate rolled on the role of media. Different media channels broadcasted it including International Media. Since terrorists targeted symbol of India's prosperity, Hotel Taj and Hotel Oberai, the entire event was called India's 9/11 by media channels, and International community came in support. America asked Pakistan, and Pakistan exercised on LeT and Jamat-udDawa. The entire coverage kept viewers informed about day to day develoepments.

The September 11 events but a profound test of the professionalism of journalists globally and, coverage appears to have been restrained, intelligent and informed. However, the manipulation of the media message by governments surges up an otherwise pressure on journalists potentially damaging the quality of coverage of the conflict.

Journalists must work in defence of governmental definitions of "patriotism" or "national interest" Meanwhile, the unprecedented debate about policing, security and civil liberties is going on. In almost every country, anti-terrorist strategies, with the possibility of damaging new laws that may threaten existing standards of personal and press freedom as well.

Index

U